Pedagogy of Hope for Global Social Justice

Advances in Education for Sustainable Development and Global Citizenship

Series Editors:

Massimiliano Tarozzi (University of Bologna)
Clare Bentall (UCL Institute of Education, UK)
Nicole Blum (UCL Institute of Education, UK)

The series provides a forum for the best current studies in Education for Sustainable Development, Global Citizenship Education and related areas. Using Education for Sustainable Development and Global Citizenship as an umbrella term for the series, encompassing terms such as global education/learning and development education, and as the framing paradigm which provides a new perspective to look at traditional educational issues.

Advisory Board

Vanessa Andreotti de Oliveira (University of British Columbia, Canada), Philip Bamber (Liverpool Hope University, UK), April Biccum (Australian National University, Australia), Douglas Bourn (University College London, UK), Pei-I Chou (Institute of Education, National Sun Yat-Sen University, Taiwan), Neda Forghani-Arani (University of Vienna, Austria), William Gaudelli (Teachers College, Columbia University, USA), Catherine Odora, Hoppers (University of South Africa, South Africa), Su-ming Khoo (National University of Ireland, Ireland), Ajay Kumar (Jawaharlal Nehru University, India), Elina Lehtomäki (University of Oulu, Finland), Silvia Moraes (Federal University of Ceara, Brazil), Tania Ramalho (State University of New York, USA), Annette Scheunpflug (University of Bamberg, Germany), Lynette Shultz (University of Alberta, Canada), Vanita Sundaram (York University, UK), Rachel Tallon (Victoria University, New Zealand), Haruhiko Tanaka (Sophia University, Japan), Carol Taylor (University of Bath, UK)

Forthcoming in the series:

Global Citizenship Education in Policy and Pedagogy: Lessons from Italy, by Sara Franch

Global Education in Ireland: Critical Histories and Future Directions, edited by Eilish Dillon, Niamh Gaynor, Gerard McCann and Stephen McCloskey

Pedagogy of Hope for Global Social Justice

Sustainable Futures for People and the Planet

Edited by
Douglas Bourn and Massimiliano Tarozzi

BLOOMSBURY ACADEMIC
LONDON • NEW YORK • OXFORD • NEW DELHI • SYDNEY

BLOOMSBURY ACADEMIC

Bloomsbury Publishing Plc, 50 Bedford Square, London, WC1B 3DP, UK
Bloomsbury Publishing Inc, 1385 Broadway, New York, NY 10018, USA
Bloomsbury Publishing Ireland, 29 Earlsfort Terrace, Dublin 2, D02 AY28, Ireland

BLOOMSBURY, BLOOMSBURY ACADEMIC and the Diana logo are trademarks of
Bloomsbury Publishing Plc

First published in Great Britain 2024
Paperback edition published 2025

Copyright © Douglas Bourn and Massimiliano Tarozzi, 2024

Douglas Bourn and Massimiliano Tarozzi have asserted their right under the Copyright, Designs and Patents Act, 1988, to be identified as Editors of this work.

For legal purposes the Acknowledgements on p. xix constitute an extension of this copyright page.

Cover design by Grace Ridge
Cover image © designtools / Shutterstock
Series logo ©-VICTOR- / iStock

This work is published open access subject to a Creative Commons Attribution-NonCommercial-NoDerivatives 4.0 International licence (CC BY-NC-ND 4.0, https://creativecommons.org/licenses/by-nc-nd/4.0/). You may re-use, distribute, and reproduce this work in any medium for non-commercial purposes, provided you give attribution to the copyright holder and the publisher and provide a link to the Creative Commons licence.

All rights reserved. No part of this publication may be: i) reproduced or transmitted in any form, electronic or mechanical, including photocopying, recording or by means of any information storage or retrieval system without prior permission in writing from the publishers; or ii) used or reproduced in any way for the training, development or operation of artificial intelligence (AI) technologies, including generative AI technologies. The rights holders expressly reserve this publication from the text and data mining exception as per Article 4(3) of the Digital Single Market Directive (EU) 2019/790.

Bloomsbury Publishing Plc does not have any control over, or responsibility for, any third-party websites referred to or in this book. All internet addresses given in this book were correct at the time of going to press. The author and publisher regret any inconvenience caused if addresses have changed or sites have ceased to exist, but can accept no responsibility for any such changes.

A catalogue record for this book is available from the British Library.

A catalog record for this book is available from the Library of Congress.

ISBN: HB: 978-1-3503-2626-2
PB: 978-1-3503-2630-9
ePDF: 978-1-3503-2627-9
eBook: 978-1-3503-2628-6

Series: Advances in Education for Sustainable Development and Global Citizenship

Typeset by Deanta Global Publishing Services, Chennai, India

For product safety related questions contact productsafety@bloomsbury.com.

To find out more about our authors and books visit www.bloomsbury.com and sign up for our newsletters.

Contents

List of Figures	vii
List of Tables	viii
List of Contributors	ix
Series Editors' Foreword	xvii
Acknowledgements	xix

Introduction: Introducing Pedagogy of Hope for Global Social
    Justice *Massimiliano Tarozzi*   1

Part I Conceptualizing Hope and Global Social Justice

1. Global Citizenship Education and Sustainability as Real Utopias *Carlos Alberto Torres*   13
2. Global Citizenship Education in Times of Pandemic: New Approaches for Transforming the World *Manuela Mesa*   30
3. Utopia, Ecopedagogy and Citizenships: Teaching for Socio-Environmental Justice, Development and Planetary Sustainability *Greg William Misiaszek and Diana Cristina Oróstegui González*   44
4. Global Values in School Curricula *Annette Scheunpflug, Martina Osterrieder, Anne-Christine Banze and Andrea Abele-Brehm*   59

Part II Global Perspectives on Global Social Justice

5. Non-Western Perspectives in Framing Global Citizenship Education: The Role of Higher Education Institutions *Mario R. Smith, Abigail Simons, Emma Wagener, Michelle Andipatin and Jose Frantz*   79
6. A Social Network Analysis of Global Citizenship Education in Europe and North America *Massimiliano Tarozzi and Lynette Shultz*   96
7. Transforming a Global Competence Agenda into Pedagogies of Intercultural Understanding and Student Voice: An Australian Case Study *Karena Menzie-Ballantyne and Miriam Ham*   110

8   How Chinese Philosophies Affect the Chinese Understanding of
    Global Citizenship Education *Jun Teng and Yuxuan Gong*   128
9   Decolonizing Citizenship, Becoming Planetary with Paulo Freire's
    Hope-in-Action in Brazilian Education *Silvia Elisabeth Moraes,
    Luiz Botelho Albuquerque and Diana Nara da Silva Oliveira*   142

Part III Applying Global Social Justice

10 Transformative Social and Emotional Learning and Digital
    Learning for Global Citizenship Education: Limits and
    Possibilities *Yoko Mochizuki*   159
11 The Evolving Development Education in Ghana: Implications for
    Social Justice Education and Pedagogies of Hope *John Kwame
    Boateng, Ellen M. Osei-Tutu, Olivia Adwoa Tiwaah Kwapong*   175
12 Global Education for Teachers: Online Continuing
    Professional Development as a Source of Hope in Challenging
    Times *Frances Hunt and Nicole Blum*   192
13 Gender Equality – The Key Role of a Pedagogy of Critical Hope
    and Global Social Justice *Lisa Ferro and Sandra Saúde*   211
14 Social Justice and Hope: Teachers' Continuing Professional
    Development in South Africa *Joyce Raanhuis*   225

Conclusion: Pedagogy of Hope for Global Social Justice *Douglas Bourn*   241

Index   253

Figures

4.1	Absolute frequencies of universalistic values according to reference horizons	66
6.1	Distribution of the organizations interviewed in Europe and North America	100
6.2	Three networks emerged in the data, based on relations and activities among the actors	103
6.3	Core-periphery mode of interaction (light= periphery dark= centre; triangle= multiscalar)	104
7.1	Three dimensions of the Australian curriculum	112
7.2	Global competence pilot data sources	116
8.1	The five elements	130
12.1	Teachers' experience, knowledge and confidence with global education	201

Tables

4.1	Percentage Distribution of Orientations Related to Social Change	65
4.2	Relative Frequencies of Universalistic Values by Reference Horizons	67
12.1	Overview of Course Participants Who Took the Survey	199
12.2	Typology of Hope	204
14.1	Overview of CPD Programmes and Objectives	229

Contributors

Andrea Abele-Brehm is Professor Emerita for Social Psychology at the Friedrich-Alexander University of Erlangen-Nuremberg in Germany. She is vice-president of the Bavarian Academy of Science and served as a president of the German Society for Psychology from 2014 to 2016. Her research focuses on social cognition, agency, well-being, values and gender aspects. She is a member of the editorial board of *Social Psychology* and the *European Journal of Social Psychology*.

Luiz Botelho Albuquerque (PhD Sociology of Education) is Professor and Supervisor at the Education Post-Graduate Programme, Federal University of Ceará (UFC) Brazil. He also teaches at the Music Programme of the Institute of Culture and Art of UFC and at the Professional Master's in Arts. His research interests are curriculum theory, sociology of art and music, teachers' education and postcolonial studies.

Michelle Andipatin holds a PhD in Psychology and currently is Deputy Dean Research in the Faculty of Community and Health Sciences. Her research interests include but are not limited to women's reproductive health, men and masculinities, alternate healing modalities, mental health and well-being, philosophical issues in science and research methodologies. Understanding social impact and the measurement thereof has become an important interest of hers.

Anne-Christine Banze is a research assistant at the Chair of Foundations of Education at the University of Bamberg, Germany. She graduated from Ludwig Maximilian University of Munich with a First State Examination in German and social sciences, and from the University of Bamberg with an MA in adult and further education. Her research interests lie primarily in the fields of teacher education, teacher professionalism, value education and qualitative educational research. She currently works on her PhD thesis on the topic of action-guiding orientations of teacher trainers.

Nicole Blum is Senior Lecturer and Associate Director of the Development Education Research Centre. Her PhD research (Anthropology; University of Sussex, UK) explored diverse forms of engagement with environmental learning and sustainable development in a rural mountain community in Costa Rica. Her research interests also include pedagogy and approaches to global learning, global citizenship education, education for sustainable development, climate change and education, online learning, internationalization and global perspectives in higher education, and the ethnography of education. Her most recent publications have been on study abroad and global citizenship.

John Kwame Boateng holds a PhD from the Pennsylvania State University (PSU, Penn State), United States. He joined the University of Ghana as Lecturer in 2013. He was a fellow of the University of Michigan's African Presidential Scholars (UMAPS) programme from August 2014 to February 2015. In 2016 and 2020 Prof. Boateng was promoted to the rank of Senior Lecturer and Associate Professor respectively. Prof. Boateng has over twenty years' experience in research, teaching and academic publishing. His research areas cover development education, educational technology, curriculum development, ICT and mobile technologies' integration into curriculum and pedagogical development, distance learning and instructional development. He was the head of the University of Ghana Learning Centres until 31 August 2021. He is a material developer and a tutor of online courses.

Douglas Bourn is Professor of Development Education at University College London, UK; author of *The Theory and Practice of Development Education* (2015), *Understanding Global Skills* (2018) and *Education for Social Change* (2022); and editor of the Bloomsbury Handbook for Global Education and Learning (2020). He was Chair of the Advisory Board for the Academic Network of Global Education and Learning (ANGEL) from 2017 to 2023 and is also Chair of Global Learning London.

Lisa Ferro has a master's degree in sustainable development and entrepreneurship and has been working in community development projects, especially in the fields of social inclusion, community participation, active ageing and migrant integration, within a non-governmental organization for development.

Jose Frantz (PhD) is Professor in the field of physiotherapy and is currently Deputy Vice Chancellor for Research and Innovation at the University of the Western Cape, South Africa. Her research interests are in faculty development and health professions education. She is also involved in leadership development through capacity development initiatives and research.

Yuxuan Gong is a PhD student from the Department of Educational Policy and Leadership in the State University of New York at Albany, United States. Being highly selective at PhD level and in the social and education sciences, Gong is China Scholarship Council Awardee from 2021 to 2025. Currently, she is the research assistant in the 'Feasibility Study on Monitoring Global Citizenship Competences in the Asia-Pacific Region'. This study is commissioned by the UNESCO Asia-Pacific Center of Education for International Understanding (APCEIU), located in Seoul Korea. She has published two papers in Japanese on policy monitoring and is preparing four English papers now. Her research interests are core competence, measurement, social emotional skills, Sustainable Development Goals and policy monitoring.

Diana Cristina Oróstegui González is an academic consultant for Santillana Colombia and Beijing Normal University pursuing a master's degree in comparative and international education from Beijing Normal University in China. Her thesis focuses on ecopedagogies within Colombia's schooling. Oróstegui González has worked for a number of years as a teacher in Medellin, Columbia. She is also working as an academic consultant for the British Council Colombia and Santillana, one of Columbia's most prominent magazines on education.

Miriam Ham is Senior Lecturer in Education on the Cairns campus of CQUniversity, Australia. She was awarded a Vice-Chancellor's Award for Exemplary Practice in Learning and Teaching in 2020. Her research and passion are to work with teachers to solve identified problems specific to their environment. Miriam's particular focus is on how teachers' beliefs and roles impact their response to change. A secondary school teacher of twenty years, Miriam draws on her classroom experience when teaching undergraduate and master's initial teacher education courses. She supervises Australian and international RHD students who are investigating teachers' beliefs and practice in their unique contexts. She works collaboratively with Karena Menzie-Ballantyne in the research cluster *Education for Global Competence and Sustainable Development*.

Frances Hunt is Senior Research Officer at UCL Institute of Education, UK, within the Development Education Research Centre. Her research has focused on global learning and global citizenship education, democracy in schools, human rights and student voice. She is also a tutor on the MA in global learning within UCL. Her most recent publications are on the role of third-sector organizations in professional development within the field of global learning and the characteristics of a global learning school.

Teng Jun has long been engaged in comparative education research. Her main research areas include international organization education policy, twenty-first-century core literacy, global competence, global education governance, international education and development education. She has maintained close exchanges and cooperation with UNESCO, the World Bank, the United States, Finland and other countries. She has led and participated in more than 20 national and provincial projects, and published more than 100 papers in *Education Research, International and Comparative Education Review* and other peer-reviewed journals, as well as in newspapers such as *China Education Daily* and *Guangming Daily*. Her doctoral thesis *The Discourse Evolution of UNESCO's Education Policy* was nominated for the 2012 National Outstanding Doctoral Thesis. Her latest monographs – *Preparing to Work in International Organization, C+ Curriculum Guideline for International Preschool in China, Reconstructing Neo-Modern Curriculum: Annual Report of Innovative Practice of International Schools in China (2020)* – have been published by Shanghai Education Press.

Olivia Adwoa Tiwaah Frimpong Kwapong is Associate Professor and Dean of the School of Continuing and Distance Education, University of Ghana, Ghana. She holds a PhD in adult education from the University of Ghana and has studied as a Special Doctoral Candidate at Harvard University. In the year 2013 she served as a Fulbright Visiting Scholar. Her research has focused on the empowerment of women through adult education, distance learning and the use of ICTs. She has published extensively in both local and international journals. She has consulted for local and international organizations that promote empowerment of women and the creation of access to tertiary education for non-traditional students.

Karena Menzie-Ballantyne is Senior Lecturer in Education at CQUniversity, based at their Bundaberg campus in Queensland, Australia. She has been researching and teaching in the fields of education for global competence, global citizenship and sustainable development for the past two decades in school, tertiary and not-for-profit sectors. Her research cluster *Education for Global Competence and Sustainable Development* explores the interpretation and implementation of the global competence, global citizenship and education for sustainable development agendas by education systems, not-for-profit organizations, schools and individual teachers in Australia, Pakistan, Indonesia, New Zealand and the UK. The cluster is particularly interested in helping amplify voices from the Global South who are teaching and research in this field.

Manuela Mesa is a pedagogue specialized in education for peace and development and in peace studies with a PhD in sociology and anthropology. She is Co-Director of the University Institute of Human Rights, Democracy, Culture of Peace and Nonviolence (DEMOSPAZ) at the Autonomous University of Madrid, Spain, and Director of the Center for Education and Research for Peace (CEIPAZ).

Greg William Misiaszek, PhD, is Assistant Professor at Beijing Normal University's (BNU), China, Faculty of Education. He is an associate director, Paulo Freire Institute, UCLA, and an executive editor of *Teaching in Higher Education* journal. His work focuses on critical, Freirean environmental pedagogies (e.g. ecopedagogy) through theories of globalizations, citizenships, race, gender, migration, Indigenous issues, linguistics and media, among others. His most recently published books focus on this analysis: *Ecopedagogy: Critical Environmental Teaching for Planetary Justice and Global Sustainable Development* (2020, Bloomsbury) and *Educating the Global Environmental Citizen: Understanding Ecopedagogy in Local and Global Contexts* (2018), www.ecopedagogy.com.

Yoko Mochizuki, is an associate member of the EDA laboratory, a multi-disciplinary research unit of Université Paris Cité (formerly the Faculty of Human and Social Sciences at Sorbonne at the University of Paris Descartes). Previously, she was Head of Policy at UNESCO Mahatma Gandhi Institute of Education for Peace and Sustainable Development (MGIEP) in New Delhi, India, Programme Specialist for Education for Sustainable Development (ESD) and Climate Change at UNESCO Paris, and ESD Specialist at the United Nations University Institute of Advanced Studies of Sustainability. She has taught the Sociology of Education at Teachers College Columbia University in New York and Keio University in Tokyo. She has a Ph.D. (with Distinction) in Comparative and International Education from Columbia University.

Silvia Elisabeth Moraes is Professor and Supervisor at the education post-graduate programme, Federal University of Ceará, Brazil. Her post-doctorate research was on Habermas's theory of communicative action, University of São Paulo. She held a Senior Internship at the Development Education Research Center, University College London. Her research interests are Freirean pedagogy, curriculum theory, citizenship, theory of communicative action and postcolonialism.

Diana Nara da Silva Oliveira is a doctoral student in education at the Federal University of Ceará; holds a master's in education and teaching by the Intercampi Academic Master in Education and Teaching; and is Substitute Professor at the

Faculty of Philosophy Dom Aureliano Matos of the State University of Ceará, Brazil. Her research interests are Freirean pedagogy, field education, school curriculum, agrarian reform, youth and adult education.

Ellen Mabel Osei-Tutu is Senior Lecturer at the Department of Adult Education and Human Resource Studies, School of Continuing and Distance Education, University of Ghana, Legon. She joined the University of Ghana after over sixteen years work experience in the field of population having worked with the National Population Council Secretariat. During this period, she worked on advocacy, youth and gender issues. She holds a PhD in population studies, MPhil in population studies, MA in population studies and BA in sociology with political science, all from the University of Ghana, Legon. Her main research areas are marriage and reproductive health issues as well as education-related issues.

Martina Osterrieder is a research assistant at the Chair of Foundations of Education at the University of Bamberg, Germany. She graduated from the University of Bamberg with a First State Examination in German, French and philosophy. Her research interests lie primarily in the fields of value education, teacher education and qualitative educational research. She currently works on her PhD thesis on the topic of value manifestations in school curricula.

Joyce Raanhuis Joyce is a Postdoctoral Research Fellow at the Department of Humanities Education, Faculty of Education at the University of Pretoria. She holds a Doctorate in Education from the Centre for International Teacher Education (CITE) at Cape Peninsula University of Technology, South Africa, and has an MA in Migration Studies from the University of Sussex, United Kingdom. The research presented in her book chapter derives from her doctoral research, which focuses on the pivot roles of teachers and professional development programmes in promoting social cohesion in post-apartheid South Africa. Her current research explores how pre-service History teachers in South Africa, Curaçao, Suriname, and the Netherlands engage with the teaching of controversial issues in History classrooms. Furthermore, she is interested in the sociology of education, social justice and equity, as well as education in post-conflict and post-colonial contexts.

Sandra Saúde has a master's degree and a PhD in sociology, with a specialization in sociology of development. She is a coordinating professor at the Polytechnic Institute of Beja (IPBeja, Portugal), a researcher at CICS. NOVA – Interdisciplinary Centre of Social Sciences (Portugal) and a member of ANGEL – Academic Network on Global Education & Learning. She has participated in and coordinated several research projects over the past twenty years, financed by Portuguese and European funds, namely in the fields of sustainable development and (post-)development. Her current subjects of scientific interest and future development, in which she has already published some papers and books, are sustainable development; global and critical citizenship education; new teaching and learning methodologies; and qualitative and mixed methods research.

Annette Scheunpflug holds the chair of foundation of education at the Otto-Friedrich-University Bamberg, Germany. Her research covers quality in education, global education and anthropology of education. She is a member of the Academy of Science in Munich, Board Member of Angel and of Global Education Network Europe (GENE).

Lynette Shultz is Professor of Educational Policy Studies at the University of Alberta, Canada. She has published widely on the topics of global citizenship, international education and the governance of education as well as education and democracy, citizenship and justice. She is the past director of the Centre for Global Citizenship Education and Research (2010–22) and has served on the executive committees of the World Council for Comparative and International Education and the Comparative and International Education Council of Canada as well as several other national and international academic and professional education organizations.

Abigail Simons is a registered research psychologist and holds a bachelor's degree in psychology and a master of arts in research psychology. Currently, Mrs Simons works as a researcher in the Centre for Diversity in Psychological Practice at the University of the Western Cape, South Africa. She is working on projects that address issues of wellness, diversity, inclusion and culture. Additionally, she is in the process of pursuing her PhD in psychology, which focuses on the imposter phenomenon in higher education among academic staff.

Mario R. Smith (PhD) is currently employed as Professor in Psychology at the University of the Western Cape, South Africa. He registered with the Health Professions Council of South Africa as a clinical psychologist. He is a former deputy dean of research and postgraduate studies and former acting director of the Division for Postgraduate Studies at the University of the Western Cape. He is also a Fulbright scholar and graduate of Columbia University, United States, and the University of the Western Cape, South Africa. Prof Smith has worked in clinical, academic and research settings locally and abroad. He has also worked in private practice and been involved in the training of health professionals for an extended period. His research interests include capacity building, clinical research and psychometrics.

Massimiliano Tarozzi is UNESCO Chair in Global Citizenship Education in Higher Education. He is Full Professor at the University of Bologna, Italy, where he is Founding Director of the International Research Centre on Global Citizenship Education (GCED). He was Co-Director of the Development Education Research Centre at UCL Institute of Education, where he is Visiting Professor. He is a member of the Advisory Board and Coordinator of Academic Network on Global Education and Learning. He has been teaching GCED in various MA programmes both in Bologna and at the Institute of Education in London, and he has been regularly invited as Visiting Professor in several international universities, including UCLA, Seattle, Harvard, USP, São Paulo and Normal Beijing University.

Carlos Alberto Torres is Distinguished Professor and Director of the Paulo Freire Institute, UCLA School of Education and Information Studies, United States. He was the inaugural holder of the UNESCO UCLA Chair on Global Learning and Global Citizenship Education, Department of Education, UCLA (2016–20); past president of the Comparative and International Education Society (CIES) 1997; past president of the World Council of Comparative Education Societies (WCCES), 2013–16; foreign fellow in the Royal Society of Canada and corresponding member of the Mexican Academy of Sciences; and has published over seventy books of scientific scholarship and half a dozen books of fiction including novels, short stories and poetry. He has published over 300 peer-reviewed articles in scientific journals.

Emma Wagener is a researcher (MA Research Psychology) who has been working across various fields since the start of her career. She has an expertise in statistics and research methodology, having been involved in various large-scale research projects as a data manager and performing complex data analyses. Emma has held positions in higher education as an educator and thesis supervisor for five years. Emma's passion lies in sound and philosophically aligned research and application of statistical analyses, which can and should be applied across disciplines, allowing for the opportunity to work across research areas. Emma is currently a researcher in the neuroscience niche area at the University of the Western Cape, South Africa. She is currently completing her PhD, which focuses on mapping the concept of executive functioning.

Series Editors' Foreword

Welcome to the first volume of the new Bloomsbury *Advances in Education for Sustainable Development and Global Citizenship* series.

The series aims to provide a forum for new and innovative studies in education for sustainable development, global citizenship education and related areas. We use education for sustainable development and global citizenship as broad umbrella terms for the series, which we see as encompassing other key related terms – such as global education, global learning, climate change education and development education – and also offering a framing paradigm through which to explore a range of contemporary educational issues.

We are keen that the series takes a broad multidisciplinary focus and that it actively promotes a wide international authorship which will increase the degree to which diverse voices and perspectives from the field are heard.

This first volume meets many of the key aims of the series through its diverse authorship and perspectives, as well as through attention to a range of theoretical concerns and examples of practice from around the world. It also links strongly to the work showcased in the existing *Bloomsbury Handbook of Global Education and Learning* (2020), also edited by Douglas Bourn. The Handbook was originally intended as the first volume in this series, but it grew so much that it became an independent project of its own. We hope that both these volumes – and those to follow – will act as an important resource for researchers, educators and learners around the world who are committed to these areas of work.

This new volume takes both an expansive and a critical focus on the role of hope in global education. The three parts – 'Conceptualizing Hope and Global Social Justice', 'Global Perspectives on Global Social Justice' and 'Applying Global Social Justice' – address a range of theoretical and empirical perspectives across diverse international contexts. As the editors' note, while these diverse contributions come from a range of disciplinary fields, approaches, and cultural and linguistic contexts, as a collection they aim to provide a mosaic of perspectives and ideas which will inspire and – and perhaps even act as a source hope in itself – to readers.

Clare Bentall, Development Education Research Centre, IOE, UCL's Faculty of Education and Society, UK

Nicole Blum, Development Education Research Centre, IOE, UCL's Faculty of Education and Society, UK

Massimiliano Tarozzi, UNESCO Chair in Global Citizenship Education in Higher Education, University of Bologna, Italy

Acknowledgements

This volume is inspired by the themes from the 2021 Academic Network for Global Education and Learning (ANGEL) international conference. Many of the papers from that conference informed a number of the chapters in this volume. We would like to thank Global Education Network Europe (GENE) for supporting that conference and in particular the comments made at that event about our work by its director, Liam Wegimont.

We would also like to thank Kester Muller from the Development Education Research Centre at University College London for his support and help with that conference and in bringing the chapters together for this volume.

Introduction

Introducing Pedagogy of Hope for Global Social Justice

Massimiliano Tarozzi

This book is about hope and its role in education, and especially in global education. We borrowed this title from the Freire's book *Pedagogia da Esperança* (Freire, 1992), *Pedagogy of Hope* (Freire, 2021), where the Brazilian philosopher of education reviewed his seminal book *Pedagogy of the Oppressed*.

Today, precisely thirty years after this book of the same name, it is still overwhelmingly urgent and timely to reiterate the role of hope not only within educational processes but also within educational policies. A critical hope is what is needed to transform social reality and to imagine possible futures. It is also particularly important in the historical time we live in, in which a whole generation of youth is coming out of the global crisis generated by the Covid-19 pandemic and the resulting economic one. A generation pervaded by deep existential malaise often with no vision of the future and unable to cultivate the feeling of hope.

But even beyond the present circumstances, the reasonable hopelessness with which the new generations view their future and that of the planet is also dictated by other structural conditions. Neoliberalism has become the dominant narrative of this century and brings with it insecurity in the labour market, wild competition and profound injustices. This social concern is coupled with one for the future of the planet projected towards an irreversible climate crisis and the disenchantment that stems from the awareness that little or nothing is being done by world governments. Still, it is precisely under these conditions, and indeed because of these conditions, that progressive educators and policymakers need to be able to cultivate and promote a not naive but critical perspective of hope for change, as one of the editors has recently argued (Bourn, 2021). Just when the dominant discourse, in the name of a cynical realism, is calling for passive acceptance that there is no other alternative to choices based on economic rationality, education for social justice must be able to nurture hope and optimism, always critical and never idealistic, for social transformation. Hope is an 'ontological need' that allows us to challenge the dominant 'pragmatic discourse that would have us adapt to the facts of reality' (Freire, 2021: p. 1).

That is why, following Freire, but also going beyond his work, the various contributions of this book agree with the position expressed by the editors and nicely summarized in the conclusions: a global perspective in education requires an ethos imbued with hope, seen as the political virtue to imagine possible worlds (Arendt, 1958), to think otherwise and to lay the foundations for a new transformative pedagogy.

In his *Pedagogy of Hope*, published in Portuguese in 1992 and the following year in Spanish, Freire raises the issue of how hope can be educated, a key issue for all progressive educators in an era dominated by neoliberalism.

The text, which has an insightful subtitle, *Reliving Pedagogy of the Oppressed*, provides this 'reencuentro' with an original autobiographical narrative. The thought of the pedagogy of the oppressed is revisited through the author's account of his childhood, and then of his early work as a popular educator in Pernambuco, and especially through the experience of exile. Then he discusses *Pedagogy of the Oppressed* and replies to some of the criticisms raised during the 1970s in order to relive and rethink experiences, encounters and travels done worldwide in the last two decades.

In the introduction, Freire describes himself as 'hopeful, not out of mere stubborness, but out of an existential, concrete imperative' (Freire, 2021: p. 1), and, to immediately dispel the risk of interpreting this formula as abstract idealism, highlights the concept of 'critical hope' and its transformative power.

From his earliest works the dimension of hope has always been closely connected with the notion of *conscientização*, conscientization. This is the critical attitude that enables individuals to become aware of the reality of oppression but also of their power to transform it. Therefore, this requires adopting a utopian stance towards the world not only cognitively but also transformatively and thus politically.

Like Freire, in this book we are hopeful as 'an existential, concrete imperative', we believe that hope can unveil contradictions, injustices, mystifications that a hopeless pragmatic fatalism tends to generate. We are in accordance with Freire when he criticizes the fatalist neoliberal ideology according to which we must accept the natural order of events, as if it were an ineluctable result of history (p. 101 ped of hope). Like Freire we believe in the political role of hope to pave the way for change by showing that another world is always possible. Like Freire we think that hope is crucial but is not enough, that there is no hope in sheer hopefulness and that 'just to hope is to hope in vain' (Freire, 2021: p. 2).

Beyond Freire, in this book we believe that a pedagogy of hope is needed both to think and to achieve a global social justice. Hope is necessary in order to conceptualize a global perspective on education that considers equality and social justice as imperative. In contrast, hopelessness and fatalism force us to intend global education only in pragmatical terms, as an efficient way to educate global elites or to spread entrepreneurial attitude worldwide. But hope is also needed to act for putting a global social justice into practice.

Unlike Freire we also maintain that terms such as 'hope', 'utopia' and 'optimism', which Freire too often uses interchangeably, are closely related but have different meanings and aim at different targets.

Therefore, a brief clarification of the terms 'hope', 'optimism' and 'utopia' that are extensively used throughout this book seems necessary.

The very concept of hope is ambiguous and sometimes entangled with strong ideological assumptions.

In many neo-Latin languages, it is embedded in the Catholic tradition, which, capitalized, is one of the three theological virtues along with Faith and Charity, the foundation of the Christian moral activity . Otherwise, in the pre-Christian Western tradition, the Greek concept of ἐλπίς seems to refer to an undifferentiated expectation towards the future, without the transformative intentionality of the subject. Accordingly, ἐλπίς, or Spes for the Romans, is worshipped as a goddess to whom one can turn to propitiate the future, a rich harvest, a marriage or a prosperous future for a newborn child. In antiquity, this mythological vision of hope was criticized on the one hand because it obscures the truth, confuses the perception of reality and the future by masking it with often unfounded and visionary expectations. On the other, it was criticized for being too emotionally bound and therefore opposed to the rational view that stoically accepts the harshness of things in the world.

Both the deification of hope in Greco-Latin mythology and hope as a Christian virtue coupled with Providence, with its saving power, end up undermining the role of individuals in creating their futures. Understood in this way, hope de-responsibilizes and subtracts agency from subjects.

Conversely, the hope we discuss in this volume, the one that can ground global social justice, is a *radical hope* (Lear, 2006; Swanson and Gamal, 2021), is also an eminently political virtue and is characterized by its great transformative power. It can inform pedagogies and educational practices and provide a perspective for change for both learners and educators.

So understood, it echoes Ernst Bloch's *The Hope Principle* (Bloch, 1986), an actual encyclopaedia of hope that attempts to combine the scientific and rational Marxian perspective with a more existential and spiritual vision. Here Bloch invites us not to take the world as it is, but through hope, to make the effort to see how things are moving, how they evolve. So hope is a cognitive and political act of anticipation of what is not yet given. But it also takes on a critical value of the present, as the sense of possibility emerges against hopelessness, routine and laziness, which are the anti-depressants that allow one to endure bourgeois life.

From this vision of hope emanates a perspective of *optimism*. Following Bertolini, every educator can only be optimistic (Bertolini, 2021), but not with the candid naiveté of Voltaire's Pangloss, but because his/her optimism originates from the intentional direction of possibility, the intrinsic capacity of every authentic educational practice to see possible futures within every educational experience and in every subject in training.

In this sense, optimism is a pedagogical virtue, structurally linked to a political perspective that evokes the Gramsci's optimism of the will. In his *Letters from Prison* (*Letter his brother Carlo*, 19 December 1929), referring to his experience in prison, Gramsci acknowledges that he was trying to overcome both pessimism and optimism as trivial concepts: 'I'm a pessimist because of intelligence, but an optimist because of will.' The latter is not just a moral virtue but is a fundamental perspective of political theory, creating the possibility to influence processes of social change.

In policy activity Gramsci discards daydreaming, abstract idealism and its consolatory style and its lack of concreteness to make a positive impact in life (Tarozzi and Torres, 2016).

His optimism does not look naively in a dreamed future, but it is firmly anchored in the present that one wants to change and in the dynamics of its possible development. The realistic understanding of the present, especially based on historical knowledge, brings with it the 'pessimism of the intellect', as the attitude to let emerge from the critical analysis of the historical reality the worst-case scenarios; a key political perspective which should be always coupled with the optimism of the will. Unlike naive utopianism and romantic idealism, the moral laziness which paved the way to Nazi-fascism, pessimism of the intellect makes people active, responsible and committed. Only from this soil can the optimism of the will, an existential but also political attitude that can be tempered by the hard trials of life and the critical analysis of reality, germinate. This optimism leads people to develop an awareness that has adequate energy and momentum to face the political challenges of change, with responsibility and ethical and political coherence.

Another key concept related to hope which plays a crucial role in Freire's and Freireans' work is *Utopia*: an ideal project, driven by good intentions, but which cannot take place. So in a strict sense the term is ill-suited to describe the political attitude of those who envision possibilities for change and act concretely to achieve them. Literally, it envisages the visionary and dreamy, and therefore surrendering, attitude, of those who take refuge in dreams rather than struggle for change. Yet, for Freire utopia is not unrealizable idealism, even if it is in fact unrealizable by definition.

Freire tries to show that for him utopia is not abstract idealism, not a vain aspiration to the unattainable, but a historical commitment, not unlike Torres when in this book describes the Sustainable Development Goals as new utopia of twenty-first century (see also in Tarozzi and Torres, 2022).

Utopia is linked to hope, since only the 'utopians can be prophetic or hopefuls' (Freire, 1972, cited in Catarci, 2016: p. 52). Against this framework, Freire evocatively defines his utopia as 'untested feasible', or *inédito viable*, also nicely presented by Torres in this volume.

Utopia is the scenario where a tension between an intolerable present pervaded by oppression and injustice and a future that has to be built collectively take place.

Against the neoliberal fatalism of passively accepting the present, Freire stands for a non-naïve critical hope: 'we need critical hope the way a fish needs unpolluted water' (Freire, 2021: p. 1)

In contrast with the neoliberal market-centred dystopian vision dominated by personal interests, where hope is only individualized, Giroux argued for an 'educated hope' as a form of militant utopianism (Giroux, 2003: p. 477) for social struggle.

A critical hope is today needed not only to encourage youth generations to overcome the effect of health, economic and environmental crises but also to avoid succumbing to fatalism in imagining global social justice. This ambitious, humanistic and progressive programme requires to overcome and contrast the conservative and neoliberal pessimism and hopelessness of TINA (There Is No Alternative), underpinning neoliberal (Shultz, 2007), economic (Oxley and Morris, 2013; Mannion et al., 2011) or entrepreneurial (Stein, 2015) models of global education and learning. A pedagogy of hope could provide a conceptual framework for Global education and learning and the role it can play in addressing current social and environmental challenges. According to bell hooks

(2003), this pedagogy of hope has been already created by educators who have struggled for social justice education and have developed new pedagogies and educational theories providing alternatives to the dominant system of racism, sexism or class elitism (hooks, 2003).

In sum following Freire, Freirean thinkers and critical theorists a pedagogy of hope has emerged in current discussion on social justice education. It can trigger social change, but it also offers to scholars and practitioners a possibility to rethink the premises of a global perspective in education and for laying the foundations for a new transformative pedagogy underpinning such an approach.

The exploration of this possibility is what emerges across the various chapters of this book which was originally based on a conference organized by the Academic Network of Global Education and Learning (ANGEL)[1] in the middle of the Covid pandemic, inviting international scholars and educators to discuss the role of hope in the dark times affected by several crises.

This exploratory journey is organized into three main areas: the first – *Conceptualizing hope and global social justice* – presents various perspectives to theoretically frame hope and global social justice; the second – *Global perspectives on global social justice* – outlines diverse angles to understand global social justice developed in different continents: Australia, Africa, Asia, Europe and North America; the third – *Applying global social justice* – provides examples of global education and learning practice in different fields and areas of the world.

Moreover, the book will discuss global social justice across different areas of the world, namely Europe and North America, by mapping the key actors promoting Global Citizenship Education (GCE); Africa by examining higher education institutions building a pedagogy of hope and global social justice; Australia and China by discussing global competences in formal education.

In the first, theoretical part, Carlos Alberto Torres explores the politics of hope and the tension between utopia and reality, which widely permeates the discussion on global citizenship education through a variety of analytical orientations, including Freire and E. O. Wright. He concludes by raising key open questions based on four provocative theses to show the limitations of school systems in achieving this utopia. Manuela Mesa addresses the role of global citizenship education in pandemic times when inequalities and injustices have been exacerbated and argues that GCE should encompass new interpretative frameworks to analyse these unprecedented times and to face its global challenges such as global public goods, epistemologies of South and feminist perspectives. 'Utopia, Ecopedagogy and Citizenships' by Greg

William Misiaszek and Diana Cristina Oróstegui González discusses the need for environmental pedagogies inspired by utopia following Freirean-based ecopedagogy teaching. The authors provide ecopedagogy as a framework to experience *unfinishedness* a key issue, according to Freire, for being able to dream and act towards achieving dreams. They argue for utopic pedagogies to disrupt neoliberal and Western-centred fatalism emergent from top-down hegemonic development and provide a case study in Colombia as an example. The chapter by Annette Scheunpflug, Martina Osterrieder, Anne-Christine Banze and Andrea Abele-Brehm provides an original empirical investigation of the preambles of the school curricula in the German province of Bavaria. The chapter reports the results of a sophisticated discourse analysis outlining the significance of politically expressed values of global relevance and it demonstrates that universalistic values do not convey what could be expected from these values in terms of climate justice, global solidarity or global social reflection beyond the immediate vicinity.

In the second part, various examples on global education and learning from a social justice education perspective are presented especially from non-Western standpoints, namely from sub-Saharan Africa, Australia and China. In particular, in 'Non-Western Perspectives in Framing Global Citizenship Education: The Role of Higher Education Institutions' the team from the University of the Western Cape, South Africa, in their chapter, presents a three-tiered framework – theory, institutional objectives and culture, student development – to engage with the conceptualization of GCE and to develop a social justice GCE agenda in sub-Saharan African universities. In their chapter Karena Menzic-Ballantyne and Miriam Ham address a case study in Australia where a group of schools experimented an innovative and collaborative way to introduce a global competence framework endorsing pedagogies of social justice, intercultural understanding and hope. Teng Jun and Yuxuan Awe, in their chapter 'How Chinese Philosophies Affect the Chinese Understanding of Global Citizenship Education', review globally related concepts rooted in Chinese philosophical tradition and especially the Chinese term *Tianxia* (Global) to discuss its implication to GCE. A Latin America perspective is then provided by Silvia Elisabeth Moraes, Luiz Botelho Albuquerque and Diana Nara da Silva Oliveira, where in the footsteps of Freire, they present a project aiming at introducing planetary citizenship as a transdisciplinary theme seeking to decolonize university curriculum in Brazilian universities. In addition, Massimiliano Tarozzi and Lynette Shultz used Social Network Analysis (SNA) to understand relationships among key GCE actors across Europe and North

America. Structural characteristics of the network and patterns of integration among members are described, and the implication of a core-periphery mode of integration is especially discussed.

The third part provides examples of concrete lessons from research in schools on most effective ways to engage learners in playing a positive role to make a more just and sustainable world. Yoko Mochizuki discusses the limits and possibilities of socio and emotional learning and digital learning, two approaches that gained great relevance during Covid-19 pandemic – in addressing SDG 4.7 from a perspective of equity, social justice and societal transformation. In their chapter, Boateng, Osei-Tutu and Frimpong Kwapong, drawing from Freire, show how pedagogies of social justice education and hope could significantly influence university reform in Ghana to respond to current global challenges such as inequality, public health and climate change. In their chapter Frances Hunt and Nicole Blum address teacher education and its role in promoting global education and learning, drawing on the case of an online course on Global Education for Teachers developed by themselves in UK. From the systematic analysis of participants' views emerge the role of global education as a source of hope. The following chapter by Sandra Saúde and Lisa Ferro examines how a pedagogy of critical hope and social justice can contribute to structurally promote gender equality, view as a key component of GCE. The analysis is carried out on the basis of a case study developed in four municipalities of Portugal. Finally, Joyce Raanhuis's chapter, drawing on empirical data, discusses how Continuing Professional Development programmes aimed at fostering a sense of hope towards social change in a post-apartheid South Africa context are experienced by teachers in diverse school contexts.

In concluding this introduction, I should eventually like to recall the conclusions by Doug Bourn, who, at the end of the journey I have just summarized, nicely unfold in a more comprehensive way the sense of hope in a broader pedagogical context and who helps put into a larger perspective the inputs collected in this book.

Ultimately, although the contributions collected in this book come from different disciplinary fields, approaches and cultural and linguistic contexts, they all together form a coherent mosaic.

We hope that this coherent conceptual framework emerging from the book may help the reader to broaden their horizons and to see in the darkness of a world plagued by deep crises, through to a glimpse of hope, the profile of a global social justice in current education.

Note

1 ANGEL is a network established in 2017 through close cooperation between Global Education Network of Europe (GENE) and the Development Education Research Centre (DERC) at the UCL Institute of Education, and built on previous collaborations between these organizations as well as the University of Bamberg, University of Oulu, University of Bologna. The network, of which the editors of this volume serve as Chair and Coordinator, arose in response to the need to establish and reinforce existing relationships among scholars and academic institutions working in global education and related areas. It also aims to bridge the gap between researchers and policymakers in search of strong research grounding for policy development, and to establish a network among early career researchers who are currently engaged in research in fields related to Global Education.

At the time of writing this introduction (July 2022) the network has more than 800 members in 79 different countries. Several large and successful conferences have been held, and a number of publications produced. More details are available in the ANGEL website www.angel-network.net.

References

Arendt, H. (1958). *The Human Condition*. Chicago: University of Chicago Press.
Bertolini, P. (2021). *L'esistere pedagogico. Ragioni e limiti di una pedagogia come scienza fenomenologicamente fondata*. Nuova edizione a cura di M. Tarozzi. Milano: Guerini.
Bloch, E. (1986). *The Principle of Hope*. Or. Ed. 1957. 3 vols. Oxford: Basil Blackwell.
Bourn, D. (2021). 'Pedagogy of Hope: Global Learning and the Future of Education'. *International Journal of Development Education and Global Learning* 13(2): 65–78.
Catarci, M. (2016). *La pedagogia della liberazione di Paulo Freire: Educazione, intercultura e cambiamento sociale*. Milano: Franco Angeli.
Freire, P. (1972). *El mensaje de Paulo Freire. Teoria y pràtica de la liberaciòn*. Madrid: Marsiega.
Freire, P. (1992). *Pedagogia da Esperança: Um reencontro com a pedagogia do oprimido*. Rio de Janeiro: Paz e Terra.
Freire, P. (2021). *Pedagogy of Hope: Reliving Pedagogy of the Oppressed*. Or. Ed. 1992. London: Bloomsbury.
Giroux, H. (2003). 'Dystopian Nightmares and Educated Hopes: The Return of the Pedagogical and the Promise of Democracy'. *Policy Futures in Education* 1(3): 467–87.
hooks, b. (2013). *Teaching Community: A Pedagogy of Hope*. New York and London: Routledge.

Lear, J. (2006). *Radical Hope: Ethics in the Face of Cultural Devastation*. Cambridge, MA: Harvard University Press.

Mannion, G., G. Biesta, M. Priestley and H. Ross (2011). 'The Global Dimension in Education and Education for Global Citizenship: Genealogy and Critique'. *Globalisation, Societies and Education* 9(3–4): 443–56.

Oxley, L. and P. Morris (2013). 'Global Citizenship: A Typology for Distinguishing Its Multiple Conceptions'. *British Journal of Educational Studies* 61(3): 301–25.

Shultz, L. (2007). 'Educating for Global Citizenship: Conflicting Agendas and Understandings'. *Alberta Journal of Educational Research* 53(3): 248–58.

Stein, S. (2015). 'Mapping Global Citizenship'. *Journal of College and Character* 16(4): 242–52.

Swanson, D. and M. Gamal (2021). 'Global Citizenship Education / Learning for Sustainability: Tensions, "flaws", and Contradictions as Critical Moments of Possibility and Radical Hope in Educating for Alternative Futures'. *Globalisation, Societies and Education* 19(4): 456–69.

Tarozzi, M. and C. A. Torres (2016). *Global Citizenship Education and the Crises of Multiculturalism*. London: Bloomsbury.

Tarozzi, M. and C. A. Torres (2022). 'Taking Global Citizenship Education Local: A Response to the Crisis of Multiculturalism, Democracy, and Citizenship', in L. I. Misiaszek, R. F. Anrove and C. A. Torres (eds), *Emergent Trends in Comparative Education. The Dialectic of the Global and the Local*, 5th edn, 77–94. Lanham: Rowman & Littlefield.

Part I

Conceptualizing Hope and Global Social Justice

Global Citizenship Education and Sustainability as Real Utopias

Carlos Alberto Torres

Introduction

The paradigms of global citizenship and sustainability taken together require an understanding of the *Weltanschauung* of the most diverse populations with the goal to find solutions to political, environmental, socio-economic and policy in a growingly interdependent world. Yet, one may ask the following question: Are global citizenship education and sustainability, key concepts emerging from the international system, analytically, normatively and politically viable?

These concepts have been heralded and nourished by the United Nations, UNESCO and other institutions of the global system as essential elements, even more a new vision for achieving Sustainable Development Goals by 2030. As part and parcel of public policy in democratic societies, both should be included in educational curricula, citizenship training and civics education.

This book is about the politics of hope in education involving a tension between reality and utopia. The purpose of this chapter is then to explore these tensions through a variety of analytical orientations.

Analytical orientations

Possible utopias

Two central traditions inspire this chapter. First, the contributions of Eric Olin Wright about possible utopias and the work of Paulo Freire in the context of its entire oeuvre. Wright told us that his *The Real Utopias Project* in the early 1990s was 'as an attempt at deepening serious discussion of alternatives to existing structures of power, privilege and inequality' (Wright, 2010: p. 11). My assumption is that both global citizenship education and sustainability policies if they are not greenwashed seek alternatives to hegemonic models of dominance. In this way they could be treated as real utopias.

For Wright,

> The idea of Real Utopias embraces this tension between dreams and practice. It is grounded in the belief that what is pragmatically possible is not fixed independently of our imaginations, but is itself shaped by our visions. . . . What we need, then, is 'real utopias': utopian ideals that are grounded in the real potentials of humanity, utopian destinations that have accessible waystations, utopian designs of institutions that can inform our practical tasks of navigating a world of imperfect conditions for social change.[1]

But what is utopia? Utopia is the ability to envision a better future, goals that are likely never to be reality but the ability to dream for a utopia is the striving to reach it, similar to that of reaching a visible horizon. It is the path to achieving utopia which is essential in education, because it allows the possibility of transformation (Wright, 2015; 2021).[2]

However, there is a dual nature of educational practices and policies. Education has the power to sustain current oppression by reproducing the current hierarchical systems or, alternatively, promoting pedagogies which ask questions and develop praxis increasing social justice. To put it in simpler terms, education functionally navigates between social reproduction and liberation.

Paulo Freire had formed a utopian pedagogy which allowed transformation through the empowerment of the conviction that social change is possible by believing in hope and giving a pedagogy that raises critical questions of oppression and focusing on social change leading to end it. See, for instance, the work of Roberts (2015); Streck (2008); Bohorquez (2008); Van Heertum (2008); Coté, Day and de Peuter (2007).

Freire's books were in essence utopian texts in which education, as a process humanization, is the key instrument to sustain or regain the ability to dream of a utopia, and this fact needs to be amplified in society or freedoms will evaporate.

Education must be full of hope that humans are transformative and have the ability to transform their society according to the path towards their conceived utopias. Criticalness in education is essential to refuse to end utopian dreaming and take up effective political-ethical action to progress to this goal.

Freire strongly contested that utopia is not what is impossible, but instead transformation without dreaming of utopia is impossible.

'Utopia' is a term used in the sense of philosopher Paul Ricoeur (1966), as *ucronia*, that is, the symbolic representation of a time reconfigured by narrative fiction. In sociology, Immanuel Wallerstein has coined the term utopistics:

> Utopistics is the serious assessment of historical alternatives, the exercise of our judgement as to the substantive rationality of alternative possible historical systems. It is the sober, rational, and realistic evaluation of human social systems, the constraints on what they can be, and the zones open to human creativity. Not the face of the perfect (and inevitable) future, but the face of an alternative, better, and historical possible (but far from certain) future. (Wallerstein, 1998: 1–2)

Utopistics, as defined by Wallerstein, can help determine how education is dealing with the death of utopian dreaming and what could be alternatives to it – a utopian dreaming in itself (Torres and Teodoro, 2007, pages 1–8). Freire was a severe critic of the cynical fatalism of neoliberalism.

One of the most debatable concepts in Freire is his definition of *inédito viable* (or untested feasible). The 'untested feasible' then, when all is said and done, is something the utopian dreamer knows exists, but know that it will be attained only through a practice of liberation – which can be implemented by way of Freire's theory of dialogical action, or, of course (since a practice of liberation does not necessarily make an explicit appeal to that theory), by way of some other theory bearing on the same ends (Bohorquez, 2008).

Freire incentivized our theoretical and practical imagination. He sets our imagination on fire. Doing so, Freire navigated the rough waters of Ideology and Utopia in education masterfully. A contemporary philosopher to Freire's life, Paul Ricoeur, and with him, perhaps unwittingly Freire, shares the profound concept of the hermeneutic of suspicious. Ricoeur said in his *Lectures on Ideology and Utopia* that

> Imagination works in two different ways. On the one hand, imagination may function to reserve an order. In this case the function of imagination is to stage a process of identification that mirrors the order. Imagination has the appearance here of a picture. On the other hand, though, imagination may have a disruptive function; it may work as a breakthrough. Its imagine in this case is productive, an imagining of something else, the elsewhere. . . . Ideology represent the first kind of imagination; it has a function of preservation, of conservation. Utopia, in contrast represent the second kind of imagination; it is always the glance from nowhere. (Ricoeur, 1966: pp. 265–6)

Political sociology of education

The second theoretical source for this chapter draws from the tradition of the political sociology of education. I have that

> Expanding capital accumulation and increasing the legitimation of the entire mode of production seem to be the principal roles of the capitalist state, a role that is in perpetual tension. Coming to grips with this tension constitutes a principal challenge for the state. Considering educational policies, programs and practices, to inquire into the reasons for the growth of a given educational level—how programs have been devised historically, by whom, for what purposes, and how they are related to the educational clientele that they are supposed to serve—is to ask for an explanation of the determinants of educational policy formation. (Torres, 1989: p. 81)

The concept of the state is crucial to understand policy formation, but it should be placed in the context of the political regime. This, in turn, is characterized mainly through the predominant modality of recruitment or access to the highest positions and roles within the state and the current mechanisms of political representation. In purely indicative terms, the state is 'the totality of the political authority in a given society (governmental or otherwise) regardless of the level – national, subnational or local – at which it operates' (Weiler, 1983: p. 259).

At this stage of late modernity there are many forms of the state at play. From the nation-state to the federal government, to state or provincial governments, to municipal or county governments, to city governments – which are particularly relevant for global cities. In the context of the global system, the role of the United Nations system plays a major role in pushing for narratives and models of policy implementation at all the above state levels. Sustainability policies and global citizenship education policies are good examples of the new utopia of the twenty-first century.

The state's political economy is organized to support the development of a commodity-production social formation. State's economic interventionism (for instance the recently passed 1 trillion infrastructure bill signed into law by President Biden in the United States) is oriented towards performing those functions which capital is unable or unwilling to accomplish for a number of reasons, including the fragmentation and political competition of different fractions of capital, or the fact that some of those investments are of such magnitude that they will not bring about a high rate of return of their investments to corporations. Yet state interventionism must also be oriented towards strengthening the legitimacy of the ruling alliance as a prerequisite to sustaining a given pattern of capital accumulation.

At an abstract level, following Claus Offe (1973; 1984; 1985), I would argue that the state is a 'self-regulating administrative system', organized by a system of selective and self-regulating rules, a process of continued discrimination generated by the state structure. In this way, the state creates the institutional apparatus and bureaucratic organizations – often defined as institutions of the public sector – and the norms and formal and informal codes that constitute and represent the public sphere of social life. In Offe's theoretical framework, there are patterns of selectivity of state action, divided into patterns of exclusion, maintenance, dependence and legitimation; modes of state intervention, distinguishing between distributive and productive modes, which depend on the appropriation and modification of the use resources; means of state intervention, which as a general rule can be grouped in three main types (fiscal, administrative rationality and mass loyalty); and distinct methods of state intervention, including state regulation, apparatus, infrastructure investment and participation (Offe, 1975; 1984). We should add repressive policies as well (Torres, 1984: pp. 21–70).

Finally, considering authoritarian and/or illiberal democratic governments, the state may be considered a pact of domination (of the social classes or fraction of the dominant class) and the norms that guarantee the domination over the subordinate strata.

Drawing from the utopian analytical tradition, and the political sociology of education, I will discuss in this chapter two factors that will require a careful analysis. One factor is the role of utopia in our lives, seeking a solution to the pressing, clearly dangerous situations we are confronted in capitalist democracies. A second factor is to situate the beginning of the implementation of global citizenship education and sustainability encapsulated in the Sustainable Development Goals, earlier anticipated by Secretary of the UN Ban Ki-moon in his much-appreciated Global Educational First Initiative or GEFI.

There is a subsidiary question of whether the utopian goal of promoting global citizenship education and sustainable development can be achieved in the context of the current global and state systems, and the way in which educational systems reproduce or transform social realities.

This second orientation opens a conundrum that requires substantive analysis. Assuming that the capitalist state pursues two quite divergent goals of promoting capital accumulation and the overall legitimation of the mode of production, one should by definition ask what role and what state is at play in pursuing global citizenship education and sustainability education and policies.

Given the relative autonomy of the state, the state is not merely a tool or instrument of the dominant classes or fractions of classes (Torres, 2009). The task of the state is not only to promote capital accumulation and political legitimation (here the role of liberal democracy is fundamental) but also to maintain the unity and cohesion of a social formation divided in classes, interest groups and political factionalism. To this extent, key institutions to achieve this cohesiveness and unity are the system of health care and education which are (or should be) formidable contributions to the common good (Velasquez et al., 2018). In short, the state has to play a major role in promoting social cohesion as indicated by Roger Dale:

> Social cohesion is in considerable part a function of the success of the state's discharge of its legitimation problem – the outcomes and processes of the distribution of prosperity and well-being. What societal cohesion adds to this is, on the one hand, a sense of a shared community of fate – in the sense of both protection from external and internal sources of risk. On the other hand, it brings a sense of national identity – both in terms of an appreciation of the 'logic of appropriateness' of the means through which these outcomes are achieved (for instance, conceptions of democratic process) and of how they relate to and define who 'we' are. (Dale, 2007)

Is this role in cohesion exclusively the product of the nation-state, or the product of the global state represented in the United Nations, the product of local governments or even global cities which have demonstrated a larger role in promoting sustainability policies? Though there is a conflation of multiple contradictions among these sources of administrative and political power, laws and multiple layers of historical-cultural understanding, this chapter will just scratch the surface of some of these problems, but does so in a provocative and hopefully illuminating way.

Utopias of governability in the twentieth century

I suspect that some historians, if it has not been done until now, will compare the utopia of the Marxist-Leninist model of governability with the utopia of neoliberalism, as a model of governability based on the fundamentalism of the markets. The concept of governability coined by Foucault and popularized in the last part of last century is defined and refers to the way in which the state exercises control over or governs its population.

As a governability alternative, the political economy of neoliberalism emerged in full force in the last quarter of the twentieth century as a model of macroeconomic stabilization, based on privatization, free trade, the 'small state' (i.e. less relevance to the role of the state as an economic actor for economic and social regulation) and reduction of the size of the external debt.

Neoliberalism is a model of globalization from above, having impacted the last three decades of the twentieth century in a direction very different than traditional liberalism, deeply affecting education and social policies (Torres, 2009) The scholar who synthesized brilliantly this situation in the United States before the turn of the century was Michael Apple when he argued

> liberalism itself is under concerted attach from the right, from the coalition of neoconservatives, 'economic modernizers,' and new right groups who have sought to build a new consensus around their own principles. Following an strategy best called 'authoritarian populism,' this coalition has combined a 'free market ethics' with populist politics. The result has been a partial dismantling of social democratic policies that largely benefited working people, people of color, and women (these groups are obviously not mutually exclusive), the building of a closer relationship between government and the capitalist economy, and attempts to curtail liberties that had been gained in the past. (Apple, 2004: p. xxiv)

Apple was prescient in a text written twelve years before the election of Donald Trump, who showed in practice how the model of authoritarian populist, taken to the extreme, fully undermines the American democratic experiment. Internationally, neoliberalism is promoted by international organization and some professional organizations of educators and researchers. It includes a drive towards privatization and decentralization of public forms of education, a movement towards educational standards, a strong emphasis on testing and a focus on accountability. That is to say, educational neoliberal reforms are based on an economic model of educational policy (Torres, 2009; Wells, 1993; Apple, 2000).

Facing the collapse of the Soviet Union in 1989, the neoliberal model was offered to the emerging countries in Eastern Europe as the recipe to transform their economies, culture and politics with the appeal of privatization, school choice, vouchers, decentralization and, in general, the business agenda for urban school reform (Rhoads and Torres, 2006; Chomsky 2003).

Human rights: The utopia of conviviality in the twentieth century

Historian Mary Nolan (2014) finds some complementarity between human rights and the fundamentalism of the market (i.e. neoliberalism). Both reclaim their universal application and despise other ideologies. Both adhere to an individualistic methodology, criticize the state and marginalize the theme of the social. Despite this description, Mary Nolan concluded that there is not an individualized relationship between human rights and market fundamentalism (Nolan, 2014: p. 7).

In many ways, human rights represent a utopia of conviviality based on a scientific humanism as predicated from some time by UNESCO and other international organizations (Singh, 2018; Pavone, 2008).

Human rights emerge in the framework of the post-war as a utopia of conviviality, based on basic human rights that should be respected. The Universal Declaration of Human Rights is a document that marks a milestone in the history of human rights and humanity per se. Elaborated by representatives of all the regions of the world with diverse juridical and legal cultures, the Declaration was proclaimed by the General Assembly of the United Nations in Paris on 10 December 1948. As we know, the Declaration established for the first time the fundamental human rights that should be protected in the whole world and has been translated to hundreds of languages.

Though timidly defended at the beginnings, while the internationalist utopia of governability based on an illiberal democratic model of the state as a central actor began to collapse, the regimen of human rights emerged slowly both as a criticism of the utopia of real socialism and as one of the faces, perhaps the human face of globalization. However, human rights need improvement. We need to find also how to include in the Universal Declaration of Human Rights the Rights of Nature. This should be a central component of the struggle for global social justice and social justice for the planet in the twenty-first century.

A new utopia for the twenty-first century: The Sustainable Development Goals

Let us focus on the proposal for global citizenship education and sustainability which are the bedrock of the 2030 agenda. The Sustainable Development Goals (SDGs) or Global Goals are a collection of seventeen interlinked global goals designed to be a blueprint to achieve a better and more *sustainable* future for all. The SDGs were set up in 2015 by the United Nations General Assembly and are intended to be achieved by the year 2030. They are included in a UN Resolution of what is colloquially known as Agenda 2030.

A central premise of this chapter is that there is an elective affinity between global citizenship and sustainability. Following the Weberian use of the notion in the field of sociology, elective affinity is a process through which two cultural forms – religious, intellectual, political or economic – who have certain analogies, intimate kinships or meaning affinities – enter in a relationship of reciprocal attraction and influence, mutual selection, active convergence and mutual reinforcement (Lówy, 2004: p. 6).

In other terms, sustainable development is a twin sister of global citizenship education. If we are in the century of sustainability and wish to achieve the seventeen global goals, we must achieve the twin goals of sustainability and global citizenship.

Sustainable development has been a concept utilized to inform thinking regarding various policies and sectors addressing the world's most pressing issues (climate change, poverty, food security, water quality, gender equality, etc.). Although the question of sustainability has risen to the top of policy agendas worldwide, there is limited theory-driven and empirical research regarding the importance that sustainable development has for education policy and practice.

Many governments have endorsed the UN Paris Climate Agreement and its guidelines for sustainable development. It is well known that the Paris Agreement is a global climate effort bringing all nations into a common cause to undertake ambitious efforts to combat climate change and adapt to its effects, with enhanced support to assist developing countries to do so.

There are key concepts developed as part of the 4.7 Goal of the UN Sustainable Development Goals (SDGs) for 2015–2030. The first concept is education for sustainable development that is founded on need to defend, protect and enhance the global commons. Moreover, this model of education is concentrated on moving our teaching training programmes from an anthropocentric model into a bio-centric model of education and training, endorsing a bio-centric ethics. The second one, which dovetails nicely with the first, is global citizenship education (Torres, 2017; Tarozzi and Torres, 2016). Both twin concepts may help to advance the defence of the global commons and social justice for the planet.

Global citizenship education is intimately related to the traditional discussion of what is citizenship education, which has been traditionally associated to 'civic education', that is, the teaching of constitutional democracy and 'obedience' to the nation-state laws. Three categories are linked to civics education. The first one is *civic knowledge*, which in the context of constitutional democracy entails the knowledge of basic concepts informing the practice of democracy such as public elections, majority rule, citizenship rights and obligations, constitutional separation of power and the placement of democracy in a market economy, used as the basic premises of civil society. The second category associated with citizenship building is *civic skills*, which usually means the intellectual and participatory skills that facilitate citizenship's judgement and actions. The last category is *civic virtues*, usually defined in Western societies around liberal principles such as self-discipline, compassion, civility, tolerance and respect.

However, within the context of the current era globalization(s) and its complex social, economic, political, cultural and environmental impacts, many questions regarding the nature of citizenship education and citizenship building remain: In what ways will global citizenship education be included into definitions of citizenship building? How has the concept of GCE been incorporated in the contemporary discourses circulating and competing in the international system, governments and academia? What is the role of UNESCO and the UN in promoting GCE and Education for Sustainable Development? Why there is an *elective affinity*[3] between the concepts of global citizenship education and sustainable development?[4] These are some of the themes that had been addressed in many publications, connecting with the dominant agendas in the multiple globalizations that we are experiencing and slowly but surely altering the way we understand education and learning in the twenty-first century (Tarozzi and Torres, 2016; Torres, 2017).

These themes are also connected to the controversies around citizenship building, diversity and the dilemmas of multiculturalism, and interact with the responsibilities of universities and adult learning systems in promoting citizenship building. There are multiple layers for understanding the meta-theoretical, theoretical and empirical implementation of global citizenship education.

The movement towards global citizenship education and education for sustainable development is impacting the institutional life, actions, policies and practices of Ministries and Secretariats of Education and Ministries of Foreign Affairs of the entire world, and therefore impacting the way teacher's training and teachers are working in diverse environments. It is imperative to know more of how programmes of teacher training are incorporating these topics in their curriculum.

The emergence of post-national citizenships questions the principles and values as well as the rights and responsibilities in which national citizenships were founded. Does this new reality reflect a crisis of classical liberalism and particularly of its neoliberal declination facing the new challenges of globalization and diversity? Multiculturalism, one of the answers to the dilemmas of citizenship and diversity, shows signs of crisis. In these contexts concepts such as cosmopolitan democracies and global citizenship education have been invoked as solutions to the possible demise of the regulatory power of the nation-state and failed citizenship worldwide. The implementation of the Global Education First Initiative (GEFI) in 2012 by the UN Secretary Ban Ki-moon sets a new programme for education, where global citizenship education is predicated as a resource to enhance global peace, sustainability of the planet and the defence of global commons.

Education and theories of social and cultural reproduction

Education is not a panacea to solve the ills of society or bring about prosperity, social mobility or income distribution. While the political sociology of education has indicated all these possibilities, the truth is that we need to consider what exactly education system does and how it may thwart the possible utopia of Sustainable Development Goals.

This analysis will be presented in a form of four short theses. I am aware that these theses as presented herein perhaps overemphasize some of the processes, routines, codes and practices that take place in education settings and that had been so well analysed through the interactions of code and control in class societies and its linguistic codes so well represented in Basil Bernstein's theory about class, codes and controls (Bernstein, 1997; Morais, 2007: pp. 121–30), as well as Pierre Bourdieu and Jean Claude Passeron theory of cultural capital (1977). Needless to say, in what follows I want to be more provocative than evocative.

Thesis one

Schooling justifies and reproduces inequalities in capitalist societies. A number of elements produce this outcome, including school tracking, racist behaviour, elite networking, disciplinary sanctions, lack of relevance of subject matter in people's life, inefficient resource allocation and lack of efficacy of schooling as measured in high dropout and repetition rates or irrelevant pro forma learning. Be that as it may, yet Apple's nuanced understanding indicates that these functions do not exhaust what schools do: 'Accumulation, legitimation, and production represent structural pressures on schools, not foregone conclusions' (Apple, 1986: 9-11).

Thesis two

If thesis one can be documented empirically, then schooling reproduces authoritarian, classist, racist, homophobic and patriarchal relationships in capitalist social formations. This is the result, among other variables, of the authoritarianism of administrators and school bureaucrats and is compounded by the authoritarianism of parents, politicians and the authoritarianism of knowledge production, distribution, exchange and consumption once it is defined as 'official knowledge' (Apple, 1998; Apple, 2000). This analysis would emphasize Bourdieu's arguments about symbolic violence (Bourdieu and Passeron, 1977).

Thesis three

Schooling and knowledge are unable to counteract the commodification of social relationships because the capitalist culture creates nothing by a culture of consumption. There are, however, contradictions. With a lovely figurative language Hartmut Rosa argues that

> For a considerable and growing part of the libido in late modern subjects seem to be directed nor toward consuming or using purchase items, but toward the act of purchase at such. Year after year, people in the affluent societies buy more books, more music instruments, more telescopes, tennis rackets, and pianos, but they read and listen to them, look thorough and play with them less and less. (Rosa, 2019: p. 254)

Thesis four

Schools have lost their edge as state instruments acting 'in locus parenti' helping children and youth to become more socialized and cultivated in the disciplines of the spirit of the body. In short, a most meaningful cultural creation of the nineteenth century and modernism may have become totally irrelevant in the twenty-first century, despite Gramsci's incisive thesis that 'Every time the question of language surface, in one way or another, it means . . . to reorganize the cultural hegemony' (Gramsci, 2000: p. 357).

What is to be done?

The spirit of this chapter is to suggest that we need to seek a new utopia between Reproduction and Liberation without giving up on the useful analytical model for social research of social reproduction so aptly implemented in the political sociology of education: Is it possible to implement GCE (global citizenship education) in our educational systems, including schooling, adult learning education and the politics of culture in late capitalism, considering the aforementioned four theses of the impact of social reproduction in schooling and education in general? How can we reconcile the ideology of the different models of the nation-state, regional state, municipal state and global cities' administrations with the utopia of the United Nations systems embodied in the Sustainable Development Goals?

In terms of research agendas, from the twin perspective of education for sustainable development and global citizenship education, the following questions merit attention:

1. What are the perceptions, aspirations, expectations and values of student-teachers, professors and administrators of teacher education programmes regarding issues of sustainability and GCE?
2. To what extent does a culture of sustainability exist within the work of teacher training institutions, and if so, how is it represented within curriculum, instruction and learning?
3. What are the challenges and controversies in teaching sustainability and GCE?
4. To define the best policies, practices and values of sustainability and GCE, what are the similarities and/or the differences between institutions with regard to the planning, teaching, evaluating and perceptions of sustainability and GCE?
5. This research will wonder if these programmes of sustainability seek to identify the principle of resonance between nature and human beings in modern culture, as strongly suggested by Hartmut Rosa in his analysis of axes of resonance (Rosa, 2019: p. 271).

Writing the first and the last sentence of any essay is the most difficult one. Let me conclude with the words of poet Martin Espada:

> The imagination is absolutely critical to political activism, illuminating the vision of a world that does not yet exist. Vision is hope, and hope is fuel for the activist. What we imagine now might become concrete reality in this lifetime or the next. There are times when we wait decades or centuries for change, and then suddenly (or so it appears), there is change. We must be able to envision a world that isn't here yet. Those who do so will be accused of utopianism. Guilty as charged. This reminds me of Eduardo Galeano's 'Window on Utopia'. Galeano writes: 'Utopia is on the horizon. I move two steps closer; it moves two steps away. I walk ten steps, and the horizon runs ten steps further away. As much as I walk, I'll never reach it. What good is utopia? That's what: it's good for walking.' Even if we don't get where we want to go, the vision moves us in the direction of justice, and ultimately makes for a more just society. (in Masciotra, 2021)

Notes

1. https://www.ssc.wisc.edu/~wright/OVERVIEW.html
2. Four projects are listed by Wright as examples of possible utopias, including participatory city budgeting, Wikipedia, the Mondragon workers cooperative and unconditional basic income. https://www.aacademica.org/erik.olin.wright/46.pdf. See also Wright, (2015; 2021).
3. The concept of elective affinity is used in three places by Max Weber in *The Protestant Ethic*. 'Weber does not define it, but one could propose the following definition, based on the weberian use of the notion: elective affinity is a process through which two cultural forms – religious, intellectual, political or economic – who have certain analogies, intimate kinships or meaning affinities, enter in a relationship of reciprocal attraction and influence, mutual selection, active convergence and mutual reinforcement. Without substituting other analytical, explanatory or comprehensive paradigms, elective affinity may offer a new approach, until now hardly explored, in the field of sociology of culture.' The Concept of Elective Affinity according to Max Weber (Löwy, 2004; p.6; d'Avray, 2010).
4. Goal 4. Ensure inclusive and equitable quality education and promote lifelong learning opportunities for all. Target 4.7: By 2030, ensure that all learners acquire the knowledge and skills needed to promote sustainable development, including, among others, through education for sustainable development and sustainable lifestyles,

human rights, gender equality, promotion of a culture of peace and non-violence, global citizenship and appreciation of cultural diversity and of culture's contribution to sustainable development.
https://sdgs.un.org/goals.

References

Apple, M. (1986). 'Ideology and Practice in Schooling'. *Boston University Journal of Education* 168(1): 9–11.
Apple, M. (1998). *Official Knowledge: Democratic Education in a Conservative Age*. New York: Routledge.
Apple, M. (2000). *Educating the "Right" Way*. New York: Routledge.
Apple, M. (2004). *Ideology and Curriculum*. Third edition. New York: Routledge.
Bernstein, B. (1997). *Class, Codes and Control, Vol. III: Towards a Theory of Educational Transmissions*. 2nd edn. London: Routledge& Kegan, Paul.
Bohorquez, I. (2008). 'Untested Feasibility in Paulo Freire: Behind the Profile of a Dream', in C. A. Torres and P. Noguera (eds), *Social Justice Education for Teachers. Paulo Freire and Education as a Possible Dream*, 177–89. Rotterdam, The Netherlands: Sense Publishers.
Bourdieu, P. and J. C. Passeron (1977). *Reproduction in Education, Society and Culture*, trans. R. Nice. London: Sage.
Chomsky, N. (2003). *Hegemony or Survival. America's Quest for Global Dominance*. New York: Henry Holt and Company.
Coté, M., R. J. F. Day and G. De Peuter, eds (2007). *Utopian Pedagogy. Radical Experiments against Neoliberal Globalization*. Toronto, Buffalo and London: University of Toronto Press.
D'Avray, D. L. (2010). *Rationalities in History. A Weberian Essay in Comparison*, 30. Cambridge: Cambridge University Press.
Dale, R. (2007). 'Globalization and the Rescaling of Educational Governance: A Case of Sociological Ectopia', in C. A. Torres and A. Teodoro (eds), *Critique and Utopia: New Developments in the Sociology of Education in the Twenty-First Century*, 25–42. Lanham: Rowman and Littlefield.
Gramsci, A. (2000). *The Antonio Gramsci Reader: Selected Writings 1916–1935*, ed. David Forgacs, with a new introduction by Eric Hobsbawm, 357. New York: New York University Press.
Lówy, M. (2004). 'The Concept of Elective Affinity According to Max Weber'. *Archives de sciences sociales des religions* 127(3): 6.
Masciotra, D. (2021). 'Poet Martín Espada: The Imagination is Absolutely Critical to Political Activism'. *Salon*, 31 March 2021. https://www.salon.com/2021/03/31/martin-espada-floaters-politics-poetry-activism/ (Retrieved 31 July 2022).

Morais, A. M. (2007). 'Basil Bernstein and the Sociology of Education', in C. A. Torres and A. Teodoro (eds), *Critique and Utopia: New Developments in the Sociology of Education in the Twenty-First Century*, 121–30. Lanham: Rowman and Littlefield.

Nolan, M. (2014). 'Human Rights and Market Fundamentalism'. Max Weber Lecture Series, MWP /02, page 7. https://cadmus.eui.eu/handle/1814/69060; https://www.youtube.com/watch?v=JJKgK4ZxLxs

Offe, C. (1973). 'The Capitalist State and the Problem of Policy Formation', in N. Lindberg, R. Alford, C. Crouch and C. Offe (eds), *Stress and Contradictions in Modern Capitalism*, 125–44. Lexington: Heath.

Offe, C. (1984). *Contradictions of the Welfare State*, ed. J. Keane. London: Hutchinson.

Offe, C. (1985). *Disorganized Capitalism: Contemporary Transformation of Work and Politics*. Cambridge: Polity Press.

Pavone, V. (2008). *From the Labyrinth of the World to the Paradise of the Heart. Science and Humanism in UNESCO's Approach to Globalization*. Lanham: Lexington Books.

Rhoads, R. and C. A. Torres, eds (2006). *The University, State and Markets. The Political Economy of Globalization in the Americas*. Stanford: Stanford University Press.

Ricoeur, P. (1966). *Lectures on Ideology and Utopia*, ed. Jorge H. Taylor. New York: Columbia University Press.

Roberts, P. (2015). 'Paulo Freire and Utopian Education'. *Review of Education, Pedagogy, and Cultural Studies* 37(5): 376–92. doi: 10.1080/10714413.2015.1091256. To link to this article: http://dx.doi.org/10.1080/10714413.2015.1091256

Rosa, H. (2019). *Resonance. A Sociology of Our Relationship to the World*. Cambridge: Polity Press.

Singh, J. P. (2018). 'UNESCO: Scientific Humanism and its Impact on Multilateral Diplomacy'. *Global Policy* 9: 53–9.

Streck, D. (2008). 'The Utopian Legacy: Rousseau and Freire', in C. A. Torres and P. Noguera (eds), *Social Justice Education for Teachers. Paulo Freire and Education as a Possible Dream*, 69–80. Rotterdam: Sense Publishers.

Tarozzi, M. and C. A. Torres (2016). *Global Citizenship Education and the Crisis of Multiculturalism: Comparative Perspectives*. London: Bloomsbury Publishing.

Torres, C. A. (1984). 'The Political Economy of Adult Education in Latin America'. *Canadian and International Education* 13(2): 61–80.

Torres, C. A. (1989). 'The Capitalist State and Public Policy Formation. Framework for a Political Sociology of Educational Policy Making'. *British Journal of Sociology of Education* 10(1): 81–102.

Torres, C. A. (2009). *Globalizations and Education. Collected Essays on Class, Race, Gender, and the State,* intro. Michael W. Apple, afterword by Pedro Demo. New York and London: Teachers College Press-Columbia University.

Torres, C. A. (2017). *Theoretical and Empirical Foundations of Global Citizenship Education*. New York: Routledge/Taylor and Francis.

Torres, C. A. and A. Teodoro, eds (2007). *Critique and Utopia. New Developments in the Sociology of Education*. Lanham: Rowman and Littlefield.

Van Heertum, R. (2008). 'Freire, Apathy and the Decline of the American Left: The Future of Utopias in the Age of Cynicism', in C. A. Torres and P. Noguera (eds), *Social Justice Education for Teachers. Paulo Freire and Education as a Possible Dream*, 129–46. Rotterdam: Sense Publishers.

Velasquez, M., C. Andre, T. Shanks, S.J. and Michael J. Meyer (2018). *The Common Good*. http://www.scu.edu/ethics/practicing/decision/commongood.html (Retrieved 31 July 2022).

Wallerstein, I. (1998). *Utopistics, or Historical Choices of the Twenty-First Century*. New York: New Press.

Weiler, H. N. (1983). 'Legalization, Expertise, and Participation: Strategies of Compensatory Legitimation in Educational Policy'. *Comparative Education Review* 27(2): 259–77.

Wells, A. S. (1993) 'The Sociology of School Choice: Why Some Win and Other Lose in the Educational Marketplace', in E. Rasell and R. Rothstein (eds), *School Choice: Examining the Evidence*, 29–48. Washington, DC: Economic Policy Institute.

Wright, E. O. (2010). *Envisioning Real Utopias*. London: Verso. https://www.aacademica.org/erik.olin.wright/46.pdf (Retrieved 31 July 2022).

Wright, E. O. (2015). 'Eric Olin Wright: Real Utopias'. https://futureswewant.net/erik-olin-wright-real-utopias/

Wright, E. O. (2021). *How to Be an Anticapitalist in the Twenty-First Century*. London: Verso.

2

Global Citizenship Education in Times of Pandemic

New Approaches for Transforming the World

Manuela Mesa

Introduction

One of the concerns of the last decade has been defining the role of education in today's world. It should be analysed by what kind of knowledge and skills people need to understand global problems and to actively participate in the pursuit of inclusive and fair solutions. Pandemics, climate change, poverty and inequality, migration, the refugee crisis caused by armed conflict and violence are issues that affect people locally, but whose causes and effects are explained by global dynamics. Each of these issues should be addressed in the educational field as part of the lifelong learning process that every person should receive.

The social, economic and political phenomena affecting citizens have their roots beyond the borders of the nation-state. The global pandemic has caused a collapse in production and employment which has pushed millions of people into poverty (UN, 2020). This situation reflected the global risks that various international studies and reports produced by academia and foresight centres had predicted for years (Sanahuja, 2020: pp. 31–2). However, the pandemic caught us unprepared and demonstrated the importance of considering scientific findings. This does apply not only to new health risks but to other threats, such as global warming, that require urgent action to ensure the survival of the planet. More than two decades ago, sociologist Ulrich Beck (2002) defined the global risk society as those risks that go beyond the confines of the state and its jurisdiction, and therefore require cooperative and concerted action at both global and local levels.

The pandemic has exacerbated some previously existing crises. Decades of neoliberal policies and the cycle of austerity that accompanied the 2008 economic crisis have caused socio-economic inequality and the weakening of health systems and public policies. Further, governmental policies that have ignored the role of multilateralism and have acted outside the institution have weakened global governance structures such as the United Nations and regional organizations. This has significantly reduced the global capacity to respond to global challenges.

One of the characteristics of the global risk society, according to Beck (2002), is the unequal distribution of its consequences among countries, territories and social groups. In a more integrated and interdependent world, global risks such as pandemics or climate change know no borders; however, these risks have a very unequal impact, defined by differences in socio-economic context and the capacity and response models implemented in each country.

The pandemic has shown those with a higher standard of living experience a much lower impact. Their situation allows them to isolate and work virtually from home; to travel by car instead of facing risk on public transport and to earn a living wage. But those who live in small and humble homes, who work in the informal sector and cannot afford to be idle for weeks at a time, and who travel in overcrowded buses are more at risk and vulnerable. Further, in many cases they do not have the health insurance that would cover their care in the event of infection. These inequalities present in all societies have shown that the consequences of the pandemic are not the same for everyone, not only within countries but also between countries.

Likewise, the closure of schools and universities due to the pandemic made educational inequalities much more visible. This situation has demonstrated how sociocultural background and family income are determining factors in access to education in times of pandemic. For example, having access to a public or private school will influence students' opportunities; moreover, those who have a computer and an internet connection will be able to continue their learning, while those without computers will have to wait for schools to reopen. Schools were closed for almost two years, and this significantly impacted the learning of the most vulnerable groups.

The pandemic caused an unprecedented disruption to education. In mid-July 2020, schools were closed in more than 160 countries, affecting more than one billion students (United Nations, 2020). For example, 45 per cent of the population in Latin America and the Caribbean does not have access to the internet, only four out of ten households have fixed broadband connection and only 50 per cent of the population has access to mobile service (UNESCO-IESALC, 2020; UNESCO, 2020). This situation is very dire, given that education is key to personal development and the future of societies and that it offers opportunities and reduces inequalities.

This chapter addresses the elements that education for global citizenship brings in the context of pandemic and post-pandemic society, from the perspective of learning, skills and values, as well as the role that education can play as a tool for social transformation. The experience of this pandemic and post-pandemic offers the possibility of incorporating new global learning, promoting values of solidarity and reviewing our priorities to achieve a more just, inclusive, solidarity-based and sustainable world. Global citizenship education has significant experience in incorporating new visions from a global and local perspective. There is moreover around the world networks of teachers linked to global citizenship education who are committed to transformative education, based on the development of innovative methodologies.

Global citizenship education: A disruptive concept in times of involution

In a time of change and great complexity, education faces the dilemma of either being a factor that reproduces dominant values and legitimizes the *status quo* or becoming an engine of change, seeking to transform an unfair and unequal world. As the Delors Report states, education is an indispensable factor for humanity to achieve the ideals of peace, freedom and social justice; education is a way to achieve a more authentic and harmonious human development, and is thus a tool to reduce poverty, exclusion, oppression and war. As such, education has a specific responsibility in building a more solidarity-based world (Delors, 1997).

The concept of citizenship has evolved throughout history and is related to the degree of equality in a society with the distribution of power and access to certain goods. Since Classical Antiquity, citizenship was based around a territory and a set of public and private goods, which necessitated a system of coexistence that defined ways of life. Citizenship conferred rights and obligations and provided a collective identity.

The concept of citizenship refers to an individual's status in relation to the community of which they are a part and with which they identify, recognizing themself as part of it. Consequently, the constituent elements of that community are assumed as one's own. As Adela Cortina (2000) states, the full concept of citizenship integrates a legal status, a set of rights, a moral status, a set of responsibilities and a collective identity in which the person feels part of a whole, with which they share a culture and values.

With the French and American revolutions, the notion of citizenship became linked to the ideas of a republic and a constitution and based upon place of birth (*ius soli*). This did not lead to the complete equality of rights, as slaves, women and non-landowners would not receive political rights until much later. In the nineteenth century, a set of nationalist ideologies emerged that connected state, nation and 'people' by considering that all citizens of a state belong to the same nation, united by ethnicity, language, culture and a common past (*ius sanguinis*).

These two legal notions of *ius soli* and *ius sanguinis*, which support different legal norms about naturalization and citizenship, illustrate the persistence of both conceptions of citizenship.

With the end of the Cold War and the intensification of globalization processes, a new notion of citizenship has emerged: global citizenship. Increasing interdependence and the transnationalization of political, economic and social interactions, as well as the growing influence of global media and social networks have changed people's experiences and the idea of political community linked exclusively to a specific territory and the idea of the nation-state. The lines between the global and the local are becoming increasingly blurred. People can participate in the various territorial and political communities that affect them – local, national and supranational – and thus can access a variety of forms of political participation and spheres of citizenship.

One definition of global citizenship has been linked to proposals for cosmopolitan democracy (Held and MacGrew, 2001; Cortina, 2000). The concepts of 'cosmopolitan democracy' and 'global citizenship' have an important normative dimension. They are ideals, or an ethical, moral and political imperative, for the reconstruction of democratic theory and practice in the age of globalization. In a globalized world, if we do not want to betray our own 'values', should we not be concerned about what happens to our own 'values' and shouldn't we be concerned about what is happening beyond our immediate environment?

Global citizenship is also related to the conception of social justice (Murillo and Hernández, 2011). Social justice is defined in relation to three concepts: distribution, recognition and participation (Rawls, 1971; Nussbaum, 2006; Fraser and Honneth, 2003). Distribution refers to the goods, material and cultural resources and capabilities in a society. Cultural recognition and respect are fundamental to achieving just relations. Finally, participation in decisions that affect people's lives is essential to building a just society (Young, 1990).

Global citizenship therefore transcends state borders and maintains an international reach. As Silveira (2000) states, 'in order not to be exclusive, citizenship must be progressively denationalized, deterritorialized, democratized, and based on criteria that respects human dignity, equal rights, and respect for differences' (Silveira, 2000: p. 32). The transnational and cosmopolitan should be conceived as an integral part of the redefinition of the national and the local, which are not opposed to each other, but related, and one refers to the other (Beck, 2005: p. 81). Global citizenship is about becoming citizens of the world without losing the link to the local or national community, through forms of local political participation that connect with global demands for peace, justice, democracy and equality. In short, it is about reaffirming that the individual has inherent rights that go beyond borders and should therefore be guaranteed by the international community. It is about building a 'universal us' that is inclusive and free of prejudice.

In this shaping of the concept of global citizenship, it is necessary to incorporate the gender perspective, and in particular, women who have traditionally been excluded from the fulfilment of their rights. The redefinition of citizenship oriented towards the expansion of rights cannot ignore a normative construction of the feminine that restricts the civil, political and social rights of half of society (Cobo, 2008: p. 46). To promote a fair and egalitarian democracy and full citizenship, it is necessary to promote rights and social and economic policies of redistribution and recognition that reduce inequalities, especially those that have structural causes and affect women (Cobo, 2008: p. 21). This requires an interpretative framework that makes visible the effects of discrimination and that incorporates women in the exercise of citizenship.

A way of looking at and knowing the world: Dilemmas and proposals

Global citizenship education provides knowledge and tools to inform people about their rights, but also to promote critical awareness of the social, economic and political dynamics that explain why these rights are not fulfilled. This is highly relevant in a context of extraordinary change and uncertainty in the face of global challenges for which different responses are possible. On one hand, responses oriented towards the protection of national interests, towards isolation, or the construction of walls that cannot solve global problems; on the other, responses that seek to move towards the elaboration of proposals that pursue the expansion of rights for all people and the consolidation of multilateralism as a form of global governance. Global citizenship can help to promote social justice and encourage the recognition of all people and the redistribution of resources and participation in society.

Another dilemma also arises: How to overcome the discourses of polarization and tension and replace them with dialogue, listening and argumentation? As Emcke (2019) considers, on the one hand it is about overcoming stereotypes based on false dichotomies which restrict the space for debate and force us to choose between what are believed to be mutually exclusive options but in reality are not; it is about promoting thinking that is open to curiosity, to new ideas and arguments from which we can learn, understand and discover (Emcke, 2019). On the other hand, it is about addressing cultural diversity as a factor of enrichment and progress, rather than as a space for confrontation between different cultural worlds, marked by the native versus the foreign. It is very important to promote educational proposals aimed at overcoming the identity markers that separate communities and that marginalize 'different' people.

These dilemmas present a major challenge for global citizenship education, committed to social transformation and social justice. Global citizenship education has to offer cognitive keys that contribute to overcoming exclusionary nationalism, or a nationalism that does not recognize the rights of foreign people and is based on a hateful, racist and xenophobic discourse. It is a matter of promoting citizenship that respects diversity and encouraging the shaping of open societies with cosmopolitan values in which multiple and dynamic identities coexist and change with time. It is about recognizing unity in our diversity, bearing in mind that we are more equal than different (de Paz, 2007: p. 70).

Global citizenship education proposes a way of looking at and knowing the world, addressing complexity, incorporating strategies that help to better understand global problems and developing actions to transform them based on justice and solidarity. It is about prioritizing the interdependence we have as human beings, the mutual link between people. It is about recognizing the vulnerability of people and the importance of care as an essential task in sustaining life. All of this allows us to try to overcome individualism as a society, to give way to the collective and the common good in a complex context that requires collective intelligence to overcome global problems.

Global citizenship education must be an effort to consolidate a new way of thinking, understanding and living the world, starting with the individual and continuing with others in a horizontal way, networking, giving confidence, security and authority to individuals and societies, exchanging with each other, overcoming mistrust, helping to mobilize people and transcend their differences, and looking at the reality of the world to reach a global perspective that can then be shared by as many people as possible.

New interpretative frameworks

Global citizenship education requires new interpretative frameworks to address global issues affecting humanity. This implies a process of redefining content in a way that enables critical understanding of the phenomena that have emerged due to globalization processes related to risks and responsiveness. It also requires the incorporation of new analytical categories to help interpret these new realities. New concepts are required to name global phenomena and to interpret them based upon cognitive frameworks that connect knowledge with capacities and values, thus shaping emancipatory narratives that put human beings at the centre.

To do so, it is necessary to deconstruct old concepts and re-signify them, overcoming essentialisms and determinisms that limit analysis and understanding. As Maria Novo (2017) argues, it is very important to overcome the mechanistic, reductionist and deterministic approaches of science, which are based on the old dual view of modernity (person-nature; mind-body). It is time to move towards a collective construction of knowledge that incorporates the knowledge of multiple actors, that seeks interdisciplinarity, a holistic vision and positive synergies; this is a knowledge that is subject to questions that can be applied in a given context and from a global approach and that can generate changes and transform reality. It is also needed to take into consideration the spatial dimension, or the relationships between the local and the global, and the temporal dimension, or the relationships between past, present and future in the analysis of global processes at political, social, cultural, environmental and technological levels (Mesa, 2019; 2020).

It is also important to incorporate what the sociologist Boaventura Sousa Santos (2011) has called the 'Epistemologies of the South', which offer a critical diagnosis of the present and propose alternatives for reconstructing, formulating and legitimizing actions aimed at a more fair and more free society. This means recognizing the diversity of knowledge, particularly that of indigenous peoples and diverse cultures, which have traditionally been excluded and disregarded, as well as the knowledge and experiences of women. This knowledge is essential to address the complexity of the present moment and in the pursuit of solutions.

For years, the feminist movement has been calling for 'care' to be placed at the centre of public policies and for all life-sustaining tasks to be properly valued. The pandemic has shown how undervalued and precarious 'care' is, and how it is mostly assumed by women. During the pandemic, the enormous burdens and risks assumed by women in care work in the home, in cleaning activities and in educational activities, who are often poor, migrant and lower-class women, have been exacerbated. This situation has renewed the importance of the recognition, value and equal distribution of these tasks. For example, in the field of health, women represent 70 per cent of the world's health personnel and 80 per cent of nursing services. They have been vital in planning and reorganizing the health system to cope with the increase in the number of infected people. Women have been on the front lines, taking the greatest risks, often with lower pay and poorer conditions, and the speed and efficiency with which they have acted has saved many lives (Oxfam, 2020; OECD, 2020). This work must be recognized and provided with the necessary financial resources.

The defence of women's rights and the principle of equality in development and peace building, as well as overcoming sexist and discriminatory stereotypes are all essential elements to incorporate into educational practice. It is necessary to show the contributions women have made in different fields of knowledge as important references in society. It is a question of building equality based upon the diversity of experiences and the recognition of women's authority, knowledge and know-how. To this end, the promotion of educational action based on co-education will be necessary, which will allow for a deeper learning of models based on equality between women and men (Asociación Pro Derechos Humanos, 1994; Cobo, 2008).

Finally, an interpretative framework that incorporates an inclusive and pacifist narrative is needed. Extreme right-wing groups have used the pandemic to expand hateful discourse, to stigmatize migrants and impoverished people, and to feed fear and anxiety. Their goal has been to gain power and weaken democracy. The pandemic cannot be used by governments or extreme-right groups to restrict rights and impose authoritarian measures which have nothing to do with managing the virus. A framework is needed that confronts fear and offers responses based on citizens' responsibility and commitment.

This requires understanding the importance of deconstructing a militaristic mindset that legitimizes the institutional theft and misuse of resources in favour of the industry of war and death, and to the detriment of human life, social justice, equity and nature. Weapons have been of little use in confronting the pandemic and ensuring our security (Mesa and Alonso, 2020: p. 90). We have moved from fighting the virus to cohabiting with it, with the resulting protective measures that this situation requires.

It is needed to delegitimize the logic of security, which entails enormous risks and implies individual and collective subordination to a higher authority, as opposed to an alternative of human cooperation. The redefinition of the classic concept of security to the concept of human security is also necessary, which promotes a focus on the planet's needs to sustain life. As has been pointed out in peace research, peace goes beyond the absence of violence and is linked to the capacity to transform conflicts through dialogue, empathy, cooperation and the promotion of universal values associated with justice, solidarity and respect for human rights (Fisas, 1998; Galtung, 1969; Lederach, 2007, Martinez-Guzman, 1995).

A society is safer when it is more equal and is built by ensuring the right to live with dignity, with access to health, education and housing, among other needs. Overcoming the structural violence that, as Johan Galtung (1969) said, prevents people from being able to develop in an integral way is essential. Further, it is important to confront symbolic and cultural violence that denies differences and diversity, that legitimizes the use of force and imposition, and that addresses dissent through polarization, hate speech and construction of the enemy.

In short, it will be necessary to promote a narrative that transcends hegemonic, patriarchal, neo-capitalist, militarist and colonial visions and that sets the basis for the future we want to build together and counterbalances the failures of the system. There are many people working from a feminist, solidarity and human development perspective. It will be necessary to give visibility to these initiatives in order to build a counter-hegemonic narrative that shows the future we want.

Global citizenship education: A way of doing and behaving in the face of global challenges

Global citizenship education proposes a way of 'doing and behaving' in the face of the great global challenges. It brings into play all the abilities human beings have to 'make peace', in the words of Martinez-Guzmán (2001), founder of the

Chair of Philosophy for Peace at the Jaume I University in Castellón. It is a way of 'networking', connecting and linking those who unite locally and internationally propose overcoming the pandemic and building a more cohesive society, in addition to promoting resilience, building from adversity and exploring new paths and ways of action.

The global pandemic has been an extraordinary challenge from which we need to learn to build a more resilient and safe society. As Boaventura Sousa Santos (2020) argues in his latest work, *The Cruel Pedagogy of the Virus*, this pandemic allows us the return of the state and the community and raises questions about the impact on people's lives of the privatization of collective social goods, such as health, education, drinking water, electricity and social security. The pandemic also allows us to learn that alternatives are possible and that societies can adapt and seek the common good, transforming the ways of living, producing, consuming and living together in the coming years (Sousa Santos, 2020: pp. 73–9).

Many people and social organizations have mobilized to meet the needs of vulnerable groups, based on solidarity and mutual support. Thousands of educational, cultural, artistic and economic initiatives have been promoted from all sides, bringing people together and creating new networks and spaces for collaboration. There is always someone who is able to find a way out of the worst situations, to generate a solution or to take action in a way that contributes to improving and offering well-being to the lives of others. This is what the peace researcher Juan Gutierrez has called 'strands of living peace': 'that network of threads that we human beings generate and enjoy by supporting one another; it is the act of pouring one's own life into the lives of others for their own good'. These are actions that, building from adversity, promote resilience and explore new paths and ways of doing (Fernández-Savater, 2016).

Some of the most innovative educational strategies are related to the concept of 'moral imagination' proposed by Jean Paul Lederach (2007). This concept proposes exploring new territories which transcend violence and injustice, break the mould and broaden the societal vision to go beyond the idea of dualities: good-evil, mind-body, nature-progress and so on. These dualities reflect the 'art of creating what does not exist' and by nature has a performative function that transforms reality. This pandemic has challenged some of the economic and social assumptions that were previously stagnant and therefore also has opened up spaces for new scenarios, inconceivable until recently, on which to build alternatives.

Finally, education for global citizenship proposes a way of 'being' in the world, feeling part of a global community and building a 'universal we' with the agency to act and commit ourselves to the future. There is nothing more transformative than calling for hope and optimism in a collective and common project for the future.

The construction of this 'universal us' requires strengthening the ties and links between people in their diversity, promoting horizontal, open and democratic structures, with relationships based on co-responsibility.

Conclusion

This chapter examined the role of education in the current international context, which is characterized by deep changes and a process of involution. The rise of extreme right-wing supremacist movements in different parts of the world, as part of a global trend, has brought back old ghosts and given way to hate speech, polarization, racism, xenophobia, misogyny, lack of solidarity and the criminalization of social movements in a context of securitization and rearmament unprecedented since the end of the Cold War.

In this situation, education for global citizenship becomes not only needed but a totally disruptive proposal that offers alternatives to this situation. It raises awareness that we live in an unfair and unequal world, which requires urgent change in the political, economic, social, cultural and environmental spheres. It seeks to promote a citizenship that can mobilize to promote human rights, the strengthening of local-global democracy, the decrease of economic inequality, the inequality between men and women, the peaceful resolution of conflicts and environmental sustainability.

Global citizenship education proposes a way of 'looking', 'doing' and 'being' to respond to the systemic crisis we are facing. It seeks to promote a new language and offer conceptual, ethical, analytical and aesthetic tools that facilitate decision-making in the face of complex problems, that help to imagine new life scenarios and that help to manage uncertainty and fear, replacing them for responsibility and commitment.

This education is a matter of defining how we as human beings will face our role on the planet and how we bring into play our capabilities to discover and 'imagine' 'possible worlds' as well as a plural 'us and we' that includes all of humanity and recognizes its diversity. This requires reconciling reason, emotion and values, in an attitude of pursuit and discovery of the visible and the invisible.

It is important to converge the experience of international solidarity, which brings people together: through pacifism and the peaceful resolution of conflicts; through feminism and its commitment to equality; and through environmentalism that emphasizes the urgency of controlling global warming before it is too late.

Global citizenship education is a commitment to hope as an engine of change and allows us to dream of a future that guarantees the rights of all, and that allows us to build alternatives for a sustainable, equal and peaceful future. Because every educational project must harbour the hope that individual, social, economic and political changes are possible, global citizenship education is a question of detecting the possibilities, even if they seem unlikely, that with persistence, society will achieve inherent alternatives to violence.

As a result, we trust that this crisis will present an opportunity for a do-over, to reinvent the future, as Federico Mayor Zaragoza, president of the Culture of Peace Foundation, points out (Mayor Zaragoza, 2021). As the American activist and pacifist, Cora Weiss (Mesa and Alonso, 2009: p. 82) states: 'When we dream alone, it is nothing more than a dream. But when we dream together, the dream can become reality.' The future is yet to come, and education for global citizenship can contribute to this process.

References

Asociación Pro Derechos Humanos (1994). *Sistema Sexo-Género*. Madrid: Libros de la Catarata.
Beck, U. (2002). *La sociedad del riesgo global*. Madrid: Siglo XXI.
Beck, U. (2005). *La mirada cosmopolita o la guerra es la paz*. Barcelona: Paidós.
Cobo, R. (2008). *Educar en la ciudadanía. Perspectivas feministas*. Madrid: Libros de la Catarata.
Cortina, A. (2000). *Ciudadanos de mundo. Hacia una teoría de la ciudadanía*. Madrid: Alianza Editorial.
De Paz, D. (2007). *Escuelas y educación para la ciudadanía global. Una Mirada transformadora*. Barcelona: Intermon.Oxfam.
Delors, J. (1997). *La educación encierra un tesoro. Informe a la UNESCO de la Comisión Internacional sobre la Educación para el siglo XXI*. Madrid: Santillana/ UNESCO.
Emcke, C. (2019). 'Falsas dicotomías'. *El Pais*, 3 de mayo 2019.
Fernández-Savater, A. (2016). 'El poder de la violencia es un mito, la paz de vida es más fuerte'. *Diario.es*. Disponible en: https://www.eldiario.es/interferencias/violencia-paz _132_3703726.html
Fisas, V. (1998). *Cultura de paz y gestion de conflictos*. Barcelona: Icaria/Unesco.

Fraser, N. and A. Honneth (2003). *Redistribution or Recognition? A Political-Philosophical Exchange.* Londres: Verso Press.

Galtung, J. (1969). 'Violence, Peace and Peace Research'. *Journal of Peace Research* 6: 3.

Held, D. and A. MacGrew (2001). *Transformaciones Globales.* México: Oxford University Press.

Lederach, J. P. (2007). *La imaginación moral: el arte y el alma de la construcción de la paz.* Bilbao: akeaz.

Martinez Guzmán, V. (2001). *Filosofía para hacer las paces.* Barcelona: Icaria.

Martinez-Guzmán, V. (1995). *Teoría de la paz. Filosofía Práctica 3.* Nau Lliabres Publisher.

Mayor Zargoza, F. (2021). *Recuerdos para el porvenir: referentes y valores para el siglo XXI.* Madrid: PPC.

Mesa, M. (2019). 'Educación y retos globales: promover la ciudadanía global en tiempos de involución', in *Ascenso del nacionalismo y el autoritarismo en el sistema internacional. Anuario CEIPAZ 2018–2019*, 61–86. Madrid: CEIPAZ-Fundación Cultura de Paz.

Mesa, M. (2020). 'Los Objetivos de Desarrollo Sostenible (ODS) y la Educación para la Ciudadanía Global. Diaz-Salazar, Rafael', in Ciudadanía Global (coord.), *Una visión transformadora de la sociedad y de la escuela*, 127–34. Madrid: SM.

Mesa, M. and A. Alonso (2020). 'Narrativas y discursos en tiempos de pandemia: como explicar la crisis del COVID-19 desde el feminismo pacifista', in Mesa (coord.), *Riesgos globales y multilateralismo: el impacto de la COVID-19. Anuario CEIPAZ 2019–2020*, 77–94. Madrid: CEIPAZ-Fundación Cultura de Paz.

Mesa, M. and L. Alonso (2009). *1325 mujeres tejiendo la paz.* Madrid: Icaria Publisher.

Murillo, F. J. and R. Hernández (2011). 'Hacia un concepto de Justicia Social'. *Revista Iberoamericana sobre Calidad, Eficacia y Cambio en Educación* 9(4): 8–23.

Novo, M. (2017). 'El papel de arte y de la educación. Cambiar en tiempos de incertidumbre', in S.m.a.r.t (Coord.), *Caminos hacia la sostenibilidad*, Capítulo 8, 256–61. C Madrid: Acciona. Disponible en: https://librosostenibilidad.files.wordpress.com/2017/12/smart_acciona_es.pdf

Nussbaum, M. (2006). *Frontiers of Justice: Disability, Nationality, Species Membership.* Cambridge, MA: Harvard University Press.

OECD (2020). 'Women at the Core of the Fight against COVID-19 Crisis'. Available: https://read.oecd-ilibrary.org/view/?ref=127_127000-awfnqj80me&title=Women-at-the-core-of-the-fight-against-COVID-19-crisis

Oxfam (2020). 'Care in the Time of Coronavirus. Why Care Work Needs to Be At the Centre of Post-COVID 19 Feminist Future'.

Rawls, J. (1971). *A Theory of Justice.* Cambridge, MA: Harvard University Press.

Sanahuja, J. A. (2020). 'Covid-19: riesgos, pandemia y crisis de gobernanza global', in M. Mesa (coord.), *Riesgos globales y multilateralismo: el impacto de la COVID-19*, 27–54. Madrid: CEIPAZ.

Silveira Gorki, H. (2000). 'La vida en común en sociedades multiculturales. Aportaciones para un debate', in *Identidades comunitarias y democracia*, 11–46. Madrid: Trotta.

Sousa Santos, B. (2011). 'Epistemologías del Sur'. *Utopía y Praxis Latinoamericana* 16(54): 17–39.

Sousa Santos, B. (2020). *La cruel pedagogía del virus*. Buenos Aires: CLACSO. Disponible en: http://209.177.156.169/libreria_cm/archivos/La-cruel-pedagogia-del-virus.pdf

UN (2020). *Shared Responsibility, Global Solidarity: Responding to the Socio-Economic Impacts of COVID-19*.

UNESCO (2020). *Impacto del Covid-19 en la educación*. https://es.unesco.org/covid19/educationresponse

UNESCO-IESALC (2020). *COVID-19 y educación superior. De los efectos inmediatos al día después*. UNESCO, 6 de abril.

Young, I. M. (1990). *Justice and the Politics of Difference*. Princeton: Princeton University Press.

3

Utopia, Ecopedagogy and Citizenships

Teaching for Socio-Environmental Justice, Development and Planetary Sustainability

Greg William Misiaszek and Diana Cristina Oróstegui González

Education saturated with possibilities of utopian futures provides the goals for student to reach for but most often never fully attaining, as Torres and Teodoro (Torres and Teodoro, 2007) give the metaphors of a distant horizon or the North Star to step towards. Paulo Freire (1992; 2000) argued that prevalent fatalism within education is inherently dehumanizing because, among other aspects, it vacates our unique ability of *unfinishedness* from being able to dream and act towards achieving dreams through reflexivity of our histories.

> If my presence in history is not neutral, I must accept its political nature as critically as possible. If, in reality, I am not in the world simply to adapt to it, but rather to transform it, and if it is not possible to change the world without a certain dream or vision for it, I must make use of every possibility there is not only to speak about my utopia, but also to engage in practices consistent with it. (Freire, 2004: p. 7)

All that comprises Earth, including living beings, adapt and evolve to their surroundings, but humans determine our actions through reflexivity of our dreams and our histories, our own and others' – hopefully most frequently ours *with* others within framings of social justice (Freire, 2000). Within ecopedagogical groundings it is also with all of Nature, as 'us' being part of Earth/Nature (Gadotti, 2008a; Misiaszek, 2012; 2020a).

Opposingly, taught fatalistic ideologies in which students are viewed as, and views themselves as, *finished* deprives them of any hope in bettering themselves, their private spheres and bettering the world. Humans' and societies' *unfinishedness* that Freire stresses allows for transformability guided by 'our' unceasing historical reflectivity and dreaming of possible futures (Freire, 2000).[1] Education absent of these characteristics is dehumanizingly fatalistic (Freire, 2000). Within ecopedagogical frameworks such education is also *deplanetarizing* by helping to sustain and intensify inseparable environmental violence and social violence (*socio-environmental* connectivity), anthropocentric ideologies of the dominance over the rest of Nature and local-to-planetary sustainability (Misiaszek, 2018; 2020a).

Freire (2000; 1992; 1997; 2004) argued that teaching, especially within banking education models, indoctrinates fatalistic ideologies that falsely justify dehumanization and deplanetarization (especially his later work (see Freire, 1997; 2004)) through teaching that touts that transforming current societal structures is impossible and such actions are 'unnatural'/'abnormal'. Banking models systematically delegitimizes students' previous knowledges and critical thinking subjects, viewing them as objects in their 'learning' (Freire, 2000). Utilizing Freire's (2000) famous title, fatalistic education are pedagogies of the oppressed – teaching that sustains/intensifies oppressions by justifying the oppressions both externally from oppressors' perspectives and internally from the Self and their socio-historically oppressed population. We argue the need to disrupt banking fatalistic models that will only continue socio-environmental injustices and planetary unsustainability.

In this chapter, we discuss the need for utopia-saturated environmental pedagogies through Freirean-based ecopedagogy teaching and scholarship to problematize education for citizenships (pluralized to indicate local-to-planetary citizenship spheres, further unpacked shortly) and education for (sustainable) development. Freire's call for education to help students to dream of possible utopias is found on the goal of education to 'better the world'. Freirean utopic education, including ecopedagogy reinvented from Freire's work, is grounded in global, all-inclusive social justice specifically as differing from education for students' goals that leads towards injustices.

Environmental consciousization (*conscientização*) for praxis will only emerge from education through critical pedagogies that unveil structural socio-environmental injustices and planetary unsustainability as fatalistically 'normal' and separatable from one another only leads to sustaining and intensifying injustices and unsustainability (Gadotti, 2008b; Gadotti and Torres, 2009; Misiaszek, 2012; 2020a). Our arguments are grounded within the work of Freire through ecopedagogical frameworks which emerged from Freire's scholarship and reinventions of his work. The topic of needing to disrupt fatalism within environmental pedagogies is complex that cannot be all-inclusively addressed in a single chapter. We argue for utopic (environmental) pedagogies to disrupt fatalism emergent from oppressive forms of citizenships (local-to-global-to-planetary); top-down hegemonic _D_evelopment (as opposed to bottom-up _d_evelopment); epistemologies of the North; neoliberalism, (neo)coloniality, and globalizations; and some specific forms of oppressions (e.g. racism, patriarchy, xenophobia). We conclude this chapter by briefly arguing these aspects in the contexts of Colombia and problematizing the ecopedagogical, utopian needs of a centre focusing on these issues.

Planetarizing utopian pedagogies, deplanetarizing fatalistic pedagogies

> Embracing the dream of a better world and adhering to it imply accepting the process of its creation. It is a process of struggle that must be deeply anchored in ethics. It is the process of struggle against all forms of violence-violence against the life of trees, of rivers, of fish, of mountains, of cities, against the physical marks of historic and cultural memories. It is also the process of struggle against violence toward the weak, the defenseless, the wounded minorities, violence toward those who are discriminated against for any reason. (Freire, 2004: p. 121)

> planetary . . . propose[s] an ecopedagogical model to give meaning to the dynamics of life as a product of educational act is exposed as such a pressing matter as hopeful when the commitment, the respect, honest interrelation and accompaniment are the fundamentals to prevent scenarios and present circumstances become modes of permanent existence. (Barriga, 2016)

Utopia within ecopedagogy is planetarizing beyond humans by teaching through possibilities of disrupting unsustainable actions because of socio-environmental justice and peace issues within the world (i.e. anthroposphere), _and_ the well-being and sustainability for the rest of Nature. In other words, ecopedagogical dreaming is not anthropocentric but planetary. Ecopedagogical work (pedagogical practices, research and methodologies) grounded in Freire's mostly later work and reinventions of his work by Freireans (e.g. Gadotti, Gutierrez, Prado, Misiaszek, Kahn). Ecopedagogy is literacy education that widens Freire's aspect of 'reading the word to read the world', to reading the world as _part_ of Earth – or 'us' are part of Nature/Earth overall (Gadotti, 2008b; Misiaszek, 2012; 2020a). Environmental pedagogies that normalize 'development' without foundational goals of ending others' suffering and injustices for *our* 'development' and/or without concern for the rest of Nature (i.e. non-anthroposphere) sustains, and often intensifies, socio-environmental violence and planetary devastation (Gadotti and Torres, 2009; Misiaszek, 2020b).

(Environmental) pedagogies are too-often absent of teaching through what Freire's (2000) argues as humans' uniqueness of self-reflectivity, historical and ability to act towards our possible utopias (Gadotti and Torres, 2009; Misiaszek, 2012). We focus on this latter aspect, but the other two allows, together and inseparably, praxis. Environmental pedagogies too-frequently fail because they are fatalistic banking education models absent of authentic dialogue full of students' dreams and collectively, dialectically sharing them, as well as through problem-posing activities. Freire argued that our histories do construct our future*s*; however, he did not mean this in fatalistic ways. Freire (2004) expressed this by using the metaphor of building a wall in which 'tomorrow' does not have to be a repletion of 'today', or yesterday, but that it is a brick in the wall nonetheless.

Teaching through ecopedagogical futures (i.e. utopias) must be rooted in globally all-inclusive socio-environmental justice *and* valuing the rest of Nature outside of humans' needs and wants. Misiaszek (2014; 2018) has termed this planarizing need, including framings of education and utopia, as world-Earth *de-distancing* by acknowledging that too much of (environmental) education distances us and our world from the rest of Earth. This includes distancing (sustainable) development from the rest of Nature, and globally-all-inclusive 'true' development.

Ecopedagogy and d/Development: Brief framings

> reality, I am not in the world simply to adapt to it, but rather to transform it, and if it is not possible to change the world without a 'certain dream or vision for it, I must make use of every possibility there is not only to speak about my utopia, but also to engage in practices consistent with it'. (Freire, 2004: p. 7)

Earth outside of humans (i.e. non-anthroposphere) can be conceptualized as *finished* in that it adapts and evolves without socio-historical self-reflectivity towards 'development'. This is highlighted by Freire (2000), stating that 'while all development is transformation, not all transformation is development' (p. 161). In short, humans transform towards development goals while the rest of Nature transforms towards equilibrium, or balance, and for immediate-to-species survival (this latter aspect is aligned with evolution).

Following are some passages on framing ecopedagogy overall and within d/Development.

> [Ecopedagogy:] Rooted in critical theories, originating from popular education models of Latin America and reinventions of the Brazilian educational scholar Paulo Freire's work, ecopedagogies are transformational environmental pedagogies centred on ending socio-environmental injustices. Although ecopedagogies have multiple definitions, they are all grounded in critical thinking and transformability to construct praxis within social-environmental justice models (Gutiérrez and Prado 2008; Gadotti and Torres 2009; Gadotti 2008c, 2000; Kahn 2010). Ecopedagogies' overall goal is for students to critically understand how environmentally harmful acts lead to oppressions for humans (anthropocentric aspects) and all else that makes up Earth (biocentric aspects), the politics of the acts, and how to problematize the acts to end socio-environmental oppressions. (Misiaszek, 2018: p. 9)

> [d/Development and ecopedagogy:] four defining factors of esD [and Development (capital and italicized 'D')]: (1) neoliberal economics as the sole factor of development analysis; (2) deprioritizing economic justice concern by ignoring how development processes sustain/increase hegemony; (3) deprioritizing planetary sustainability for Earth's balance; and (4) local framings of development are disregarded for globally constructed ones 'from above' (e.g. Western Development models), denoted by the lower-case, underlined, and italicized 'd'. (Misiaszek, 2020b: p. 16)

> I utilize the lower-cased development and upper-cased Development to indicate, respectively, empowering versus oppressive, holistic versus hegemonic, just versus unjust, sustainable versus unsustainable, and many other opposing framings of who is included within 'development' and framings of d/Development goals. There are no absolute origins or framings differentiating between d/Development, but rather the essence and outcomes of their framings.. . . . Constructs of development that counters growth towards and emergent from Development. (Misiaszek, 2020a)

Freire's discussions on unfinishedness provide utopic ideologies that can lead to development and, in turn, counter Development, with the understanding that world-only development cannot be untethered. Utopic development is inclusive of not denying others' unfinishedness and development, *and* Earth's sustainability.

Teaching for praxis for development

> Critical theories in education have the utopian goal to end oppressions through actions constructed from deeper reflection through holistic understandings – praxis – with the realizations that societies are fluid, transformative, and conflictive. (Gadotti, 1996) (Misiaszek, 2018: p. 98)

As true for all critical pedagogies and research (Apple, Au and Gandin, 2009; Gadotti, 1996), ecopedagogical work is for praxis with just gaining 'environmental knowledge' as not enough without action. Freire (1992; 2000) argued for the need of teaching through students-constructed generative themes which deconstructed the barriers, which he named 'limit situations', to achieve a better world (Gadotti, 1996). Determining a 'better world' is impossible within fatalism indoctrinated within (environmental) pedagogies because the world is only taught to be seen how it is currently, including all global present oppressions and planetary unsustainability. Below, Freire discussed the connections of neoliberalism (in which <u>D</u>evelopment is rooted from) and fatalistic education.

> I cannot avoid a permanently critical attitude toward what I consider to be the scourge of neoliberalism, with its cynical fatalism and its inflexible negation of the right to dream differently, to dream of utopia. My abhorrence of neoliberalism helps to explain my legitimate anger when I speak of the injustices to which the ragpickers among humanity are condemned. It also explains my total lack of interest in any pretension of impartiality. I am not impartial or objective; not a fixed observer of facts and happenings. I never was able to be an adherent of the traits that falsely claim impartiality or objectivity. That did not prevent me, however, from holding always a rigorously ethical position. (Freire, 1998: p. 22)

It is education that is '[f]ull with hope and guided by utopics' that can have 'students determine how they see their socio-environmentally utopic view and what are the current realities' (Misiaszek, 2018: p. 202).

Without hope within teaching ecopedagogical praxis is impossible. For example, banking models systematically silence students' dialogue on possibilities to 'overcome' limit situations. Education as tools for 'remaking the world' needs 'faith in humankind' (Freire, 2000: pp. 90–1), teaching 'through conscientization that subjects assume their historical commitment in the process of making and remaking the world, within concrete possibilities, also making and remaking themselves' (Freitas, 2012: p. 70). Utopic dialogue within ecopedagogical spaces is critical problematizing what are the utopias for everyone within the spaces and bringing local-to-global voices/perspectives outside the space. Emergent ecopedagogical praxis must not shift socio-environmental oppressions to 'others' but towards ending them globally holistically within planetarization.

Development and citizenships

> [We teach to] understand history as a possibility and not as a fatality. That is why, educate for another possible world is to educate for breakthroughs, for non-conformity, for refusal, for saying 'no', for yelling, for dreaming with other possible worlds. Announcing and denouncing. Neoliberalism conceives education as market good, reducing our identities to mere consumers, disregarding public spaces and the humanistic dimension of education. Opposing itself to this paradigm, education for another possible world respects and co-exists with differences, promoting 'intertransculturality' (Padilha, 2004). The center of neoliberal conception of education is to deny dream and utopia. That is why, an education for another possible world is, first of all, education for a dream, for hope. (Gadotti, 2008a: p. 21)

Disrupting (environmental) teaching which normalizes the masses as hosts and commodifies the rest of Nature for a few to _D_evelop requires teaching to disrupt the normalization of such instilled notions as without alternatives. This includes disrupting false, fatalistic notions of _D_evelopment as 'natural' and _d_evelopment as 'unnatural' or 'abnormal'. Such disruptions are difficult because of the treadmill of hegemony sustained from these taught notions _and_ these notions further entrenched from neoliberal education bolstered from hegemony. Freire (2000) discussed this difficulty by asking how can the oppressed as divided, unauthentic beings participate in developing the pedagogy of their liberation. Utilizing Hegel's Master-Slave dialectic, Freire (2000) argued that liberation can only occur when the oppressed 'discover themselves to be "hosts" of the oppressor can they contribute to the midwifery of their liberating pedagogy' (p. 48). Freire explains the utopian need through the (re)constructions and (re)imaginations of citizenship, as follows:

> The ability to observe, to compare, and to evaluate, in order to choose, through deciding, how one is to intervene in the life of the city and thus exercise one's citizenship, arises then as a fundamental competency. If my presence in history is not neutral, I must accept its political nature as critically as possible. If, in reality, I am not in the world simply to adapt to it, but rather to transform it, and if it is not possible to change the world without a certain dream or vision for it, I must make use of every possibility there is not only to speak about my utopia, but also to engage in practices consistent with it. (Freire 2004: p. 7)

There are almost endless aspects needed to unpack with Freire's answer here; we will focus on collective utopianism necessary for such liberation that, in turn, counters fatalistic divisions.

These divisions, in part, are caused by taught distancing ideologies of 'us' versus 'them', with the 'them' inclusive of Nature overall. Distancing most frequently aligns with socio-historical oppressions (e.g. racism, patriarchy, heteronormativity, xenophobia, Global South/North); in this short chapter we will briefly focus on citizen: non-citizen distancing. We argue the need for utopic, critical global citizenship education (GCE) in which there is no 'non-citizen' *with* planetary citizenship education (PCE) that has citizenship as inclusive of all of Earth, as well as Earth as a citizen.

> To teach students to become citizens of the world requires critical understanding of the global processes affecting society, creating oppressions upon other societies and upon the world holistically. It is to understand the actions within and across the world to construct possible utopias through observations, comparisons, and evaluations that end oppressions to determine how to act toward making the utopias realities. Another facet of this is a widened perspective of being a citizen of the World – a citizen of Earth. (Misiaszek and Torres, 2019: p. 476)

A key aspect of ecopedagogical work is conceiving of citizenship in the pluralized citizenships to 'indicate[s] the multiple spheres of citizenship, with specific attention to its education and the complicated connections with environmental pedagogies and praxis' (Misiaszek, 2020a: p. 6).

This aligns with the following quote by Gutiérrez and Prado (2008/1989) (who wrote the first book naming ecopedagogy) and Freire (1997) writing that he was a citizen of his home city of Recife and of Brazil and of the world.

> The meaning itself, the sense that personal or collectively we can guide our path, it is the cornerstone on which significance must rest of planetary citizenship. This rationale it opens wide the door of possible and hopeful relationships. Our existence should no longer be an a priori imperative of obligations to fulfill, but a being open to the new reality, full of suggestions and possibilities. This dimension of openness and flexibility puts us in front of an education conceived as the creation of new and possible relationships. [CITE (p. 40)]

Ecopedagogically teaching and reading through the commonalities and differences of self-to-planetary utopias emergent from local-to-global citizenships collectiveness within our world *with* local-to-planetary collectiveness and beyond anthropocentric understandings is essential for praxis towards a just, peaceful and sustainable world.

Absolute knowledge of the world-Earth should be the utopic goal of environmental teaching ecopedagogical work through citizenships helps towards gaining this utopic goal of understanding through multiple and diverse citizenship spheres. The valuing of diversity grounding of critical GCE and PCE, as opposed to traditional citizenship's homogeneous goals, encourages diverse, inclusive and new-to-the-learner ways to understand each other and all of Nature (Misiaszek, 2015). This includes Santos's (2018) arguments of needing reflexivity and teaching through *ecologies of knowledges* to counter epistemologies of the North rooted in coloniality, patriarchy and capitalism. Pedagogies saturated in hope is essential for students to construct goals to guide their actions towards a better world, countering engrained fatalism from teaching through epistemologies (e.g. epistemologies of the North (Santos, 2016; 2018; Takayama, Sriprakash and Connell, 2017) which sustain/intensify hegemony and dominance of Nature. Educating for another possible world must include a pedagogy of absences. As said by Boaventura de Souza Santos (2018) it means to show what has been absented historically by dominant cultures, what started to be considered strange due to over-valuing of what is scientific over non-scientific and by non-recognition of knowledge that comes from practice. There is no social justice without epistemological justice.

Case study: Colombia

Colombia is considered one of the world's megadiverse nations, with nearly 10 per cent of the world's biodiversity as almost a utopia in the country of magical realism,[2] but is also the world's deadliest place for environmentalists.[3] Columbian national environmental policies have included educational aspects since the mid-1990s. However, we argue that there are numerous aspects not reflected in the resulting pedagogical projects, including socio-environmental justice aspects and, directly connected to this chapter's topic, utopic ecopedagogical teaching as previously discussed. To deconstruct these issues, we utilize the case study of the new Sustainable Development Goals Center for Latin América (CODS – Centro de los Objetivos de Desarrollo Sostenible para América Latina) in Bogotá by problematizing the ecopedagogical importance of current popular education and democratic participation, environmental movements and possible connections with utopic teaching.

More often than not, students have been taught to memorize Colombia's diverse range of ecological, climatic, biological and ecosystem elements through banking pedagogies. Although environmental teaching has also adopted a *naturalist current*, as termed by Suavé (2005), many Colombians also are taught by being immersed within their richly diverse ecosystems daily. Utopic ecopedagogy is far from easy and uncomplicated as Columbians deal with the harsh realities of industrial agriculture practices, illicit drug trade and land disputes. These are a few of the many limit situations for environmentalism and teaching it.

The CODS, housed at the Universidad de Los Andes and part of the United Nations Sustainable Solutions Network (SDSN),[4] plans to transform the socio-environmental landscape through innovative and investigative educational strategies. CODS aspires to be a global meeting place for universities, businesses, governments and civil society organizations throughout Latin America and the Caribbean to discuss and debate the implementation of the UN SDGs through teaching, monitoring and evaluation. As well, CODS will conduct interdisciplinary research through interuniversity teams and networks. Our question is how this centre will provide possibilities for local-to-planetary transformability with our argued needed utopic ecopedagogical elements, if at all.

For CODS to be successful their work must be through diverse, complex and often contesting local-to-planetary perspectives. The centre's stated focus on incorporating sustainability in daily life tasks must coincide with Gutiérrez and Prado's (2016) defining factors of ecopedagogy of teaching the significance of things in everyday life with (new) relationships between ourselves, the Earth and other humans. In essence, the work needs to be world-Earth de-distancing with the rest of Earth as 'not a strange and distant being, but it is our home, the place where we live and we coexist' (Pérez & Rojas, 2016, p. 100). Teaching and research through this grounding for students' students to ground their praxis must be both CODS's utopic goal and saturated with possible of utopic in their work – within their teaching, research, leadership, governance, activism and other activities.

We argue that this work needs utopic possibilities to rethink environmental pedagogies towards ecopedagogical models. In Colombia where at least 105 human rights defenders were killed between 2017 and early 2018, primarily community leaders, defenders of the right to land, territory and environment, and individuals who participated in campaigns for signing the final agreement with the FARC (Ramírez-Hernández & Leguizamon-Arias, 2020).[5] As argued previously in this chapter, rethinking educational approaches, practices and structures for students and teachers to unlearn fatalism. The previously harsh realities cannot be absent, but this does not mean that another world, or future, is not possible and teaching must be saturated in this ideology. To be successful, CODS's work must be educationally all-inclusive, through formal, informal and non-formal models (e.g. social-environmental movements, public pedagogy such as from local to-global-media), and epistemologies (e.g. Indigenous, global Southern).

Columbia's widespread environmental devastating in the name of Development indicates the need for ecopedagogy to counter fatalistic notions that development is impossible. Teaching to ecopedagogically read the destruction of Andean forests and the Amazon (e.g. due to mining, extensive livestock, pollution) for different futures for development is essential. These are some specific issues CODS is taking up. As argued previously, critical global citizenship and planetary citizenship pedagogies are essential for education for development to be successful because their teachings counter citizen: non-citizen and world-Earth distancing. Planetary citizenship education 'includes ethical obligations that link us so much with society as with the natural resources of the planet according to our social role and perspective sustainable development' (Pérez & Rojas, 2016, p. 16).

Teaching to radically disrupt Development includes utopian imagining of development through critical, diverse and democratic dialogue. Quimbayo-Ruíz (2014) found that in municipal debates, especially in Bogotá, only a select few have a formal voice within them (e.g. those from social movements, government, academia and/or private economic sectors) rather than the overall population who are in/directly affected by the debates' outcomes. Concerns are focused on their perceptions of safety, mobility and public transportation, as well as their enjoyment of a decent urban space, outside of these social dynamics (Quimbayo Ruiz, 2014), such as socio-environmental justice issues and non-anthropocentric aspects. But there is hope as Pérez (2019) has argued that the Latin American region has a higher level of participatory citizenship guiding socio-environmental movements. Many of Colombia's social movements are creating networks for increasingly democratic futures through collective efforts through praxis to confront exploitation and domination.

For example, the movement 'Sueña Colombia'[6] in Santander protested against underground exploitation of minerals in páramos because of the negative impact on the region's water resources and ecosystems. Thanks to lawsuit actions initiated from public pressure aided by this and other movements,[7] Columbia's Supreme Court declared the river to be a 'subject of rights' and entitled to special constitutional protection. These social movements exemplify the need and power from integrating people from diverse cultures and backgrounds, especially those who are often deemed powerless, to reimagine what is needed *and* what is possible to end socio-environmental oppressions. CODS will need to diversify voices through, in part, working with heterogeneous social movements for achieving such effective ecopedagogical public pedagogy. In the following concluding section, we give four key issues that we argue are essential for institutions, such as CODS, to focus upon.

Conclusion

Teaching through ideologies of fatalism with our world viewed as 'finished' – a singular future of endlessly continuing current oppressions, dominance and unsustainability – are pedagogical tools of oppressions and unsustainability. Ignoring students' fatalistic notions that have been instilled in them through their (in/non)formal education is equally negative; teaching to actively counter these false notions is essential for students' praxis grounded in socio-environmental justice and planetary sustainability. In other words, disrupting fatalism is crucial to unlearn false normalization of unsustainable environmental violence.

In this chapter, we specifically focused on utopic teaching to counter unjust, unsustainable *D*evelopment which is further entrenched in (environmental) education by intensifying neoliberal globalization. Education is influenced by the 'commonsense of development', and vice versa in constructing development goals that mark our 'progress', or not. Utilizing the terminology utilized throughout this chapter, teaching for opposing *d*evelopment both requires utopian teaching and is essential for imaginaries of goals required *for* utopian teaching. We argued the need for ecopedagogical work throughout all of education which innately has utopic groundings from its Freirean foundations throughout its whole-curricula, transdisciplinary approaches. This includes, as unpacked in this chapter, critical utopic citizenship education that actively counters previously taught ideologies that nullify the valuing of *d*evelopment for 'non-citizens' and/or Nature beyond the anthroposphere. Our chapter is far from including all aspects of utopia and education within the areas we wrote on. However, we view this chapter as initiating dialogue emergent on how utopianism must, and can, be saturated throughout all of education towards justice and balance with all of Nature. By providing the case study of Colombia, we hope to enrich such dialogue by exemplifying our theoretical arguments and allow for readers to critically compare with theirs and others' contexts.

We argue CODS and similar centres need to work towards integrating academia and communities to construct utopian environmental teaching for praxis, especially for those who have been historically excluded from educational decisions and decision-making processes. The most important and challenging goals for Colombian educators, including CODS's and similar centres' largely centring environmental pedagogical work, is engaging students and the overall public in meaningful environmental learning experiences that are relevant to them, respond accordingly and respectively, and that transformation towards a better world and sustainable planet is possible. These aspects align with key utopian tenets of ecopedagogy. We conclude by giving the following four key issues that institutions, such as CODS must focus upon: (1) making the unequal environmental impacts of _D_evelopments more transparent and public; (2) help strengthen and empower socio-environmental movements; (3) increase all-inclusive access to quality education that are rooted ecopedagogies; and (4) widen overall work, collaborations and meaningful dialogue to be all-inclusive and, for example, education beyond formal schooling.

Notes

1 Future_s_ is plural to indicate the utopic idea of possible multiple futures, rather than a fatalistically determined future.
2 Colombia is one of the world's richest countries in terms of marine wealth, and the country's biological diversity is the highest in the Andean habitats, which are home to many endemic species, followed by the Amazon rainforests and humid ecosystems of the Chocó biogeographical region. https://www.cbd.int/countries/profile/?country=co, https://www.colombia.co/en/colombia-country/environment/environment-environment/colombia-second-greatest-biodiversity-in-the-world/.
3 Colombia is the world's deadliest place for environmentalists. https://justiceforcolombia.org/news/more-than-twice-as-many-environmental-activists-killed-in-colombia-as-anywhere-else-in-2020/, https://www.nytimes.com/2021/11/18/opinion/colombia-environmental-defenders.html.
4 https://cods.uniandes.edu.co/. This centre, which inaugurated on 21 September 2018, is expected to be a specialized centre that promotes sustainable development throughout Latin America and the Caribbean. It was established in Bogotá with the goal of providing solutions to the region's growth and conservation challenges, fostering the training of leaders and academics on these issues, and influencing Latin American governments' policies.
5 Final Agreement to End the Armed Conflict and Build a Stable and Lasting Peace between the National Government of Colombia and FARC-EP (Fuerzas

Armadas Revolucionarias de Colombia - Ejército del Pueblo) to bring an end to the Colombian conflict. Ramírez-Hernández and Leguizamon-Arias (2020) affirm the need to recognize nature as victim of the armed conflict and as a victim of a structural violence in Colombia.

6   https://www.vanguardia.com/area-metropolitana/bucaramanga/la-lucha-por-proteger-el-paramo-de-santurban-llego-a-canada-JE3240083.

7   The 'Tierra Digna' organization has filed lawsuits to stop such projects (see https://www.elespectador.com/colombia/mas-regiones/un-salvavidas-para-el-atrato-article-691575/).

References

Apple, M. W., W. Au and L. s. A. Gandin (2009). 'Mapping Critical Education', in M. W. Apple, W. Au and L. s. A. Gandin (eds), *The Routledge International Handbook of Critical Education*, 3–20. New York: Routledge.

Amaro Barriga, M. J. (2016). Prólogo a la edición mexicana. F. G. Pérez & C. P. Rojas (Eds.), Ecopedagogia e cidadania planetária. De La Salle Ediciones, Mexico, UCR, DeLaSalle editions, p.9.

Freire, P. (1992). *Pedagogy of Hope*. New York: Continuum.

Freire, P. (1997). *Pedagogy of the Heart*. New York: Continuum.

Freire, P. (1998). *Pedagogy of Freedom: Ethics, Democracy, and Civic Courage*. Lanham: Rowman & Littlefield.

Freire, P. (2000). *Pedagogy of the Oppressed*. New York: Continuum.

Freire, P. (2004). *Pedagogy of Indignation*. Boulder: Paradigm Publishers.

Freitas, A. L. S. d. (2012). 'Conscientization [Conscientização]', in D. R. Streck, E. Redin and J. J. Zitkoski (eds), *Paulo Freire encyclopedia*, 69–71. Lanham: Rowman & Littlefield Publishers.

Gadotti, M. (1996). *Pedagogy of Praxis: A Dialectical Philosophy of Education*. Albany: SUNY Press.

Gadotti, M. (2008a). *Education for Sustainable Development: What We Need to Learn to Save the Planet*. São Paulo: Instituto Paulo Freire.

Gadotti, M. (2008b). 'What We Need to Learn to Save the Planet'. *Journal of Education for Sustainable Development* 2(1): 21–30. doi: 10.1177/097340820800200108

Gadotti, M. and C. A. Torres (2009). 'Paulo Freire: Education for Development'. *Development and Change* 40(6): 1255–67. doi: 10.1111/j.1467-7660.2009.01606.x

Gutiérrez, F. and C. Prado (1989). *Ecopedagogia e cidadania planetária. (Ecopedagogy and planetarian citizenship)*. São Paulo: Cortez.

Gutiérrez, F. and C. Prado (2008). *Ecopedagogia e cidadania planetária*. San Paulo: Instituto Paulo Freire.

Kahn, R. (2010). Critical pedagogy, ecoliteracy, and planetary crisis: The ecopedagogy movement (Vol. 359). New York: Peter Lang. (city is New York City is needed (i.e., New York, New York))

Misiaszek, G. W. (2012). 'Transformative Environmental Education within Social Justice Models: Lessons from Comparing Adult Ecopedagogy within North and South America'. in D. N. Aspin, J. Chapman, K. Evans and R. Bagnall (eds), *Second International Handbook of Lifelong Learning*, vol. 26, 423–40. London: Springer.

Misiaszek, G. W. (2014). 'Learning from Southern Environmental Education Models: Borrowing Ecopedagogy through Processes of Globalization from Below'. *Éducation Comparée* 10: 209–41.

Misiaszek, G. W. (2015). 'Ecopedagogy and Citizenship in the Age of Globalisation: Connections between Environmental and Global Citizenship Education to Save the Planet'. *European Journal of Education* 50(3): 280–92. doi: 10.1111/ejed.12138

Misiaszek, G. W. (2018). *Educating the Global Environmental Citizen: Understanding Ecopedagogy in Local and Global Contexts*. New York: Routledge.

Misiaszek, G. W. (2020a). *Ecopedagogy: Critical Environmental Teaching for Planetary Justice and Global Sustainable Development*. London: Bloomsbury.

Misiaszek, G. W. (2020b). 'Ecopedagogy: Teaching Critical Literacies of "development", "sustainability", and "sustainable development"'. *Teaching in Higher Education* 25(5): 615–32. doi: 10.1080/13562517.2019.1586668

Misiaszek, G. W. and C. A. Torres (2019). 'Ecopedagogy: The Missing Chapter of Pedagogy of the Oppressed', in C. A. Torres (ed.), *Wiley Handbook of Paulo Freire*, 463–88. Hoboken: Wiley-Blackwell.

Padilha, P. R. (2004). *Curriculo intertranscultural: Novos itinerários para a educação*. São Paulo: Cortez/Insituto Paulo Freire.

Pérez, F. G. and C. P. Rojas (2016). *Ecopedagogia e cidadania planetária*. Costa Rica: De La Salle Ediciones.

Pérez Cubero, M. E. (2019). 'La participación ciudadana de los movimientos socioambientales en América Latina'. *Revista Colombiana de Sociología*, 42: 135–56. http://www.scielo.org.co/scielo.php?script=sci_arttext&pid=S0120-159X2019000100135&nrm=iso

Quimbayo Ruiz, G. A. (2014). 'Movimientos sociales, políticas y conflictos ambientales en la construcción de ciudad: El caso de Bogotá'. *Ecología Política* 47: 104–7. Retrieved from http://www.jstor.org/stable/43528421

Ramírez-Hernández, N. E. and W. Y. Leguizamon-Arias (2020). 'La naturaleza como víctima en la era del posacuerdo colombiano'. *El Ágora USB* 20(1): 259–73.

Santos, B. d. S. (2016). 'Epistemologies of the South and the Future'. *From the European South: A Transdisciplinary Journal of Postcolonial Humanities* 1: 17–29.

Santos, B. d. S. (2018). *The End of the Cognitive Empire: The Coming of Age of Epistemologies of the South*. Durham: Duke University Press.

Sauvé, L. (2005). 'Currents in Environmental Education: Mapping a Complex and Evolving'. *Canadian Journal of Environmental Education (CJEE)* 10(1): 11–37.

Takayama, K., A. Sriprakash and R. Connell (2017). 'Toward a Postcolonial Comparative and International Education'. *Comparative Education Review* 61(S1): S1–24. doi:10.1086/690455

Torres, C. A. and A. Teodoro (2007). *Critique and Utopia: New Developments in the Sociology of Education in the Twenty-First Century*. Lanham: Rowman & Littlefield.

4

Global Values in School Curricula

Annette Scheunpflug, Martina Osterrieder, Anne-Christine Banze and Andrea Abele-Brehm

Introduction

Curricula convey values that are considered significant by a society. On the one hand, they are an expression of societal value configurations; on the other hand, they influence values in schools. Irrespective of whether curricula really shape the reality of teaching, the underlying values are therefore of interest as an expression of what a society feels to be important and worth to be passed on to the next generation. This applies in particular to the preambles of curricula, which refer to the general tasks of schools but do not take the perspective of different school subjects, their traditions and tasks.

This chapter analyses global values that can be found in the preambles to the curricula of four types of schools in Bavaria. It is about identifying the significance of global values within the entire spectrum of values. In addition, these values are subjected to a content analysis: Which topics are associated with them? What understanding of globality is expressed by these terms?

This study is part of a research project on figurations of social value communication,[1] including a study on values in programmes of political parties (Müller and Séville, 2022) as well as different studies on the general spectrum of values in curricula (Osterrieder et al., under review). As main results, curricula support values of 'openness to social change', propagate fearless education and pursue the idea of achievement less centrally than it would have been expected based on the values of society as a whole. In addition, the value profile of different types of schools in the tracking school system was compared (Scheunpflug et al., under review). Curricula leading to certificates entitling university access address more often values associated with self-direction and explain the paradoxical requirements of complex value configurations. However, curricula that lead to vocational training tend to address less complex value configurations, and self-realization is less often the focus; in these curricula values of achievement and care are found there all the more intensively (Scheunpflug et al., under review). As such, these results are already relevant to globalization issues because they subtly perpetuate existing educational injustices.

This chapter focuses on the values that are related to issues of education for sustainable development or 'global learning' in the broadest sense. Subsequently, we understand 'global learning' to be the pedagogical reaction to the development of world society (Scheunpflug, 2001: p. 87) and thus follow the Maastricht Declaration of 2002 (see the section 'Current state of research and research desideratum' in this chapter).

In the following, first of all the state of research on global learning in curricula will be reported (see Section 'Current state of research and research desideratum'). Against this background, the theoretical focus will be developed (see Section 'Theoretical background: Operationalization of value discourses') followed by the explanation of the methods used for the empirical research (see Section 'Method'). Then the results will be presented (Section 'Results: Global values in curricula') and these findings will be explained concerning their relevance to 'Global Learning' and a 'Pedagogy of Hope' (Section 'The content of universal values'). This study points beyond the specific case of schools in Bavaria in understanding the complexity of 'global values' and proposing a research instrument for hidden values. Research on curricula, which has so far focused purely on the content of learning, focusing the underlying value configurations, interprets curricula less in terms of their importance for school learning and more as markers for societal debates.

Current state of research and research desideratum

With the present study, we combine several research strands that have so far largely run separately, curriculum research on global learning (1), value research (2) and the discourse on 'global values' (3). The research question then becomes apparent from the overview (4) of these strands.

(1) From the point of view of curriculum research on global learning, several aspects are important. On the one hand, there are numerous studies that reflect the anchoring of topics of global learning in the curricula for different countries (Schreiber and Siege, 2016; for universities Killick 2020). Overall, the topic has been implemented at least to some extent with regard to the curricula in recent decades (cf. Ferguson-Patrick, Reynolds and Macqueen, 2018; Bentall et al., 2014;

Tarozzi and Mallon, 2019; Tarozzi and Inguaggiato, 2018). Reviews for Europe also show increasing awareness of the issue. Implementation has progressed to different degrees in individual European countries (cf. for Europe the reviews of the Global Education Network Europe: https://www.gene.eu/peer-reviews).

The study presented here goes beyond these aspects when elaborating the values associated with global learning in curricula. It is about the configurations of values implicitly associated and invoked with curricula. This ties in with studies that interpret texts of curricula less as a statement about the school, the lessons or even as determined teaching input, but as an expression of societal expectations towards schools (cf. Künzli, 1986; Künzli et al., 2013; or the summary in Terhart 2021, cf. on the associated decision-making processes Biehl, Ohlhaver and Riquarts, 1999).

(2) Second, questions of value research are taken up. In value research, values are described as ideal concepts of what is desirable that guide social actors in how they make decisions about action, assess people and events, and interpret and justify their decisions and actions (e.g. Schwartz, 1999). Values are cross-situational goal orientations and decision criteria that are hierarchized and prioritized according to their importance, acting as guiding principles in the conduct of life (Schwartz, 1999: pp. 24–5). These explicit and implicit value orientations are passed on, expressed and consolidated by the members of society through communication, everyday dealings with customs, laws, norms and organizational structures.

Necessarily, values are conceptually fuzzy and fluid (Sommer, 2016: p. 83 ff.). It is precisely through this conceptual fuzziness that they develop their orienting function (cf. Luhmann, 1997: p. 341; on the function of semantic fuzziness Scheunpflug and Affolderbach, 2019). By communicating about values, expectations are formulated that control actions and cooperation and enable orientation in complex social contexts. Schools, in the way they are organized and with the communication embedded in them, are significant institutions of the implicit transmission of societal values. This communication encompasses far more than just curricula; however, the expectations towards schools are giving visibility in these texts like in a burning glass.

(3) Global values, which are related to global learning, bundle motivational dispositions to deal with complexity at different levels. They help to develop an attitude to actively deal with global challenges. The aforementioned understanding of education and learning in a globalized world is linked to 'global learning', to use the definition of the Maastricht Declaration of the 2002 GENE/European Council: 'Education that opens people's eyes and minds to the realities of the world, and awakens them to bring about a world of greater justice,

equity and human rights for all' (Maastricht Declaration, 2002; Nygard and Wegimont, 2018; cf. Bourn, 2014; 2018; Lehtomäki, Moate and Posti-Ahokas, 2016; Räsänen, 2009; or Tarozzi and Mallon, 2019). This is an umbrella concept that covers 'global citizenship education' (i.e. Shultz, 2010; Grobbauer, 2014; or UNESCO, 2015), and related concepts, and that identifies the necessity of considering social justice in human relations in a globalized world as foundation. This concept combines (1) the normative focuses of greater social justice and sustainability in the world, as well as (2) the perspective that social relations in a global perspective should be addressed.

In this study, these very different strands of research are seen together. The implicit social values embedded in and transported through curricula have hardly been examined with regard to the importance of global learning. Therefore, this research asks for the embedded global values in curricula and develops an operationalization to investigate implicit values.

Theoretical background: Operationalization of value discourses

The following criteria were decisive for the selection of the empirical instruments: (1) the theoretical frame of reference should have already been used for empirical investigations, (2) it should cover the value discourse as broadly as possible, and (3) provide comparative data for the classification of the findings (this criterion does not report any relevance for the findings here).

After reviewing the relevant literature, we discussed two approaches: the 'Refined Theory of Basic Individual Values' by Schwartz et al. (2012) and the 'Values in Action Inventory of Strengths' by Christopher Peterson and Martin Seligman (Peterson and Seligman, 2004; Park, Peterson and Seligman, 2004; Peterson and Park, 2004; Peterson, 2006). Schwartz's value theory takes into account the value prioritization and hierarchization of values by individuals and groups and systematically relates them to one another. It has been empirically tested, and data from international studies are available (Schwartz, 1992; 1999; Schwartz et al., 2012; Knafo et al., 2011; Drahmann, Cramer and Merk, 2020). Individual values are represented on a motivation continuum.

Schwartz (2012) distinguishes the following values:

1. self-determination in thinking (self-direction thought)
2. self-determination in action (self-direction action)

3. stimulation
4. hedonism
5. achievement
6. power over other people (power-dominance)
7. power over resources (power-resources), face, personal security (security-personal)
8. social security (security-societal)
9. tradition
10. rule-related conformity (conformity-rules)
11. group-related conformity (conformity-interpersonal)
12. humility
13. benevolence as dependability (benevolence-dependability)
14. benevolence as concern for others (benevolence-caring)
15. universalism concern (universalism concern)
16. nature-related universalism (universalism nature)
17. universalism as a tolerant attitude (universalism-tolerance)

For this study, the relationship of universalism to other values or the entire range of values is of special interest.

This spectrum is to be understood as a motivation continuum that relates to different basic needs. Linking back to these basic needs leads to a circular order that determines the self and social reference of values, and visualizes four basic attitudes (Schwartz et al., 2012: pp. 668–70) – namely openness to change (motivated by self-direction and stimulation), self-enhancement (motivated by achievement and power), conservation (motivated by security, tradition, conformity) and self-transcendence (motivated by benevolence and universalism). Values that are opposed to each other in different types of motivation can be clearly distinguished from each other (cf. Schwartz, 1994: p. 25). While Schwartz's measuring instruments for both the investigation of shared cultural values and the collection of individual values are based on questionnaire evaluations with self-reports from individuals, the present study uses the concept for a text analysis.

Method

Basic methodological decision: As the research intends to reflect implicit and explicit values in texts, the method of content analysis (Kuckartz, 2014) was chosen. The texts to be analysed were divided into analysis units and assigned to Schwartz's value categories in an iterative process with coders independently of each other. Those units that were placed in the same categories were further processed (detailed herein).

Data basis: Based on the research objectives, the study used the introductory texts of the curricula of four types of general education in Bavaria in the current version[2] (primary school and secondary tracking schools: *Hauptschule [leading to vocational training], Realschule [leading to professional colleges]* and *Gymnasium [leading to higher education/university]*) as basic documents. Each curriculum of a school type contains preambles on the 'Educational Mission' (*Bildungs- und Erziehungsauftrag*) and 'Overarching Educational Goals' (*Schulart- und fächerübergreifende Erziehungs- und Bildungsziele*). This is about fifty pages of text.

Data collection: The texts were imported into MAXQDA (Kuckartz, 2014) and then divided into units of analysis. A unit of analysis usually consists of a complete sentence, more rarely of a heading or the bullet point of a listing. Overall, the chapters consist of N = 876 analysis units, in the following called segments (primary school N = 358; *Hauptschule* N = 178; *Realschule*, N = 187; *Gymnasium* N = 153).

Coding process: The category system used to analyse the segments is based on Schwartz's model of nineteen fundamental values. The categories deductively obtained from the theory were operationalized by means of text passages and processed into a coding manual in which definitions, key word aids, anchor examples and references are presented. In addition, problematic classifications and important distinctions to other values were outlined. The coding manual was developed stepwise in discussion of the working group and coders were trained for using the coding manual. After finalizing the coding manual (Osterrieder and Banze, 2021) two independent coders coded the entire material two times again.

Lexical search: In addition, lexical searches were performed and manually filtered according to semantic affiliation. The terms 'sustainability'/'sustainable', 'globalization'/'global' were examined about their use and the respective contexts.

Results: Global values in curricula

The formal status of addressing universalistic values

Of the above 876 segments, N = 472 (53.9 per cent) were consistently coded as containing at least one value. The remaining 404 segments contained no value reference and were not further considered. The value-related segments received between one and nine codes, N = 317 (67.2 per cent) received one value code, N = 97 (20.6 per cent) received two, N = 41 (8.7 per cent) three and N = 17 (3.5 per cent) received more than three value encodings. There were no differences between the coders in the average number of codes, chi² < 1. The intercoder agreement was calculated using Cohen's kappa and was κ = .90. The agreement varied between 76 per cent (power over other people; power over resources) and 94 per cent (nature-related universalism). The values 'face' and 'humility' were never coded.

(1) The importance of universalistic values: High overall importance with low importance of nature

Overall, values related to universalism make up 17.2 per cent of all mentions. This value range is thus in second place of the ten central values according to Schwartz. A higher percentage can only be found for self-direction values (29 per cent) (cf. Osterrieder et al., under review). Values of universalism are given high priority.

Of the parts of the text tagged with universalism, 8 per cent of the mentions refer to social values in the sense of a commitment to equality, justice and security. 1.4 per cent of the mentions relate to the topic of 'nature' in terms of protecting the natural environment and the climate, and 7.8 per cent relate to tolerance in terms of acceptance and understanding for people who are different from oneself.

(2) Openness to change and self-transcendence

The value structure mentioned by Schwartz (1994) results from the assignment of values to specific underlying motivational orientations. In the following, the values are summarized according to their position on the axes 'openness to change' versus 'conservation', and 'self-transcendence' versus 'self-enhancement' (cf. Table 4.1).

Table 4.1 Percentage Distribution of Orientations Related to Social Change

Motivational orientation	Frequency (%)
Openness to change	33
Conservation	17
Self-transcendence	35
Self-enhancement	16

The findings show that the curriculum texts place a stronger focus on 'openness to change' and 'self-transcendence', and thus values of conservation and ego-related values of 'self-enhancement' play a lower role.

(3) Levels of values manifestation

The values address different levels of manifestation in the curriculum preambles. The segments coded with the three dimensions of universalism, additionally, were inductively coded according to the horizon in which the values are located.

(1) Values that are directly related to teaching, that is, which are located at the micro level of individuals
(2) Values that manifest themselves in school, that is, which are located at the meso level of the institution
(3) Values that appear in a context of society, that is, which are located at the national macro level
(4) Values that are reflected in global society, i.e. which are located at a global level.

The following figure shows the allocation of the different universalistic values according to reference horizons in absolute frequencies (cf. Figure 4.1). Table 4.2 presents the findings in their percentage frequencies.

The value configurations on the social concern mainly show a national focus. Second, it becomes apparent that the social challenges of an increasingly

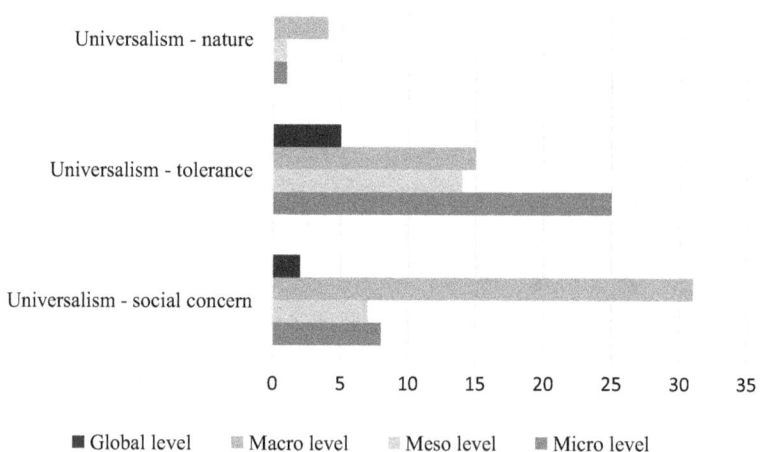

Figure 4.1 Absolute frequencies of universalistic values according to reference horizons.

Table 4.2 Relative Frequencies of Universalistic Values by Reference Horizons

Reference horizon	Universalism – social concern (%)	Universalism – tolerance (%)	Universalism – nature(%)
Micro level	17	42	17
Meso level	15	24	17
Macro level	65	25	67
Global level	4	8	0

heterogeneous society are placed in the immediate vicinity of the students and that they are called upon to be tolerant as individuals. Third, the prospects for protecting the environment are predominantly placed in the horizon of social action. Fourth, it is consistently apparent that the global social horizon of value configurations is largely absent.

The content of universal values

(1) Universalism – concern: equality among those present

There are thirty-eight references to 'universalism – concern' in the analysed preambles to curricula. The content of the value 'universalism – social concern' manifests itself predominantly at the level of society. The school should represent this value in its institutional constitution.

In these texts, the commitment to equality, justice and security for all people worldwide is mainly reduced to the commitment to the equality of all children in the respective school (LP GYM, 64): 'The curriculum for the Bavarian Gymnasium ensures for the pupils of the Gymnasium equivalent educational opportunities throughout Bavaria and should at the same time avoid obstacles for a possibly necessary change of school';[3] as well as LP MS, 36; LP GS, 34; LP GS, 105, LP GYM, 21. In addition, the right to education through the school is discussed (LP GS, 5): 'One of the main tasks of responsible education policy is to offer all children the best possible educational experiences and opportunities at an early stage. The focus is on the child's right to education from the very beginning' (LP RS, 35, LP GS, 105). Justice is reflected in particular with regard to educational equity and equal opportunities in the respective school (LP Gym, 71, LP RS, 121; LP GS, 62–3).

Equal opportunities and justice are only addressed insofar as pupils should find 'room for personal development' in their diversity. School should also be a place where democratic values are lived, including justice, equal opportunities and freedom. Furthermore, other elements of the free-democratic basic order are paraphrased: 'The rights of minorities', the prevention of discrimination and 'consideration for the weaker' (LP GYM, 71).

Equality, justice and safety are outlined in the curriculum texts for the people who are directly present in the school. A global perspective on justice and equal opportunities is not discernible. Ultimately, the curricula do not address these values as relevant for political action but only call for their importance in the respective social school environment.

(2) Universalism – nature: Sustainable thinking and acting for privileged students

For 'universalism – nature' there are thirty-eight references in the preambles to the curricula. 'Responsibility for nature and the environment' is explicitly named as an educational goal for all school types (LP GS, 84, LP GYM, 7; LP RS, 15-16; LP MS, 6). What this exactly consists of is not explained further. Concern about nature and climate change tends to be trivialized when the topic is discussed as one of several extra-curricular activities and as a topic outside of the classroom: 'Furthermore, working on the school newspaper, taking part in competitions, helping and contributing to Church services, the commitment to protecting and caring for the environment as well as social, cultural and political commitment are of great importance' (LP RS, 156).

Only the preamble to the curriculum for Gymnasium, that is, for those students who receive admission to university after leaving school, is this educational goal specified in the sense of 'a reflected value orientation for acting in social, ecological and economic responsibility' (LP GYM, 11–12). Only privileged students are confronted with responsibility towards environment and sustainability. In the context of this quote, ecologically responsible action is mentioned as an objective that is equivalent to socially and economically responsible action. This implicitly addresses the three-pillar model of sustainable development with the triad of ecology, economy and social affairs.

A lexical search was also carried out to examine the understanding of 'sustainability' that is reflected in the curricula. Terms related to 'sustainab*' are mentioned nineteen times in the four curricula examined. This term refers eighteen times to 'sustainable learning' in the sense of 'the development of permanent knowledge bases'. Just one passage in the primary school curriculum suggests thinking about education for sustainable development: 'In primary school, pupils get to know their living space with its historical, geographical, natural, cultural and social characteristics that are worth protecting and preserving. In exchange with others, a basis is created for actively shaping sustainable developments in space and society. The students relate their own environment to other regions and cultures in Europe and the world' (GS 125–6). This passage indicates the beginnings of thinking about environmental protection globally, but also remains in the conservative mode that is related to values of *conservation*.

In summary, environmental and climate problems are represented in a simplified way. The topic is not only clearly under-represented in terms of the frequency of mentions. It is hardly specified and with regard to taking responsibility for environmental issues and climate protection; it is only designed for high school students. Pupils from other school types are not addressed as subjects who assume responsibility. The topic is not described related to global justice, for example regarding the unequal distribution of the consequences of man-made climate change. Protection of the environment and nature in the situation of a global threat from the consequences of climate change also means securing human existence. However, this relation is not mentioned.

(3) Universalism – tolerance: Othering as a continuous perspective

The value 'universalism – tolerance' is the most frequently found of all three universalism values with fifty-five references. Tolerance values such as the promotion of understanding others, a change of perspective, peaceful conflict resolution and openness to new things are addressed in all curricula. A particular thematic focus is on the heterogeneity of the student body (e.g. LP GS, 105, 152; LP MS, 36, 52, 92). However, these universal values are often hedged in by conservative values of preserving tradition and the associated 'othering', as for example in this passage: 'Education and upbringing at the Realschule are based on the values of Western cultural tradition and sensitize the pupils to other cultures and ways of life' (LP RS, 331). This passage of text names the 'occidental cultural tradition' as a resource for orienting standards of value from which 'other forms of life' come into view. The term 'occidental cultural tradition' is used in conservative discourses to differentiate it from a Muslim cultural tradition that is not further differentiated (the Orient, the 'morning country').

The 'own' is contrasted here against the 'other'; and an approach from what is assumed to be the majority 'own' to 'the foreign' is imagined. The associated notion of cultures as clearly definable, essentialized identities does not take into account the understanding of hybrid culturality (Bhabha, 1994). Similar attributions of 'othering' show the assumption that students are involved in 'the most diverse social and family relationships' separated from those of the teachers (LP RS, 9). Teachers are obviously imagined in traditional family constellations, so they should be reminded of the diversified social and family constellations of the students.

Hybrid identities only addressed with regard to the primary school: 'Children have an emotional connection to the people, cultures and places with which they grow up or with which they feel connected. In the exchange with others and against the background of cultural diversity, they learn that the children in the class and school have different experiences and connections in this regard' (LP GS, 124). This position is also immediately caught up with culture essentializing: 'They [= the children] experience and understand that new surroundings can become homes and that many people are connected to several homes' (LP GS, 124).

Such an understanding of tolerance cannot exist on its own, but needs to be safeguarded: 'For a thriving coexistence of all groups involved in school life, mutual respect, respect and tolerance, but also clearly agreed rules are indispensable' (LP RS, 138). Here, the 'but' rhetorically creates an antinomy between the values of 'mutual respect, respect and tolerance' on the one hand and 'clearly agreed rules' on the other. Tolerance is contrasted with the value 'conformity – rules'.

Only for the Gymnasium social interactions are also described as essential, but as opening up new perspectives: 'Learning foreign languages enables a deeper understanding of other cultures and opens up new perspectives. The reciprocal relationship to English, but also to other modern foreign languages, is particularly evident in those grammar schools where bilingual teaching in subjects is part of the school profile' (LP GYM, 35).

Tolerance values described remain narrow and related to differentiation from others. The texts focus on the immediate vicinity, the experienced migration and the differentiation of life forms. A change of perspective with regard to difference criteria such as poverty, different legal systems and forms of society, environmental conditions and transculturality is omitted.

(4) Missing the global perspective

The lexical search for global perspectives yielded only two references:

> For secondary school students, learning in the 21st century means facing the challenges and needs of a rapidly changing society in a global world. The competences young people need today to achieve their goals require more than mastering a few narrow skills and abilities. Rather, they need strategies to cope with an increasingly complex society and world of employment, in which

independent planning and action are indispensable key competencies. (LP RS, 7–8)

The text refers to the increase in complexity in the context of globalization. In this context, however, no universalism values or considerations of justice are invoked, but rather the reference to self-determination and performance values is established. Pupils have to adapt to globalization, but cannot shape and influence globalization itself, for example with regard to questions of sustainability, climate policy or justice.

In another part of the curriculum, the assumed social heterogeneity is opened up as a perspective. Through intercultural education, students should be 'prepared for globalized structures in politics, business and society' (LP MS, 93). Here, too, the adaptation of the students is addressed.

Hence, global social challenges are not reflected in the manifested values. The formulation of universalism-values remains related to the school and its vicinity (e.g. LP MS, 105): 'Both joint celebrations and events as well as an appropriate and suitable culture of discussion and conflict resolution are further aspects of participation. All members of the school community have a stake in decisions, feel responsible and identify with their school'; see also LP Gym, 27 or LP RS, 34.). The cosmos in which values are reflected begins with the individual student and ends at the borders of Germany (e.g. LP GYM, 7: 'The students are to be educated in the spirit of democracy, in love for the Bavarian homeland and for the German people and in the spirit of international reconciliation'; see LP GYM 11–12). The way universalism values are manifested neglects the global perspective.

Summarizing reflection

The findings of this study are multiple. On the one hand, it became clear that universal themes have a relatively high priority in the texts of the curricula. A more detailed analysis of the individual text passages showed, however, that the way in which these value configurations were addressed did not convey what could be expected from these values in terms of climate justice, global solidarity or global social reflection beyond the immediate vicinity. Rather, it became obvious

1. that equality and justice are only reflected among those present and that the 'distant neighbour' does not come into view,

2. that urgent human issues with regard to climate and global justice are not addressed,
3. that these values are forms of discriminatory and exclusion of responsibility, and
4. that the understanding of values identified in this study encompasses an essentializing understanding of culture that promotes 'othering'.

The subject of universalism values therefore remains simplified in view of global social, political and economic challenges. Ultimately, this means that – despite high values of universalism – global values are not implemented. Despite all the lip services, the social transformation has not progressed so far that school learning is reflected in the horizon of the one world and the requirements of sustainability. This is not supporting a 'pedagogy of hope' and not in line with the needs of students related to their own future and the future of the planet.

This study provides a stimulus to enable further empirical research on global value discourses. The selected instruments can be applied to different types of texts that are an expression of social characteristics and at the same time shape society, such as textbooks, party programmes or mission statements of institutions. Especially in view of the universal relevance of the Sustainable Development Goals of the United Nations in different social contexts and the requirements for an 'education of hope', such forms of analysis seem indispensable. Curriculum texts not only say something about the school but also reflect the discourse of a society. By this, they serve as a seismograph about the values architecture, which might not be explicit. The study foreshadows that there might be a challenge to consider adequately the implementation of the global values in curricular guiding principles.

List of abbreviations

LP GS: *Bayerische Leitlinien für die Bildung und Erziehung von Kindern bis zum Ende der Grundschulzeit, Bildungs- und Erziehungsauftrag der Grundschule, Übergreifende Bildungs- und Erziehungsziele- guidelines and educational goals for primary schools*

LP MS: *Bildungs- und Erziehungsauftrag der Mittelschule, Übergreifende Bildungs- und Erziehungsziele- educational goals for middle schools*

LP RS: *Bildungs- und Erziehungsauftrag der Realschule, Übergreifende Bildungs- und Erziehungsziele- educational goals for secondary schools*

LP GYM: *Bildungs- und Erziehungsauftrag des Gymnasiums, Übergreifende Bildungs- und Erziehungsziele- educational goals for grammar schools*

Notes

1 This study was part of the 'Ad Hoc Working Group on Future Values' (*Ad Hoc-Arbeitsgruppe Zukunftswerte*) at the Bavarian Academy of Sciences, subgroup community-interest versus self-interest. Andrea Abele-Brehm, Frank Fischer, Dieter Frey, Michaela Gläser-Zikuda, Annette Scheunpflug, Peter Schwardmann, Astrid Séville and Monika Schnitzer were involved in the concept and discussion of the study. We thank the Bavarian Academy of Sciences for funding the project.
2 These curricula are called 'Curriculum Plus'. The designation 'Curriculum Plus' indicates that the educational standards agreed by the Conference of Ministers of Education (KMK) were taken into account and that the curriculum is formulated in a competence-oriented manner. The primary school curriculum has been in effect since the 2014/15 school year in grades 1 and 2, from the 2015/16 school year in grade 3 and from the 2016/17 school year in grade 4. For the other three school types, the Curriculum Plus gradually came into force from the 2017/18 school year. See also https://www.isb.bayern.de/schulartueberfallendes/paedagogik-didaktik-methodik/kompetenzorientation/; retrieved in October 2021.
3 All quotations are own translations from the German original text.

References

Bentall, C, D. Bourn, H. McGough, A. Hodgson and K. Spours (2014). 'Global Learning for Global Colleges: Creating Opportunities for Greater Access to International Learning for 16–25 Year Olds'. *Journal of Further and Higher Education* 38(5): 621–40. https://doi.org/10.1080/0309877X.2013.817001

Bhabha, H. (1994). *The Location of Culture*. London: Routledge.

Biehl, J., F. Ohlhaver and K. Riquarts (1999). 'Sekundäre Lehrplanbindungen. Vergleichende Untersuchung zur Entstehung und Verwendung von Lehrplanentscheidungen'. Endbericht zum DFG-Projekt. Available online: https://www.lehrplanforschung.ch/wp-content/uploads/2011/11/DFGEndbericht-Gesamt1.pdf (accessed 11 April 2022).

Bourn, D. (2014). *The Theory and Practice of Development Education: A Pedagogy for Global Social Justice*. London: Routledge.

Bourn, D. (2018). *Understanding Global Skills for 21st Century Professions*. Cham: Palgrave MacMillan. https://doi.org/10.1007/978-3-319-97655-6

Drahmann, M., C. Cramer and S. Merk (2020). *Wertorientierungen und Werterziehung. Ergebnisse einer repräsentativen Studie zur Perspektive von Lehrpersonen und Eltern schulpflichtiger Kinder*. Tübingen: Universität Tübingen.

Ferguson-Patrick, K., R. Reynolds and S. Macqueen (2018). 'Integrating Curriculum: A Case Study of Teaching Global Education'. *European Journal of Teacher Education* 41(2): 187–201. https://doi.org/10.1080/02619768.2018.1426565

GENE (= Global Education Network Europe) (2019; 2018). *The Stage of Global Education in Europe*. Dublin: GENE.

Grobbauer, H. (2014). 'Global Citizenship Education – Politische Bildung für die Weltgesellschaft' ['Global Citizenship Education: Political Education for the World Society']. *Zeitschrift für Internationale Bildungsforschung und Entwicklungspädagogik* 37(3): 28–33.

Killick, D. (2020). 'Beyond Competencies and Silos: Embedding Graduate Capabilities for a Multicultural Globalizing World across the Mainstream Curriculum'. *Research in Comparative and International Education* 15(1): 27–35. https://doi.org/10.1177/1745499920901946

Knafo, A. S. Rocco and L. Sagiv (2011). 'The Value of Values in Cross-Cultural Research. A Special Issue in Honor of Shalom Schwartz'. *Journal of Cross-Cultural Psychology* 42(2): 178–85.

Kuckartz, U. (2014). *Qualitative Text Analysis. A Guide to Methods, Practice and Using Software*. New Castle: Sage.

Künzli, R. (1986). *Topik des Lehrplandenkens. Architektonik des Lehrplans: Ordnung und Wandel*. Kiel: Mende.

Künzli, R., A. V. Fries, W. Hürlimann and M. Rosenmund (2013). *Der Lehrplan – Programm der Schule*. Weinheim: Beltz Juventa.

Lehtomäki, E., J. Moate and H. Posti-Ahokas (2016). 'Global Connectedness in Higher Education: Student Voices on the Value of Cross-Cultural Learning Dialogue'. *Studies in Higher Education* 41(11): 2011–27. https://doi.org/10.1080/03075079.2015.1007943

Luhmann, N. (1997). *Die Gesellschaft der Gesellschaft*, 2 vols. Frankfurt/M.: Suhrkamp.

Maastricht Global Education Declaration (2002). *A European Strategy Framework for Improving and Increasing Global Education in Europe to the Year 2015*. GENE.

MAXQDA, Software für qualitative Datenanalyse (1989–2022). *VERBI Software. Consult*. Sozialforschung GmbH, Berlin, Deutschland.

Müller, J. and A. Séville (2022). 'Paradoxe Kopplungen. Die Wertekommunikation von Bündnis 90/Die Grünen als Ansprache und Fürsprache einer neuen Mittelklasse'. *Leviathan. Berliner Zeitschrift für Sozialwissenschaft* 50(1): 90–117.

Nygaard, A. and L. Wegimont (2018). *Global Education in Europe: Concepts, Definitions and Aims in the Context of the SDGs and the New European Consensus on Development*. Dublin: GENE.

Osterrieder, M. and A.-C. Banze (2021). *Kodierhandbuch Lehrplanuntersuchung, Universität Bamberg*. non-published document.

Osterrieder, M., A. Scheunpflug, A.-C. Banze and A. Abele-Brehm (submitted under review). *Self Direction and Universalism: Value Manifestations in German School Curricula*.

Park, N., C. Peterson and M. E. P. Seligman (2004). 'Strengths of Character and Well-Being'. *Journal of Social and Clinical Psychology* 23: 603–19.

Peterson, C. and N. Park (2004). 'Classification and Measurement of Character Strengths. Implications for Practice', in P. A. Linley and S. Joseph (eds), *Positive Psychology in Practice*, 443–6. Hoboken: Wiley.

Peterson, C. and M. E. P. Seligman (2004). *Character Strengths and Virtues: A Handbook and Classification*. Washington D.C.: American Psychological Association.

Peterson, C. E. (2006). 'The Values in Action (VIA) Classification of Strengths', in M. E. Csikszenthihalyi and I. S. E. Csikszenthihalyi (eds), *A Life Worth Living: Contributions to Positive Psychology*, 29–48. New York: Oxford University Press.

Räsänen, R. (2009). 'Transformative Global Education and Learning: Teacher Education in Finland'. *International Journal of Development Education and Global Learning* 1(2): 25–40.

Scheunpflug, A. (2001). 'Die globale Perspektive einer Bildung für nachhaltige Entwicklung', in O. Herz, H. Seybold and G. Strobl (eds), *Bildung für nachhaltige Entwicklung*. Wiesbaden: VS Verlag für Sozialwissenschaften. https://doi.org/10.1007/978-3-322-93257-0_7

Scheunpflug, A., A. Abele-Brehm, M. Osterrieder and A.-C. Banze (submitted under review). 'Gesellschaftliche Wertekonfigurationen im gegliederten Schulwesen'.

Scheunpflug, A. and M. Affolderbach (2019). 'Zur Funktion unscharfer Begriffe. Ein Plädoyer für einen reflexiven Blick auf Explikationen'. *Vierteljahrsschrift für wissenschaftliche Pädagogik* 95(2): 187–98.

Schreiber, J. R. and H. Siege, eds (2016). *Curriculum Framework Education for Sustainable Development*. Bonn/Berlin: Cornelsen.

Schwartz, S. H. (1992). 'Universals in the Content and Structure of Values. Theoretical Advances and Empirical Tests in 20 Countries', in M. Zann (ed.), *Advances in Experimental Social Psychology*, vol. 25, 1–65. Orlando: Academic.

Schwartz, S. H. (1994). 'Are there Universal Aspects in the Structure and Contents of Human Values?'. *Journal of Social Issues* 50: 19–45.

Schwartz, S. H. (1999). 'A Theory of Cultural Values and some Implications for Work'. *Applied Psychology. An International Review* 48(1): 49–72.

Schwartz, S. H. (2012). 'An Overview of the Schwartz Theory of Basic Values'. *Online Readings in Psychology and Culture* 2(1): 3–20. DOI https://doi.org/10.9707/2307-0919.1116

Schwartz, S. H. J. Cieciuch, M. Vecchione, E. Davidov, R. Fischer, C. Beierlein, A. Ramos, M. Verkasalo, J-E. Lönnqvist, K. Demirutku, O. Dirilen-Gumus, & M. Konty (2012). 'Refining the Theory of Basic Individual Values'. *Journal of Personality and Social Psychology* 103(4): 663–88.

Shultz, L. (2010). 'What Do We Ask of Global Citizenship Education? A Study of Global Citizenship Education in a Canadian University'. *International Journal of Development Education and Global Learning* 3(1): 5–22.

Sommer, A. (2016). *Werte. Warum man sie braucht, obwohl es sie nicht gibt*. Stuttgart: Metzler.

Tarozzi, M. and C. Inguaggiato (2018). 'Implementing Global Citizenship Education in EU Primary Schools: The Role of Government Ministries'. *International Journal of Development Education and Global Learning* 10(1): 21–38. https://doi.org/10.18546/IJDEGL.10.1.03

Tarozzi, M. and B. Mallon (2019). 'Educating Teachers towards Global Citizenship: A Comparative Study in Four European Countries'. *London Review of Education* 17(2): 112–25. https://doi.org/10.18546/LRE.17.2.02

Terhart, E. (2021). 'Zukunftsthemen der Schulforschung', in D. Fickermann, B. Edelstein, J. Gerick and K. Racherbäumer (eds), *Schule und Schulpolitik während der Corona-Pandemie: Nichts gelernt?' Beiheft Die Deutsche Schule*, 147–75. Münster: Waxmann.

UNESCO, ed. (2015). *Global Citizenship Education: Topics and Learning Objectives*. UNESCO.

Part II

Global Perspectives on Global Social Justice

5

Non-Western Perspectives in Framing Global Citizenship Education

The Role of Higher Education Institutions

Mario R. Smith, Abigail Simons, Emma Wagener, Michelle Andipatin and Jose Frantz

Introduction

The aim of this chapter is to provide an alternate conceptual framework of global citizen education that espouses social justice principles through a three-tiered approach. This formulation posits that the triangulation of the three tiers provides a critical lens and robust framework to develop a global citizen education (GCE) agenda for universities within sub-Saharan Africa (SSA). The first tier consists of theory; the second, institutional objectives and culture; and the third tier incorporates student development. Each of these tiers contains operational strategies that can be incorporated into the conceptualization of global citizenship education to achieve contextual sensitivity and local relevance.

The projected population growth in SSA suggests an increase to 1.4 billion in 2030 and more than 2 billion in 2050 (UN, 2019). However, the proportional participation in higher education for the population of SSA, as estimated by higher education enrolments (HEE), is not commensurate with this projected population increase. The related concern is the impact this has on sustainable economic development, as the growth rate of participation in higher education within SSA is below 12–15 per cent (Calderon, 2012). Currently, only 7 per cent of school leavers in Africa progress into the higher education space (Morris, Perry and Wardle, 2021).

The landscape of higher education in SSA is complex, and there are some major trends indicating the need for action in the field of higher education. Provision is inadequate by world standards despite the number of higher education institutions (HEIs) in SSA mushrooming. HEE in SSA is expected to increase from 8.8 million in 2020 to 13.6 million in 2030 (Calderon, 2018). While there has been rapid growth in enrolments, systems remain insufficient, making this a very competitive space. The demand for higher education currently exceeds its capacity, and, in some instances, this has resulted in overcrowding which in turn has led to concerns about quality assurance. Given the limitations in terms of access and opportunity, it becomes imperative for institutions to reflect on their role in providing transformative, inclusive education. This is true particularly if our intention is to equip our students with the requisite critical thinking skills so that they are able to take their places in the global village to work collaboratively on addressing some of the major challenges facing contemporary society (Bringham, 2011).

The increased demand for access and participation in higher education prompted massification, that is, an increased enrolment that placed a substantial burden on infrastructure, human and material resource capacity and quality assurance. GCE is thought to contribute to the development of graduate attributes and regulation of institutional cultures that will enhance the adoption of innovative learning and teaching strategies (Shultz, 2007). Similarly, policy directives in SSA, such as the South African National Development Plan 2030, promote a regional focus and skills acquisition that will result in graduates being transformative agents with the capacity to impact local and global social challenges. Thus, the approach to research and postgraduate education must be focused on an interdisciplinary understanding of problems rather than only a disciplinary one. This is consistent with Freire's (2009) mandate for universities to be critically engaged in the service of the popular classes, without loss of seriousness and rigour. In this way, social justice and pedagogy of hope must be prioritized. GCE has been heralded as a means to achieve such outcomes.

The future leadership of higher education in SSA is at risk due to an ageing research and development cohort and a slow rate of graduate production, especially at the doctoral level.

In response to these challenges, governments in SSA have launched several programmes to address the need for succession planning. An attitude of global citizenship is thought to be instrumental in the pursuit of these goals and the success of these initiatives. For example, in South Africa programmes included the future professors' programme, the Black Academics Advancement Programme (BAAP), the University Staff Doctoral Programme (USDP) and the Nurturing the Emerging Researcher Programme (NESP). These programmes focused on developing capacity through completion of postgraduate qualifications, the development of leadership skills and exposure to various aspects of university management and governance.

Several initiatives from the global North attempted to strengthen doctoral education, increase mobility and build supervisory capacity in research and instructional staff at universities in the global South and SSA specifically. The United Nations Educational Scientific and Cultural Organisation (UNESCO) firmly placed GCE on their agenda as a vehicle for transformation and inclusion. GCE is a strategic area of UNESCO's education sector programme that aims to instil values, attitudes and behaviours in learners and graduates that support responsible global citizenship (UNESCO, 2015).

Global citizenship education at universities in SSA must promote an attitude of critical engagement in their local and regional realities (Frantz et al., 2020). Thus, contextual sensitivity and relevance must be incorporated into the conceptualization of global citizenship and GCE in order to ensure that there is a coherent framework for learning, teaching, research and community engagement. There is unfortunately no consensus on the conceptualization of global citizenship which impacts application and implementation (Oxfam, 2015). Current conceptualizations do not systematically provide a critical lens and a robust formulation for this purpose. Thus, there is a need for alternate conceptualizations. Current conceptualizations systematically excluded non-Western perspectives and, therefore, it is important to explore non-Western perspectives for applications to higher education in SSA.

Traditional conceptualizations of global citizenship

A citizen is someone who lives in a nation-state, has rights and privileges and performs duties in accordance with the state (Banks, 2014). Citizenship refers to the rights, duties and identities which link an individual to the nation-state (Koopmans et al., 2005). Global citizenship aims to expand the definition of citizenship to promote the principle of inclusion. It does not entail a legal status and refers more to a sense of belonging (UNESCO, 2013). In contrast, citizenship is a product of diversity rather than an institutional tool serving particular groups (Abdi and Shultz, 2008). Several scholars proposed the notion of global citizenship which advocates empathy for and solidarity with all people, along with the rights and responsibilities that are valid across national boundaries (Oslar and Vincent, 2002; Marshall, 2007; Horey et al., 2018). A global citizen respects and values diversity, understanding the presence of a wider world and how it functions (Oxfam, 2006). Essentially, global citizens are aware of their role in the world. Thus, taking it upon themselves to be an active part of the community, both locally and internationally.

The concept of global citizenship is influenced by conflicting disciplinary interpretations including influences from psychology, education, politics, economics, culture, social studies, environmental studies and moral/spiritual dimensions. For example, educational theorists Davies (2006) and Haigh and Clifford (2010) highlight the notion of 'global awareness', whereas philosophical theorists Hanson (2010) and Stoner et al. (2014) emphasize moral and ethical components of global citizenship. From an economic perspective, global citizenship is viewed as a business model that gauges an individual's fiscal knowledge and abilities to operate cross-nationally (Millar et al. 2019).

There is currently no consensus on the definition of global citizenship, as it is ill-defined and lacks sufficient clarity and comprehensiveness (Caruana, 2014). Different models of global citizenship have emerged that specify elements and suggest how a global citizenship identity is developed. The lack of consensus on the definition of global citizenship influences how it is operationalized in educational practice (Reysen and Katzarska-Miller, 2013). Thus, there is a need to examine the theoretical tenets underlying various models of and approaches to global citizenship education, especially the extent to which it considers non-Western perspectives.

Global citizenship education

Global citizenship education (GCE) has become a focus of study in a diverse range of academic fields over the past two decades. According to Parmenter (2011), GCE emanates from the joining of two or more existing topics of concern within the area, so that literature on the topic is embedded in existing research within the field while being linked to transdisciplinary trends in knowledge production and societal change. For example, in the field of education, GCE is rooted in the two distinct fields of global education and citizenship education. Osler and Vincent (2002: p. 2) define global education as

> encompassing the strategies, policies and plans that prepare young people and adults for living together in an interdependent world. It is based on the principles of co-operation, non-violence, respect for human rights and cultural diversity, democracy and tolerance. It is characterised by pedagogical approaches based on

human rights and a concern for social justice which encourage critical thinking and responsible participation. Learners are encouraged to make links between local, regional and world-wide issues and to address inequality.

Over the years, GCE has been critiqued by a number of academics who often referred to the term as being ambiguous and holding explicit Western assumptions. This led to the development of many typologies which enabled scholars to identify, articulate and assess the goals of GCE. For example, Dill (2013) identified two main approaches to GCE from which two differing goals can be identified. First, the global competencies approach aims to provide students with the necessary skills to compete in a global society. The second approach, global consciousness, aims to provide students with a global orientation, empathy and cultural sensitivity, stemming from human values and assumptions (Dill, 2013).

Schattle (2008) suggested a framework that categorized GCE into four ideologies: (1) moral cosmopolitanism, (2) liberal multiculturalism, (3) neoliberalism and (4) environmentalism. Gaudelli (2009) proposed a multidimensional framework for examining and constructing different forms and understandings of global citizenship. This comprised neoliberal, national, Marxist, cosmopolitan and world justice and government models. Another scholar, Shultz (2007), identifies three underlying understandings of GCE, that is, neoliberal, radical and transformationalist models.

Torres (2017) suggests three justifications for including GCE in a modern educational institution. First, GCE supports global peace. Second, it encourages interventions addressing economic, social and cultural inequality and could potentially reduce global poverty; and third, GCE provides a framework and guidelines supporting civic virtues that will result in more democratic societies. These traditional conceptualizations underpinned capacity-building initiatives by the 'global North' that entailed investing of resources into resource development and global citizenship education. North–South collaborations must draw on reciprocal learning that incorporates non-Western perspectives.

The role of HEIs in SSA becomes critical as active partners in the process of capacitation and transformation towards a global and local social justice through GCE. HEIs in SSA must provide the voice and articulation that will make it possible to start from and respect the local reality in order to raise consciousness (Thomas, 2009). HEIs in SSA must engage in dialogue in the Freirean sense which is a prerequisite for change. These institutions must balance the dialectic between validation of what is (current) and what can be (change) (Reimers and

Marmolejo, 2022). As a region, they must embrace and articulate their realities before they can embrace continental and global realities and initiatives. The following sections will present an alternative conceptual framework to develop GCE in SSA. This framework consists of three tiers, containing strategies to empower students and academics to become responsible and active global citizens. The framework ultimately constitutes a theory of change for global citizenship education in SSA.

Tier 1: Theory of change

GCE requires a framework or a theory of change that institutions must adopt intentionally in order to achieve its goals. There must be a theoretical underpinning to the change we wish to achieve through GCE. Theory must be used to formulate relationships between various factors that influence the development of students' interest and their participation in civic activities. Theoretical approaches contribute to the ongoing discourse on finding complementary approaches to promote students' interest and participation in civic activities, especially in HEIs (Reimers and Marmolejo, 2021). Owusu-Agyeman and Fourie-Malherbe (2019) concluded that the university environment remains an appropriate space for augmenting students' civic knowledge and skills, diverse experiences and social responsibility. A supportive university civic environment has the potential to foster interaction during civic activities, engagement with communities and special activities that deepen the students' understanding of volunteerism and civic engagement (Reimers, 2021). In order for the university to take on these qualities, an intentional and clear theory of change must underpin the conceptualization of global citizen education.

Traditional conceptualizations of global citizenship are focused on international exchange and mobilization that can have neoliberal undertones (Goddard et al., 2016). Aktas et al. (2017) proclaimed that many education institutions approach global citizenship as something to be earned by completing a checklist of requirements rather than developing critical reflexive skills. For example, Zemach-Bersin (2012) describes the nature of global citizenship in the US context as a licence that universities hand out to students who study abroad. The neoliberal view of global citizenship is focused more on the drive to increase transnational mobility of knowledge and skill, with the goal of linking global citizenship to global economic participation. Given the expansion of GCE, it is crucial to understand how HEIs promote GCE programmes.

In the SSA region and within the respective SSA countries, there is such oppression, inequality, variation in class and relative privilege that serves as an impetus for developing a global citizen identity evidenced by the appreciation of group differences, intergroup empathy and the need to act in response to inequality (Freire, 2009). UNESCO (2013) has been promoting education for peace and sustainability development focusing on transformative education by empowering individuals to engage and assume active roles to face and resolve global challenges. Thus, HEIs in SSA have a strong social justice agenda, promote equity and celebrate diversity. These institutional values and foci often reflect implicit theories of change. These theories must become explicit in order for institutions to optimally harness theoretical tenets and to develop clear links between theory and operational strategies and institutional operational plans. Thus, GCE must allow for an articulation of institutional values that already have transformational agendas.

An important theoretical departure point in SSA is the implicit construction of students as partners in the promotion of social responsibility and cultural diversity. Individuals are constantly influenced by transitional, cross-cultural, multicultural and multi-ethnic interactions. HEIs consequently develop campus climates that enhance students' interest and participation in civic activities (Khodabocus, Bahadur and Armoogum, 2022). The theoretical underpinning of such activities and initiatives must be leveraged in order to achieve a greater level of intentionality and directed monitoring and evaluation of implemented activities. The ability of students to enter into partnerships could foster a sense of social responsibility, as well as their engagement with peers from diverse cultural groupings (Thomas, 2009). The theoretical departure would be that experiences with cultural diversity at the core promote civic activities among students in HEI settings, especially in developing countries and multicultural environments. To create an effective GCE programme to encourage students to be active citizens within their communities in SSA, the HEIs should provide opportunities to reflect the complex identities within a growing diverse world (Banks, 2014). A direct outflow of such a theoretical position would be a commitment to establish a strong institutional civic culture that has the potential to enhance the development of students' civic knowledge and skills through common norms and group ideals.

Another important theoretical tenet is that personal and collective agency can develop civic knowledge and skills. As such, institutions in SSA must promote the development of agency at the personal and the collective level through all aspects of the institutions. For example, the individual student must develop a sense of mastery and capacity to impact his or her environment. The university context becomes a space where this skill can be practised and honed through engagement with staff, administration, governance structures and fellow students. Once acquired, this skill can be generalized to other areas of his or her life where there is or may be oppression and inequality. At a collective level, groups of students, student associations, discipline groups or interest groups may embark on particular actions in areas of interest (Lewis, 2012). Through this process, students learn the power of collective agency. The democratization of countries in SSA is replete with examples of student action that impacted the micro- and macro-political context. Through the core and co-curricular activities students are educated and learning takes place. This education is not politically neutral. Hooks (2014) argues that our methods of teaching as educators must be living examples of our politics and how we would like the world to be. She writes about teaching to transgress by pushing against the boundaries, to challenge racism, sexism, classism and all forms of oppression in the world. In a transgressive approach to education, educators support others and themselves to achieve the freedom to live fully in the world (Hooks, 2003). We can only progress and develop if we create learning spaces to develop our capacity for critical thinking about ourselves and our lives. Thus, theory must become explicit and promote critical thinking followed by action in pursuit of social justice. Moreover, there must be a commitment to approach global citizenship education from an interdisciplinary focus, to critically engage the canon of theory within disciplines and to intentionally incorporate critical theory from the liberation stable (Sewell, 2013).

Tier 2: Institutional objectives and culture

One of the key objectives of GCE is to bring about transformation within institutions. HEIs have thus been deliberate in their attempts to address GCE. According to Popescu (2015), institutional strategic planning has to provide evidence of intentions and attempts to integrate GCE and GC in the operational plans of the institution. In other words, HEIs must pursue GCE at an institutional level and create an enabling environment for the development of a global citizenship identity. Within an enabling environment, the institution is able to use various strategies to provide its stakeholders with information that facilitates the understanding of social, environmental, economic and political processes globally, thus developing critical thinking in students and staff and allowing them to think broader than local but more globally. The institutional objectives can invariably dictate the trajectory of GCE. HEIs are often motivated by the goal of increasing the global dimension of the institution rather than developing global citizen identification among students and staff. The culture and values of the school/unit and the management at different levels determine the global initiatives that HEIs get involved in (Oxfam, 2015).

Among universities in the South, the thinking of globalization may be influenced by the thinking of the North. Popescu (2015) observed that global dimensions are often operationalized in North–South collaborations as active engagement in the development of global research partnerships and scientific research infrastructure, by participation in research projects and competitive applications for international funding. HEIs in SSA have strong traditions of collaboration and have demonstrated the importance of being equal partners and collaborators in initiatives rather than being passive recipients of capacitation initiatives. Frantz et al. (2014) highlighted the impact of a North–South collaboration between HEIs in not only building research capacity but also developing intra- and interdisciplinary partnerships that resulted in maximizing the capacity-building efforts that enhanced the individual and institutional capacity. The voice of the South must not be lost, but cultivated, so that the 'global South' will be able to advance the equity required to develop with GCE.

The extent to which internationalization and GCE are incorporated into the agenda of an institution will be reflected in the curriculum and programming qualification mix. The aim of credit-bearing programmes to assist in driving CGE and its principles has been highlighted in the literature. Aktas et al. (2017) identified that credit-bearing global citizenship programmes in HEIs in SSA were located within various faculties, with a quarter of programmes located in a department specifically dedicated to GCE. Four observations were made about global citizenship programmes within SSA.

The first observation was that internationally, programmes or courses on global citizenship include mobility as a requirement. This approach to global citizenship is based on the assumption that students have the means, financially and circumstantially, to travel. Aktas et al. (2017) identified that only 25 per cent of programmes at HEIs in SSA required *international travel* for the completion of the programme, although mobility was strongly encouraged. The authors state that by making travel optional, institutions can account for practical and financial restrictions. This stance is sensitive to the lived realities of students. It resonates with the Freirean notion that 'hope born in the creative unrest of the battle, will continue to have meaning when, and only when, it can in its own turn give birth to new struggles on other levels' (Freire, 2009: p. 185). In consultation with student leadership, a solution was found to make travel optional. However, out of this solution, another source of inequality was born. There might be equal access to the programme, but this option creates the potential for inequalities within the institution where some students are able to travel abroad, and others are not. Thus, differential experiences among students in the same programme result that are patterned along racial, gendered and economic lines.

The second observation was the *language requirements* in foreign languages that were noted in international programmes as a prerequisite. In programmes at SSA institutions, the language requirement was set as a prescribed degree or programme requirement. This provided students with an opportunity to acquire a foreign language and develop proficiency as part of the degree programme. Making language a requirement could be to the advantage or disadvantage of the students as learning a new language may be difficult for some. Another approach was to group language study into the broader area of communication (Aktas et al., 2017). This allowed for flexibility that focused on learning about effective communication strategies rather than language acquisition per se. The second approach highlighted may be more conducive for applicants from the South.

The third observation was the requirement of *engagement and service-learning* is a common feature of international programmes. Within the SSA context, 79 per cent of institutions required engagement. Interestingly, 71 per cent of programmes specified both local and global engagement and action. The focus on both local and international engagement emphasized global citizenship as active engagement, rather than an academic understanding. The most prominent form of engagement was identified as service-learning, with the majority (67 per cent) of programmes listing service-learning as an optional component. Service-learning requires a high level of coordination, planning and accountability from the institution. Setting it as an optional activity reduces the pressure on the institution to manage the requirement. This provides a solution to the limited infrastructure and resources within institutions in the SSA region but creates a differential uptake that is often patterned along racial, gendered and economic lines. However, incorporating an aspect of engagement can assist in developing social responsibility in those students or staff moving between countries.

Finally, GCE must be articulated in the *learning outcomes and curriculum content*. In the SSA context six general learning outcome areas were identified among institutions: self-reflection (75 per cent), social responsibility (67 per cent), employability (58 per cent), leadership (38 per cent), problem-solving (33 per cent) and entrepreneurship-oriented outcomes such as divergent thinking (8 per cent). The most frequently observed area of the curriculum was social justice and human rights (63 per cent), followed by business and economics (58 per cent). Sustainable development, politics and international relations were all equally present, within 54 per cent of programmes.

Research indicated that internationalizing higher education and the curriculum were placed prominently in the institutional operational plans of HEIs in the SSA region (Clifford and Montgomery, 2017; McGrath, Thondhlana and Garwe, 2019). Clifford and Montgomery (2017) highlighted that coloniality continues to pervade many countries and education systems, and institutional inertia and investments in the status quo fuel resistance to change. There remains a lack of indigenous, minority and diaspora voices in Western-generated discussions of internationalization of the curriculum and the need for them to become integral to the discussion of future tertiary education policies and curricula. McGrath, Thondhlana and Garwe (2019) state that it is likely that lower-income countries are likely to perceive IHE as a contributing factor to achieve national development strategies. The emphasis on entrepreneurship over employment also needs to be considered in ways which 'situate entrepreneurship strongly in civic engagement rather than atomised individualism' (p. 17). These understandings also reflect the pan-African tradition of 'self-reliance'. Thus, institutional strategy and culture assists in building the values of global citizenship.

Tier 3: Student development

Strategies to promote global citizenship among students must be prioritized. Three strategies employed in HEIs in SSA were identified. Walker and Loots (2016) evaluated the 'Undergraduate Leadership Programme', implemented in a South African university in 2010, which focused on diversity, citizenship and leadership. First-year students were selected to visit universities to experience models of integration across lines of culture, colour and language. The programme involved exposing groups of students comprising mixed races, genders and fields of study, to different cultures, lifestyles and beliefs away from the familiarity of home (Walker and Loots, 2016). This programme intended to foster leadership development by facilitating new ways of thinking, and engagement among students from different backgrounds.

The programme was successful in various aspects. Students noted that being placed with new people in an unfamiliar space created an opportunity for them to find common ground with each other. Students also reported being more 'open-minded' after the programme and were able to engage with privilege and related issues with more courage. Students reported diversity awareness increased through exposure to a structured environment. Students were able to develop increased sensitivity to others from different racial groups, by acknowledging the role and impact of history and family on their own and others' attitudes. This was largely facilitated by the group discussions and deliberations required around issues of diversity. Being able to speak up about issues of racism is understood by Walker and Loots as a form of civic action, by challenging the notions and subtleties that continue to maintain racist perspectives. Walker and Loots (2016) concluded that the Undergraduate Leadership Programme supported the importance of universities as spaces for the formation of individual citizenship capabilities and functioning and democratic citizenship values.

The study-abroad programme involved three weeks abroad, at one of ten participating universities in the United States. The trip was fully funded and aimed to expose students to the academic, social, cultural and residential lives of the students at the host university. Selected students participated in a short preparatory programme around leadership, dialogue and diversity. Students were required to provide reflections on their experience that facilitated personal growth and introspection.

Social networks can play a role in the transitional experiences of international African doctoral students in South Africa (Herman and Meki Kombe, 2019). Academic networks were an important site for building social networks, as involvement in 'research commons' where postgraduate students are able to get together, academic support from other students and text-based communication through email or WhatsApp. A second network identified was the religious network, where international students reportedly were provided with a stable social network through attending mosque or church. A third and essential social network was that of co-nationals, where students could find familiarity and support from other international students. Interestingly, students also reported that South Africa felt too Westernized, and did not feel as though it was a part of Africa anymore.

Herman and Meki Kombe (2019) further reported that South African students did not benefit from the rich experiences offered by their international doctoral fellows. This raises some concerns as doctoral studies should not only be about getting the degree, but it is important that students develop intercultural skills, become global citizens and develop strong international networks. The separation of local and international students on campus may further hinder this goal. Herman and Meki Kombe (2019) highlighted the role that South African HEIs played over the past few years, particularly during the post-apartheid era. South African institutions have seen a steady increase in enrolment of regional students, particularly at a postgraduate level. South African institutions have an important role to play in integrating international students within the institutional culture and for South African students to be orientated on internationalization and its importance in bringing together diversity within campus life.

Akudolu, Ugochukwu and Olibie (2017) identified that while students possess virtual learning competencies, only a few engaged in virtual learning applications. When looking at the competencies possessed, researchers identified that these were not the core competencies needed for virtual learning. The low engagement with virtual learning limited their engagement in opportunities to acquire global citizenship and develop as global citizens. Akudolu, Ugochukwu and Olibie (2017) recommend that to foster global citizenship through virtual learning, universities need to provide reliable virtual learning platforms or software, governmental increase in the provision of digital technologies to universities. O'Dowd (2019) further elaborated that in order to enhance virtual learning abilities, lecturers and staff should model virtual learning for students, and students should engage in self-development programmes to increase virtual learning competence.

Conclusion

An alternate conceptualization framework of global citizenship education that would promote a pedagogy of hope and social justice can be found in a three-tiered formulation. This formulation triangulates theory, institutional objectives and culture, and student development. Each of these tiers includes operational strategies that can be used to implement global citizenship education that is sensitive and relevant to the local and regional context of SSA. The triangulation of the three tiers approximates the Freirean mandate for universities to be critically engaged in the service of the popular classes, without loss of seriousness and rigour. In this instance universities in SSA must be critically engaged in their local and regional realities in order to take up the role of teaching, training, researching and seeking an interdisciplinary understanding rather than only a disciplinary one (Freire, 2009). Thus, the three-tiered triangulation forms a robust framework to develop a global citizenship education agenda in Southern African universities.

References

Abdi, A. A. and L. Shultz, eds (2008). *Education for Human Rights and Global Citizenship*. Albany: State University of New York Press.

Aktas, F., K. Pitts, J. C. Richards and I. Silova (2017). 'Institutionalizing Global Citizenship: A Critical Analysis of Higher Education Programs and Curricula'. *Journal of Studies in International Education* 21(1): 65–80. https://doi.org/10.1177/1028315316669815

Akudolu, L. R. I., S. E. Ugochukwu and E. I. Olibie (2017). 'Preparing University Students in Nigeria for Global Citizenship through Virtual Learning'. *International Journal of Curriculum and Instruction* 9(1): 47–62.

Banks, J. A. (2014). 'Diversity, Group Identity, and Citizenship Education in a Global Age'. *Journal of Education* 194(3): 1–12. https://doi.org/10.1177/002205741419400302

Bringham, M. (2011). 'Creating a Global Citizen and Assessing Outcomes'. *Journal of Global Citizenship & Equity Education* 1(1): 15–43.

Calderon, A. (2012). 'Massification Continues to Transform Higher Education'. *University World News*. Issue No. 237. Retrieved from http://www.universityworldnews.com/article.php?story=20120831155341147

Calderon, A. (2018). 'Massification of Higher Education Revisited'. http://cdn02.pucp.education/academico/2018/08/23165810/na_mass_revis_230818.pdf

Caruana, V. (2014). 'Re-thinking Global Citizenship in Higher Education: From Cosmopolitanism and International Mobility to Cosmopolitanisation, Resilience and Resilient Thinking'. *Higher Education Quarterly* 68(1): 85–104. https://doi.org/10.1111/hequ.12030

Clifford, V. and C. Montgomery (2017). 'Designing an Internationalised Curriculum for Higher Education: Embracing the Local and the Global Citizen'. *Higher Education Research & Development* 36(6): 1138–51. https://doi.org/10.1080/07294360.2017.1296413

Davies, L. (2006). 'Global Citizenship: Abstraction or Framework for Action?' *Educational Review* 58(1): 5–25. https://doi.org/10.1080/00131910500352523

Dill, J. S. (2013). *The Longings and Limits of Global Citizenship Education: The Moral Pedagogy of Schooling in a Cosmopolitan Age*. New York: Routledge.

Frantz, J. M., L. Leach, H. Pharoah, S. Basset, N. Roman, M. Smith and A. Travill (2014). 'Research Capacity Development in a South African Higher Education Institution through a North-South Collaboration'. *South African Journal of Higher Education* 28(4): 1216–29.

Frantz, J. M., N. Roman, M. Smith, M. Du Plessis, T. Sokupa, M. Andipatin, F. Dambula, B. Chisanga, D. Mabetha, L. M. Sichimata, S. Karonga, T. Simelane, T. Ntshalintshali, L. Mdleleni, C. Jansen van Vuuren, A. Simons, I. Sonn, E. Wagener, Z. Mvelase and J. Marais (2020). 'Theme 4: We Are all in this together: The Barriers and Facilitators of Global Citizenship Education to Exercise Collective Intention in the Fight against

COVID-19'. Researchers Challenge #openupyourthinking. https://www.jet.org.za/resources/sadc-researchers-challenge-theme-4-gced-final-report-1.pdf

Freire, P. (2009). 'From Pedagogy of the Oppressed'. *Race/Ethnicity: Multidisciplinary Global Contexts* 2(2): 163–74.

Gaudelli, W. (2009). 'Heuristics of Global Citizenship Discourses towards Curriculum Enhancement'. *Journal of Curriculum Theorizing* 25(1): 68–85.

Goddard, J., E. Hazelkorn, L.Kempton and P. Vallence (2016). *The Civic University: The Policy and Leadership Challenges.* Elgar Publishing. ISBN: 9781784717711

Haigh, M. and V. A. Clifford (2010). 'Widening the Graduate Attribute Debate: A Higher Education for Global Citizenship'. *Brookes eJournal of Learning and Teaching* 2(5). https://vuir.vu.edu.au/id/eprint/7530

Hanson, L. (2010). 'Global Citizenship, Global Health, and the Internationalization of Curriculum: A Study of Transformative Potential'. *Journal of Studies in International Education* 14(1): 70–88. https://doi.org/10.1177/1028315308323207

Herman, C. and C. L. Meki Kombe (2019). 'The Role of Social Networks in the Transitional Experiences of International African Doctoral Students at One University in South Africa'. *Higher Education Research & Development* 38(3): 508–21. https://doi.org/10.1080/07294360.2018.1556618

Hooks, B. (2003). *Teaching Community: A Pedagogy of Hope*, New York: Routledge.

Hooks, B. (2014). *Teaching to Transgress.* New York: Routledge.

Horey, D., T. Fortune, T. Nicolacopoulos, E. Kashima and B. Mathisen (2018). 'Global Citizenship and Higher Education: A Scoping Review of the Empirical Evidence'. *Journal of Studies in International Education* 22(5): 472–92. https://doi.org/10.1177/1028315318786443

Khodabocus, F., G. K. Bahadur and S. Armoogum (2022). 'Innovative Teaching and Learning Methods at the University of Mauritius', in *ICT and Innovation in Teaching Learning Methods in Higher Education*, vol. 45, 31–49. Bingley, England: Emerald Publishing Limited.

Koopmans, R., P. Statham, M. Giugni and F. Passy (2005). *Contested Citizenship: Immigration and Cultural Diversity in Europe*. Minnesota: University of Minnesota Press.

Lewis, T. E. (2012). 'Teaching with Pensive Images: Rethinking Curiosity in Paulo Freire's Pedagogy of the Oppressed'. *Journal of Aesthetic Education* 46(1): 27–45.

Marshall, H. (2007). 'Global Education in Perspective: Fostering a Global Dimension in an English Secondary School'. *Cambridge Journal of Education* 37(3): 355–74. https://doi.org/10.1080/03057640701546672

McGrath, S., J. Thondhlana and E. Garwe (2019). 'Internationalisation of Higher Education and National Development: The Case of Zimbabwe'. *Compare: A Journal of Comparative and International Education* 51(6): 1–20. https://doi.org/10.1080/03057925.2019.1684241

Millar, C., L. B. Carey, T. Fortune, B. A. Mathisen, A. E. Hill, J. Dukhno and B. McKenzie (2019). 'Global Citizenship: Defining Capabilities for Speech-Language

Pathology'. *International Journal of Speech-Language Pathology* 21(3): 317–24. https://doi.org/10.1080/17549507.2019.1607902

Morris, R., T. Perry and L. Wardle (2021). 'Formative Assessment and Feedback for Learning in Higher Education: A Systematic Review'. *Review of Education* 9: e3292. https://doi.org/10.1002/rev3.3292

O'Dowd, R. (2019). 'A Transnational Model of Virtual Exchange for Global Citizenship Education'. *Language Teaching* 1–14. https://doi.org/10.1017/S0261444819000077

Osler, A. and K. Vincent (2002). *Citizenship and the Challenge of Global Education*. Stoke-On-Trent: Trentham Books.

Owusu-Agyeman, Y. and M. Fourie-Malherbe (2019). 'Students as Partners in the Promotion of Civic Engagement in Higher Education'. *Studies in Higher Education* 1–15. https://doi.org/10.1080/03075079.2019.1666263

Oxfam (2006). *Getting Started with Global Citizenship: A Guide for New Teachers*. Oxfam.

Oxfam (2015). 'Education for Global Citizenship', in *Why Do We Educate? Renewing the Conversation*. Oxfam. https://doi.org/10.1002/9781444307214.ch6

Parmenter, L. (2011). 'Power and Place in the Discourse of Global Citizenship Education'. *Globalisation, Societies and Education* 9(3–4): 367–80. https://doi.org/10.1080/14767724.2011.605322

Popescu, F. (2015). 'South African Globalization Strategies and Higher Education'. *Procedia-Social and Behavioral Sciences* 209: 411–18. https://doi.org/10.1016/j.sbspro.2015.11.212

Reimers, F. M. (2021). 'Can Universities Help "build back better" in Education? The Socially Embedded University Responds to the Covid-19 Pandemic'. *Frontiers in Sustainability* 2(636769). https://doi.org/10.3389/frsus.2021.636769

Reimers, F. M. and F. Marmolejo (2021). 'Leading Learning during a Time of Crisis. Higher Education Responses to the Global Pandemic of 2020 in University and School Collaborations during a Pandemic'. https://doi.org/10.3389/frsus.2021.636769

Reimers, F. M., and F. J. Marmolejo (2022). *University and School Collaborations During a Pandemic: Sustaining Educational Opportunity and Reinventing Education*. London: Springer Nature.

Reysen, S. and I. Katzarska-Miller (2013). 'A Model of Global Citizenship: Antecedents and Outcomes'. *International Journal of Psychology* 48(5): 858–70. https://doi.org/10.1080/00207594.2012.701749

Schattle, H. (2008). 'Education for Global Citizenship: Illustrations of Ideological Pluralism and Adaptation'. *Journal of Political Ideologies* 13(1): 73–94. https://doi.org/10.1080/13569310701822263

Sewell, J. (2013). 'bell hooks on Critical Thinking: The Successes and Limitations of Practical Wisdom'. *Electronic Theses and Dissertations* 4924. https://scholar.uwindsor.ca/etd/4924

Shultz, L. (2007). 'Educating for Global Citizenship: Conflicting Agendas and Understandings'. *Alberta Journal of Educational Research* 53(3). https://doi.org/10.11575/ajer.v53i3.55291

Stoner, L., L. Perry, D. Wadsworth, K. R. Stoner and M. A. Tarrant (2014). 'Global Citizenship Is Key to Securing Global Health: The Role of Higher Education'. *Preventive Medicine* 64: 126–8. https://doi.org/10.1016/j.ypmed.2014.05.006

Task Force on Higher Education and Society (2000). *Higher Education in Developing Countries: Peril and Promise*. The World Bank. https://doi.org/10.1596/0-8213-4630-X

Thomas, D. P. (2009). 'Revisiting Pedagogy of the Oppressed: Paulo Freire and Contemporary African Studies'. *Review of African Political Economy* 36(120): 253–69.

Torres, C. A. (2017). *Theoretical and Empirical Foundations of Critical Global Citizenship Education*. New York: Routledge.

UNESCO (2013). 'Global Citizenship Education: An Emerging Perspective'. Available at http://unesdoc.unesco.org/images/0022/002241/224115E.pdf

UNESCO (2015). 'Global Citizenship Education: Topics and Learning Objectives'. Available at https://unesdoc.unesco.org/ark:/48223/pf0000232993

United Nations (2019). *World Population Prospects 2019*. Available from: https://population.un.org/wpp

Walker, M. and S. Loots (2016). 'Social Citizenship Formation at University: A South African Case Study'. *Compare: A Journal of Comparative and International Education* 46(1): 48–68. https://doi.org/10.1080/03057925.2014.884920

Zemach-Bersin, T. (2012). 'Entitled to the World: The Rhetoric of U.S. Global Citizenship Education and Study Abroad', in V. Andreotti and L. M. Souza (eds), *Postcolonial Perspectives on Global Citizenship Education*, 87–104. New York: Routledge.

6

A Social Network Analysis of Global Citizenship Education in Europe and North America

Massimiliano Tarozzi and Lynette Shultz

Introduction

In the last decade global citizenship education (GCED) has developed in Europe and North America (EUNA) through conceptual, political and pedagogical negotiations among policymakers, educators and community members. According to UNESCO's geo-scheme, EUNA is one of five world regions, together with Africa, Arab states, Asia and the Pacific, Latin America, through which UNESCO organizes the world to provide programmes and activities that are supposed to be tailored to the needs of specific territories. While we use this descriptor of the region, we also recognize that it does not capture the intra-regional geopolitical relations that influence relations which is beyond the scope of this study. While it is very diverse, EUNA is a geographic area understood as 'the global north', therefore its actors are positioned within complex global relations with much of this complication related to the history of colonialism, and this is definitively an unavoidable prerequisite of every perspective of GCED as global social justice. Therefore, it is relevant to enquire about the way in which organizations from other parts of the world see EUNA as a cohesive region regarding approaches to GCED and the extent to which organizations in these countries collaborate on GCED activity, and if so, what is the nature of these collaborations. Our study findings support insights shared by key actors early in the planning stages of the research that Europe and North America are not often conceived of as one region by people within these areas. However, data showed that there is a strong network formed by organizations working in GCED.

Many studies conducted in Europe and/or North America have mapped how North–South relations have shaped GCED (see, for example, Andreotti and de Sousa, 2008; Shultz, 2007; Gaudelli, 2009; Pashby et al., 2020; Pashby and da Costa, 2021). In the United Kingdom, Continental Europe, Canada and the United States much of the work of GCED is related to larger development education that in some cases supports, but, in other cases, seeks to dismantle established norms of 'global north' to 'global south' transfer of ideas and activity (Acharya, 2004). Against this framework, GCED is practised in ways that inform, support and sometimes offer challenge to education policy and practice, bringing transformational justice potential in communities and their global relationships.

The study we present in this chapter is located in this complexity, in the entangled network of significant relationships through which GCED policy and practices take shape. We understand the manifoldness of GCED work in the EUNA region to be aimed at very different goals, audiences, funding models and policy processes impacts. In spite of these differences, the region, collectively, has had a powerful impact on GCED in the world.

GCED has been widely taken up in the EUNA region over the past two decades. Studies have looked at curriculums, pedagogies, policies and theoretical foundations, and have identified a range of GCED actors including multilateral organizations, national and local civil society organizations, schools, universities and many non-formal organizations working within and beyond state boundaries. GCED has had many different frames, goals and imaginaries (see, for example, Yemini, Tibbitts and Goren, 2019; Bosio, 2021; Bourn, 2020). Drawing on the results of a social network analysis (SNA), this chapter is a contribution towards understanding patterns of relationships among key GCED actors across the region.[1]

After a brief methodological section on SNA, this chapter addresses some of the results of a larger study aiming at mapping relationships that connect GCED key players as a network of GCED providers in Europe and North America. Based on maps created through SNA procedures, four main relevant results are presented here which contribute to making sense of the network, especially as a knowledge network. Finally, we conclude by identifying within this network a space for global social justice, by proposing to read the maps with the participants as social cartographies highlighting power relations intrinsic to them.

Adopting social network analysis[2]

Global citizenship is an idea or cluster of ideas (Oxley and Morris, 2012) that is a movable feast, conceptually rich in an increasingly interconnected world but with a tendency for conceptual drift in different contexts and with different actors, leaving it difficult to study through specific curriculum guides or policy statements or organizational reports. Mandates from policy authorities, for example UNESCO or state education ministries, look very different when implemented in the diverse educational settings across the EUNA region. This is why the significance of ideas travelling through networked relations provided a novel way to understand the fluidity and diversity of GCED policy and practice. This is particularly important to our overall concern that GCED work, especially in the global North, was not achieving its transformational potential towards social, economic, environmental, epistemological, decolonial or any other aspects of justice.

According to a social network perspective, a social, political or educational phenomenon cannot be understood if it is segmented or isolated from social relations (Kadushin, 2012; Knoke and Yang, 2008). Using SNA to study relationships in a field of organizations that act as a network makes visible how these relations contribute to the enactment of particular social, cultural and political norms. While in recent years some research has explored the role of both offline and digital networks (Schuster, Jörgens and Kolleck, 2021) in shaping educational policy, GCED has not been investigated specifically. With the exception of a study combining SNA and discourse analysis (Kolleck and Yemini, 2020), SNA has never been used to investigate GCED educational policy and practice. This chapter aims to fill this gap, by analysing the structural and functional effects of GCED enactment, where social relationships are prevailing over organizational characteristics.

We understand the parameters of our study as a field, in line with Bordieu's concept of *field* (1975) where social actors – in our case, organizations – are positioned within the field as a result of interactions and particular power relations. Within organizational studies, an organizational field is made up of agents that represent a recognized area of institutional life and a focus on some particular social action (Di Maggio and Powell, 1983; Dian, 2015). GCED within the EUNA region forms a field of practice that is shaped by social structures, networks of relationships and historical contexts that locate organizations in particular ways in the network. The social capital dimension (Bourdieu, 1986) that emerges from these relationships appears to be a strategic lens through which we look at the material benefits and resources generated by the possession of a stable network of relationships, or by being part of a group and sharing the capital collectively owned. As power moves within these networked relationships there are dynamic shifts in competition, collaboration and positioning among organizations in the network to remain relevant and active in the field. In addition, this network is crossed not only by power relations but also by the flow of knowledge about GCED. It is therefore also significant to explore how knowledge moves and what knowledge moves within this field.

The starting assumption of the SNA methodological framework is that individual characteristics (attributes) are not enough to capture the complexity of the phenomenon we aim to observe (Scott and Carrington, 2011). SNA methods enable the measurement and description of the structure of relations (*ties*) among social entities (*nodes*). In this study of GCED, we investigated the structural characteristics of the network and were able to make visible the main features of the patterns of collaboration, information exchanges and meetings among the networked organizations.

In sum, the main goal of the study was to map multiple ties among active promoters of GCED in Europe and North America, where promotion is understood broadly to include funding, education, programming, policy development, networking, research and teacher education.

To build the dataset for data collection, the research team selected a list of organizations based on the following criteria:

1. *Geographical location*. Each participating organization conducts their work or should be based in Canada, the United States, Europe or the United Kingdom.
2. *Influence*. Each organization has contributed to shape GCED implementation in the region through its work.
3. *Conceptualization of GCED*. Each organization plays a role in the conceptualization and/or defining of GCED through its work.
4. *Promotion*. Each organization is active in disseminating, promoting and fostering GCED in the region or worldwide.
5. *Education*. Each organization provides courses, programmes, research, guidelines or reports about GCED at any level of education which may include formal, non-formal and informal education activities.

The limitation of this sampling process it that less visible organizations were not included. In order to address this and include actors outside the mainstream but which provided significant contribution to GCED promotion, we designed our survey questions to include the opportunity to identify additional organizations with whom they had GCED relationships. Eventually we identify fifty-six key organizations, forty-five of them accepted to be interviewed. The sample included different typologies of actors, as shown in Figure 6.1.

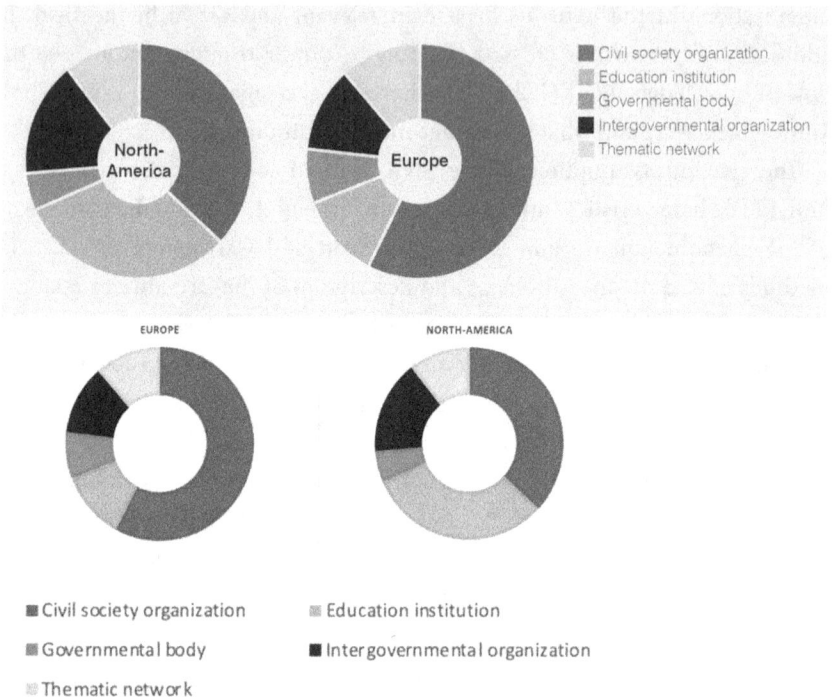

Figure 6.1 Distribution of the organizations interviewed in Europe and North America.

After receiving ethical approval from the Research Ethics Board at the University of Alberta, we developed a questionnaire ensuring it captured the attributes (individual characteristics), ties and nodes (relations) among organizations. After a pilot phase, six researchers carried out structured interviews via Zoom with leading figures in each organization.

The structured interview was organized into five parts:

1. Description of the organization;
2. The views of the organization on global citizenship education;
3. The organization relationships with other key actors;
4. The organization affiliation to regional networks;
5. The organization values and beliefs about GCED (qualitative open-ended questions).

We also used a digital method approach as parallel and complementary strategy to trace the links between GCED actors on both (a) organizational websites, and (b) Twitter, using crawler techniques. But in this chapter, due to the space limits we narrow our report to some of the results of the SNA investigation which can provide a critical perspective on the space of global social justice in the regional debate surrounding GCED.

Three networks emerged in the data, based on relations and activities among the actors: namely, technical information sharing, mutual collaboration and meetings between organizations. Each was one-mode network (actor to actor) and based on direct ties between the organizations. One network related to the use and sharing of information and knowledge. A second formed around activities of mutual or reciprocal collaborations such as providing support to another organization on a policy issue and receiving support in return. The third network was based on organizational relations that included face-to-face meetings about GCED (including using online platforms during the global pandemic).

Maps from these networks were processed and visualized using data gathered in the interviews through the UCINET software.

Making sense of the maps

In examining the maps and the multiple ties among active GCED promoters, instead of an 'egocentric' study, we adopted a *whole network* design. We were interested in the structural properties of the whole network, rather than in the position of single actor in the network. Moreover, this seems to be confirmed by the fact that the network cannot be easily divided into smaller subgroups based on common characteristics of the organizations.

This is important because 'network properties' have implications for understanding how information flows and organizations interact.

In this chapter, we will discuss some of the structural properties of the network based on a number of network measures such as density, connectedness, network closure, emerging from our analysis which can be helpful to understand and to further improve this network.

Due to space limitations, we will just report here four main results that stand out for their relevance in unfolding the features of the complex map of relations that connect them as a network.

A first consideration concerns the possibility of considering EUNA as a uniform region with regard to the enactment and promotion of GCED. While a group of actors has close connections across the two geographical areas, a regional homophily tends to prevail, which indicates the propensity of actors to create ties with others that have the same geographical location and therefore the division of two geographical areas is clearly visible in the network graphs.

In Figure 6.2, the node colours indicate the same geographical region with European organizations coloured dark and North American coloured light. The node size indicates the percentage of resources allocated to GCED. The larger circle means the organization devotes more than 50 per cent of its resources to GCED. The position of the node is determined by the number of ties with other organizations. The nodes with the higher number of ties are the most central in the map, while the organizations that are in the periphery have fewer ties. The graphs are spatialized according to the Multi-Dimensional Scaling in UCINET[3] which overlaps organizations that have a similar pattern of ties.

A knowledge network becomes visible

Among the three networks we analysed based on relations and activities among the actors, the relations were most dense in activities of *knowledge sharing*. This indicates an important feature of the network and of GCED in the EUNA region. A strong *knowledge network* is formed around the work of GCED with dense knowledge sharing relations evident in the maps. In particular, actors positioned at the core of the network tends to be at the centre of intense knowledge sharing processes, but innovation and original knowledge tend to come from periphery.

Core-periphery

Looking at the ties depicted in the map in Figure 6.3, it is evident that the network cannot be easily divided into smaller subgroups based on common characteristics of the organizations. So, while organizations tend to connect with others from the same geographical area there is a low level of clustering. This suggests that even though there are differences in the number of connections among organizations at the centre of the network (orange) and those with fewer connections (green), it was not possible to divide the network into smaller subgroups based on common characteristics. Therefore, the maps also show an important set of relations that in SNA is described as a core-periphery model of interaction (Borgatti and Evertt, 2000). The main characteristic of a core-periphery network map is that a small group of densely connected actors are located in the centre of the network and a larger group of actors are in in the periphery, characterized by a lower level of exchange. The organizations that are at the core of the network generally benefit from a dense flow of information exchange, collaboration and meetings. It is at the core where we find organizations sharing similar conceptualizations of GCED and more mainstream and sanctioned activities. However, looking at the whole network, we see a different pattern.

GCED in Europe and North America 103

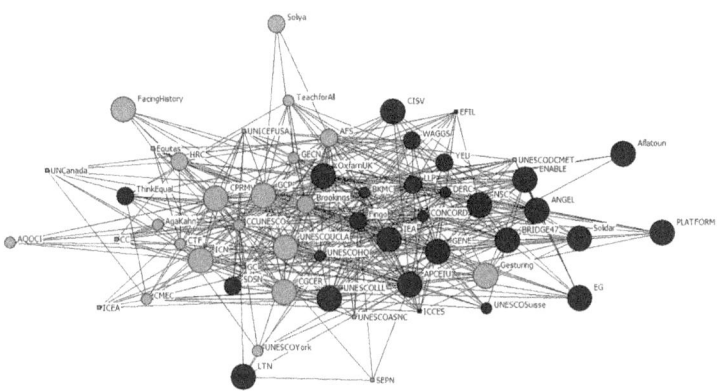

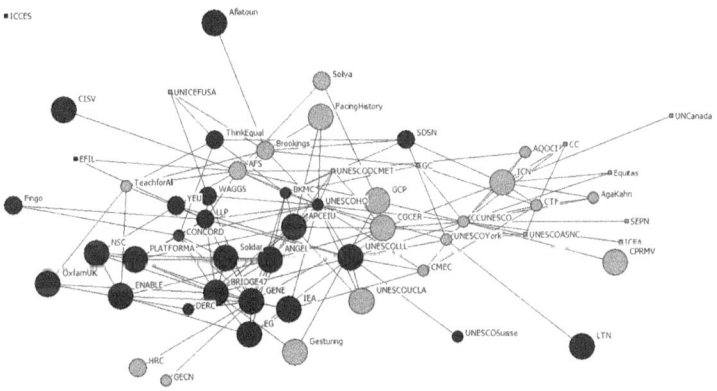

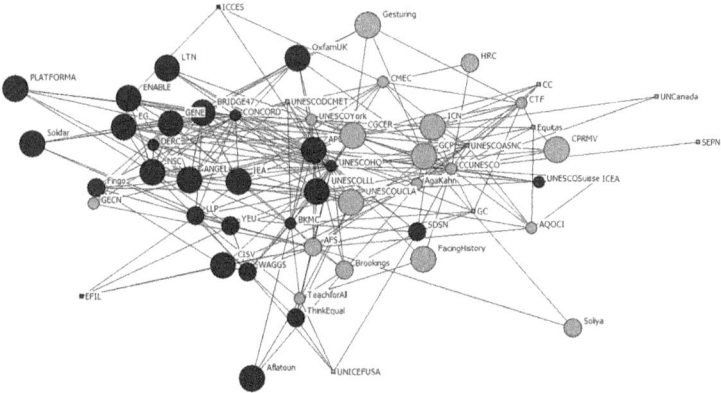

Figure 6.2 Three networks emerged in the data, based on relations and activities among the actors.

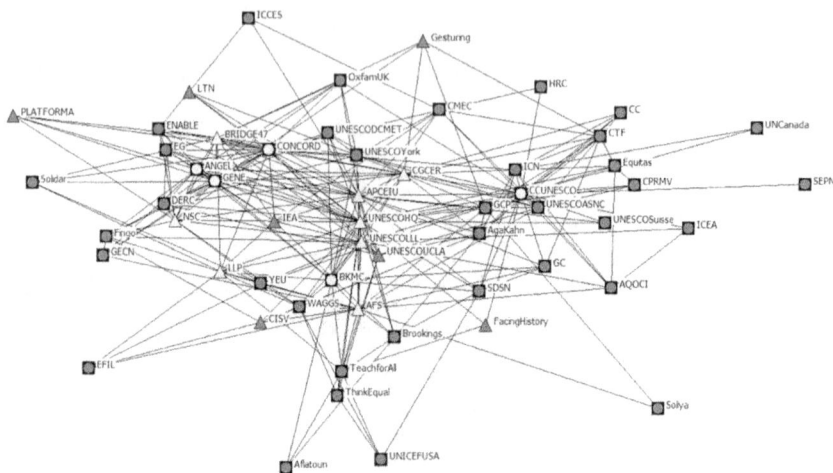

Figure 6.3 Core-periphery mode of interaction (light= periphery dark= centre; Triangle= multiscalar).

While in many cases the amount of resources available determines the size of an organization's impact in a network, our study shows there is no clear pattern related to the resources devoted to GCED. This suggests that the centrality of organizations within the network is not a function of the resources devoted to GCED. It is also notable that the majority of organizations that are in the core of the three networks are 'multiscalar' (triangle node shape in Figure 6.3), so they are working at local, national and international levels providing a density of ties that position them centrally. These organizations were of varied sizes, so the location in the network core was not a result of large financial resources. In addition, the data suggest the organizations located on the periphery do not play a diminished role in the network, even though they have fewer ties. While this seems a contradiction, when we looked at the extent that these ties were strongly related to knowledge exchange where organizations on the periphery played important roles in providing technical and scientific knowledge to the network. In particular, we can see the importance of the organizations working outside the centre in the provision of new ideas outside the mainstream. New ideas and experiences can be moved into the network from positions on the periphery.

Networking

Organizations tend to have a higher number of outgoing than incoming ties. This is especially evident for multiscalar actors positioned at the core of the network. This seems to indicate that actors in this sector consider networking an important activity and they are aware of the material benefits and resources generated by the possession of a stable network of relationships, or by being part of a larger group.

Networking is perceived as crucial: efforts to strengthen the network without forcing a homogenizing agenda on GCED can contribute to stronger GCED work at the individual organization level as well as a sector. Similarly, multi-stakeholder collaborations seem to be well established in this network, especially in Europe. This collaborative environment, if not just created by the need to share resources and increase one's lobbying and advocacy power, can be used to deepen and expand the important contributions of GCED to education policy and practice.

GCED conceptualizations across the network

Alongside quantitative data, we also collected some qualitative data through open-ended questions. Qualitative data included the organizations' definitions of global citizenship and GCED provided by participants in the interviews.

We then used 'networked keyword analysis' to investigate these definitions seeking patterns of conceptual relations among GCED actors. Our preliminary data in this part show that there is much diversity in the language used by organizations, indicating diverse positions, an intermixing of goals, actions, concepts, orientations, issues and future visions. We saw no overarching guiding or shared definition of GCED, although there was evidence of cohesive use of language related to Agenda 2030 and SDG Target 4.7, which is especially evident among the actors located at the core of the network. Significantly, many organizations have developed individual or nuanced definitions. This provides important information given the strong role of knowledge sharing in this network. The organizations appear to support and value sharing new ideas through relations of knowledge exchange where the ties are both dense and reciprocal. This suggests the organizations do not simply use the network to broadcast their own organization's ideas or that there is support for only dominant knowledge. In particular, as we noted earlier, when we combine the core-periphery maps with the GCED conceptualization, we can see the network data where novel ideas and experiences can be moved into the network from positions on the periphery or radiated out from core organizations.

Conclusion: Significance of the EUNA GCED network

A main objective of this chapter was to explore the social network of organizations working on GCED and located in the EUNA region from the concern for global justice as an educational practice. Through the methods of SNA, we were able to carefully build maps of the network of organizational relationships. These maps made the relationships visible, and we are able to see that the network 'works' as a knowledge network where knowledge moves mainly through informal relations and less through formal structures such as meetings, shared resources and specific project collaborations. Instead, this network is highly engaged in sharing ideas. Global social justice is definitively one of these ideas, but it is not the only one, nor is there shared and broad consensus on its definition. This echoes the very nature of GCED, which is the result of conceptual, political and even pedagogical negotiations. So this network is not just *about* GCED; it *is* GCED. The educational aspect of the knowledge sharing is significant.

We understand that social relations are not neutral and are embedded in power relations that, in turn, enable or constrain particular ideas, actors and actions. These relations reflect key justice concerns of how and by whom GCED is undertaken. While SNA, as a predominantly quantitative methodology, does not seek to examine relations of power or justice, the maps that are created can serve as potential social cartographies (see Paulson, 2000; Andreotti et al., 2016) that can be engaged by communities, practitioners and policymakers for generative projects for justice. Therefore, as a research team we are planning to extend this to dialogues with organizational representatives to develop even deeper understanding of this dynamic network through future research.

There are many studies that have provided descriptions of different approaches to GCED (see, for example, Andreotti and deSouza, 2007; Shultz, 2007; Pashby et al., 2020; Pashby ad da Costa, 2021; Torres, 2017). These studies position different aspects of GCED as highly contested and in conflict, often set up as dichotomous to the degree that there is little overlap or even communication between actors holding opposing views. Our data confirmed there were significantly different conceptualizations of GCED related to different geographies, organizational types and organizational sizes. Organizations that worked with an economic focus on education named relationships with organizations that challenged the very foundation of these same economic structures; organizations that challenged global scaled efforts as directly in conflict with local experiences showed ties of knowledge exchange. However, despite the differences, dense ties indicate a strong network exists.

It will take further research to understand the dynamics of the network over time and what kind of mimetic or isomorphic pressures are exerted as different and difficult knowledge is presented to the network. More research is also needed to explore the link between different GCED conceptualizations and types of actors. This study makes clear that networking is perceived by the study participants as crucial. Efforts to strengthen the network without forcing a homogenizing agenda on GCED can contribute to stronger GCED work at the individual organization level as well as a sector. The network showed many characteristics of a transnational advocacy network, a network that advocated for the idea of global citizenship. Further study with organizations outside of the EUNA region would provide another view of how networked relations 'work' in GCED. They would also provide a different and critical way to understand GCED and the way in which EUNA, the 'global north', can be regarded as a cohesive region promoting the mainstreaming idea of global citizenship. To replicate a similar study in other regions of the world could represent an important step forward not only for comparative research but also to use evidence to facilitate relationships within and across various regions of the world and expand the movement of ideas across a global knowledge network.

There are, of course, limitations to this study, not the least that it was conducted during the global pandemic where there were almost universal lockdowns and restrictions disrupting organizations, along with profound personal disruptions in the lives of our team and the study participants. We are grateful to all who supported and participated in the study.

But the very fact of having conducted this research at such a complex juncture and of having found full and convinced cooperation from the diverse community of GCED actors in these difficult times is in itself a reason for hope.

Notes

1 This report is based on a research project funded by Asia-Pacific Centre of Education for International Understanding and Ban Ki-moon Centre for Global Citizens led by Lynette Shultz (Centre for Global Citizenship Education and Research, university of Alberta) and Massimiliano Tarozzi (International Research Centre on Global Citizenship Education, university of Bologna) as principal investigators. The research team was composed of Carrie Karsgaard (university of Alberta) and Carla Inguaggiato (university of Bologna), experts in SNA and digital research methods.
2 For a full description of the methodological approach, data collection and analysis, see the full research report (Shultz et al., 2021).
3 Graphs in Figures 6.2 and 6.3 have been developed with UCINET by Carla Inguaggiato.

References

Acharya, A. (2004). 'How Ideas Spread: Whose Norms Matter? Norm Localization and Institutional Change'. *International Organisation* 58(2): 239–75.

Andreotti, V. and L. M. de Sousa (2008). 'Translating Theory into Practice and Walking Minefields: Lessons from the Project "Through Other Eyes"'. *International Journal of Development Education and Global Learning* 1(1): 23–36.

Andreotti, V., S. Stein, K. Pashby and M. Nicolson (2016). 'Social Cartographies as Performative Devises in Research on Higher Education'. *Higher Education Research & Development* 35(1): 84–99. doi: 10.1080/07294360.2015.1125857

Borgatti, S. P. and M. G. Everett (2000). 'Models of Core/periphery Structures'. *Social Networks* 21(4): 375–95.

Bourdieu, P. (1975). 'The Specificity of the Scientific Field and the Social Conditions of the Progress of Reason'. *Social Science Information* 14(6): 19–47.

Borgatti, S. P. and M. G. Everett (2000). 'Models of Core/periphery Structures'. *Social Networks* 21(4): 375–95.

Bourdieu, P. (1986). 'The Forms of Capital', in J. Richardson, *Handbook of Theory and Research for the Sociology of Education*, 241–58. Westport: Greenwood.

Bourn, D. (2020). *The Bloomsbury Handbook of Global Education and Learning*. London: Bloomsbury.

Bosio, E., ed. (2021). *Conversations on Global Citizenship*. London: Routledge.

De Sousa Santos, B., ed. (2007). *Cognitive Justice in a Global World. Prudent Knowledges for a Decent Life*. Plymouth: Lexington Books.

Dian, M. (2015). *The Cement of Civil Society: Studying Networks in Localities*. Cambridge: Cambridge University Press.

Di Maggio, P. and W. Powell (1983) 'The Iron Cage Revisited: Institutional Isomorphism and Collective Rationality in Organisational Fields'. *American Sociological Review* 48(2): 147–60.

Gaudelli, W. (2009). 'Heuristics of Global Citizenship Discourses towards Curriculum Enhancement'. *Journal of Curriculum Theorizing* 25(1): 68–85.

Kadushin, C. (2012). *Understanding Social Networks: Theories, Concepts and Findings*. Oxford: Oxford University Press.

Knoke, D. and S. Yang (2008). *Social Network Analysis*. Los Angeles: Sage Publications.

Kolleck, N. and M. Yemini (2020). 'Environment-Related Education Topics within Global Citizenship Education Scholarship Focused on Teachers: A Natural Language Processing Analysis'. *The Journal of Environmental Education* 51(4): 317–31. doi: 10.1080/00958964.2020.1724853

Oxley, L. and P. Morris (2013). 'Global Citizenship: A Typology for Distinguishing Its Multiple Conceptions'. *British Journal of Educational Studies* 61(3): 301–25.

Pashby, K. and M. da Costa (2021). 'Interfaces of Critical Global Citizenship Education in Research about Secondary Schools in "global North" Contexts'. *Globalisation Societies and Education* 19(3): 1–14.

Pashby, K., M. da Costa, S. Stein and V. Andreotti (2020). 'A Meta-Review of Typologies of Global Citizenship Education'. *Comparative Education* 56(2): 144–64.

Paulston, R. G. (2000). *Social Cartography: Mapping Ways of Seeing Social and Educational Change*. New York: Garland.

Schuster, J., H. Jörgens and N. Kolleck (2021). 'The Rise of Global Policy Networks in Education: Analyzing Twitter Debates on Inclusive Education using Social Network Analysis'. *Journal of Education Policy* 36(2): 211–31.

Shultz, L. (2007). 'Educating for Global Citizenship: Conflicting Agendas and Understandings'. *Alberta Journal of Educational Research* 53(3): 248–58.

Shultz, L., M. Tarozzi, C. Karsgaard and C. Inguaggiato (2021). 'Europe and North America Regional GCED Network Research Report'. https://bankimooncentre.org/?s=europe+and+north+america+GCED

Scott, J. and P. J. Carrington, eds (2011). *The Sage Handbook of Social Network Analysis*. Los Angeles: Sage Publishing.

Torres, C. (2017). *Theoretical and Empirical Foundations of Critical Global Citizenship Education*. New York and Oxon: Routledge.

Yemini, M., F. Tibbitts and H. Goren (2019). 'Trends and Caveats: Review of Literature on Global Citizenship Education in Teacher Training'. *Teaching and Teacher Education: An International Journal of Research and Studies* 77(1): 77–89.

7

Transforming a Global Competence Agenda into Pedagogies of Intercultural Understanding and Student Voice

An Australian Case Study

Karena Menzie-Ballantyne and Miriam Ham

Introduction

Achievement of the United Nations Sustainable Development Goals (2015) and Freire's (2021) vision of a system that educates students to be critical and knowledgeable actors capable of intervening in the world pivots around one word: agency. Article 12 of the UN Convention on the Rights of the Child (1989) enshrines the right of children to be heard on matters affecting them, and there is consensus in the field of global citizenship education that a fundamental key to success is the belief that one can bring about change (OECD, 2018; Oxfam GB, 2015; Peterson, 2016; Reimers et al., 2016; Reysen and Katzarska-Miller, 2013), Despite this, systems and schools persist in imposing outdated top-down power relationships. Aspirational language of graduating global citizens can be seen in international, national and state policy documents (such as the Mparntwe Declaration, 2019; Pakistan National Review, 2019; OECD, 2018; UNESCO, 2017) providing the potential for inclusion of voice and agency in curricula around the world, yet educational systems continue to dictate content-focused 'banking' (Freire, 1980) or 'gas tank' (Robinson, 2011) models of education. Reimers (2020) argues that one of the reasons global educational approaches remain aspirational for teachers and seldom a reality for students is because 'more time has been spent examining what it is than discerning how to teach it' (p. 107).

For this reason, this chapter takes a very practical approach to exploring how one Australian state disrupted this top-down, content-focused model at system and school level to co-design and trial their own global competence framework. It aims to provide insights into how the collaborative process empowered individual schools and educators with agency to co-create the framework and trial it in action research projects relevant to their contexts. The chapter explains how this approach saw an ostensibly neoliberal agenda (Vaccari and Gardinier, 2019) driven by the addition of a global competence assessment to the Organisation for Economic Co-operation and Development's (OECD) Programme of Student Assessment (PISA) transformed into pedagogies of intercultural understanding and student voice. Presented through the lens of the authors, who acted as participant observers and critical friends throughout the pilot, the chapter does not aim to present a shining example or even a finished product, rather to examine how the educators' beliefs and situational frameworks (Kelchtermans, 2005; 2009; Marz and Kelchtermans, 2013) impacted the process. To inform, and hopefully empower, others undertaking a similar journey, the chapter also presents school-based case studies and real-world advice from the pilot schools as to the steps they took, the challenges they faced and how the process transformed pedagogical approaches and school culture, and enhanced student voice.

The Australian educational context

The Australian education environment over the past two decades can best be described as a dichotomy. The country's federated structure means that responsibility for the enactment of education and schooling, including mandated school priorities and recommended pedagogical approaches, lies with the individual states. In 2013, however, a national curriculum was introduced to which all states subscribe, albeit with their own additions and interpretations. The Australian curriculum provides a three-dimensional approach to teaching and learning (see Figure 7.1), including eight key learning areas, three cross-curriculum priorities and seven general capabilities (Australian Curriculum Assessment and Reporting Authority, 2021).

Despite this, the focus and political rhetoric around education has been framed by a 'back to basics' emphasis on literacy and numeracy (Fahey, 9th November 2020) and strident nationalist voices (Buchanan, Burridge and Chodkiewicz, 2018). The second goal of the Alice Springs (Mparntwe)

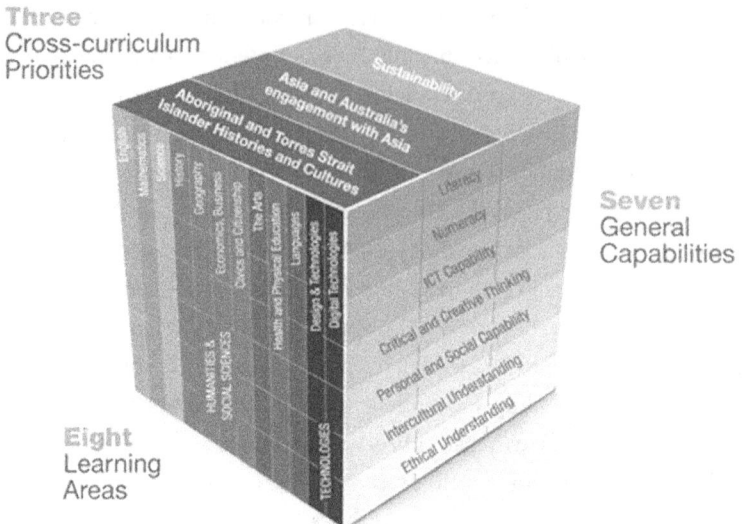

Figure 7.1 Three dimensions of the Australian curriculum.

Education Declaration (Education Services Australia, 2019) is that all young Australians become confident and creative individuals who are active and informed members of their local and global communities; however, individual and school comparatives are centred on the results of a national literacy and numeracy assessment (NAPLAN) (Australian Curriculum Assessment and Reporting Authority, 2019).

Surrounding this dichotomy is evidence of frustration with the political direction of the country and a resurgence of grassroots action, exemplified by the swing away from major parties towards the Greens and independents in the 2022 election and the high numbers of Australian students taking part in the School Strike 4 Climate Change (Menzie-Ballantyne and Ham, 2022). There are also growing numbers of schools supporting students in abstaining from NAPLAN or expressing concern as to its impact on students' well-being (Heffernan, 2018) and significant support for greater emphasis on the general capabilities and cross-curriculum priorities, despite an overcrowded primary curriculum (ACARA, June 2020, Scoular et.al. 2020).

Add to this scenario, in 2018, the addition of a global competence assessment to PISA (OECD, 2018). Here was a neoliberal, economically and assessment-driven vehicle (Vaccari and Gardinier, 2019) that was talking about the knowledge, skills, values and attitudes of global citizenship. Here was a mandate for grassroots education to enact pedagogies which amplify the elements of the curriculum that focus on real-world issues of equity, social justice, intercultural understanding and sustainability (Bourne, 2022, Heggart, 2015, Reynolds, MacQueen and Ferguson-Patrick, 2019).

There have been previous attempts to highlight the potential for global citizenship education inherent in the Australian curriculum and upskill teachers in global education approaches, but, like in many other countries, these programmes have been dependent on the political agenda of the time and were often driven or implemented by not-for-profit organizations such as the Global Learning Centre, Oxfam and Caritas (Reimers et al., 2016; Reynolds, MacQueen and Ferguson-Patrick, 2019; Sant et al., 2018). As result, many of the programmes, such as the Department of Foreign Affairs AusAID-funded Global Education Project (Gilbert, 2012), evolved from a development education approach, echoing the Millennium Development Goals perspective of building understanding and assistance for 'developing' countries. More recent initiatives have been economically driven, such as the Asia Education Foundation (Asia Education Foundation, 2021). Established in 1992 by Asialink, the foundation was influential in the curriculum's 'Asia literacy' focus (ACARA, 2012).

Despite the apparent commitment to the knowledge, skills, values and attitudes of global citizenship evident in the curriculum and policy documents, these programmes have to date been seen as 'nice to have' additions or complements to the curriculum rather than core learnings (Reynolds, MacQueen and Ferguson-Patrick, 2019; Sant et al., 2018). They were commonly viewed as developing the 'soft skills' rather than foundational skills such as literacy and numeracy (Menzie-Ballantyne and Ham, 2022). The 2013 change to the federal government meant a significant reduction in funding for these and other such programmes with some, such as the Global Education Project, cancelled completely. By contrast, the strong influence of PISA (Cobb and Couch, 2018; Rautalin, Alasuutari and Vento, 2019; Sjoberg, 2016) has brought the concept of education for global competence to the fore in many Australian states (at the time of writing, it was too soon to tell if the change of government will see similar priority given to the agenda at national level). What follows is a case study of how this PISA-driven agenda was enacted in one state and how giving agency to the educators transformed the agenda into one of hope, student voice and intercultural understanding. It is acknowledged upfront that 'global competence' is a contested term; however, it is used here as this was the terminology of the department in creating and presenting their pilot programme.

Co-designing an education for global competence framework

In 2019, after extensive stakeholder consultation, one Australian state released a strategic plan acknowledging that education systems have to stay relevant in the age of globalization and provide

> young people with the intercultural understanding and global mindset needed to respond positively to internationally competitive work opportunities and more inclusive societies and to contribute to [the state's] future prosperity. (reference withheld for de-identification, 2019)

In this statement, three important elements of an education for global citizenship/global competence agenda are acknowledged:

- that students need specific knowledge, skills, values and attitudes to effectively engage in and contribute to a globalized world;
- that education systems and therefore the educators within them need to adapt their curriculum and pedagogical approaches to foster the required knowledge, skills, values and attitudes;
- and that such education has both global and local impact.

Interestingly this strategic plan and the subsequent pilot programme were driven by the international division of the state education department. Discussions with the division manager acknowledged that there were both commercial and educational objectives to the programme, including:

- fostering the global competence of the state's domestic students to ensure they graduated with the knowledge, skills and dispositions needed in the globalized world;
- creating a climate which would attract international students to state schools and ensure they felt safe and included;
- and developing a framework and resources that could be sold to other countries and education systems.

Although initiated and funded by the international division, the pilot involved personnel from the state schools curriculum division through workshops and inclusion in the development process of the framework and associated resources, particularly unit and lesson plan exemplars. At time of publication, it was too early to determine the degree to which the global competence framework and agenda was successful in becoming a mainstream focus for other department divisions, and for schools other than the pilot schools. This is being examined as a longitudinal study.

The pilot

The Global Competence pilot programme was initially run in two phases over two years, 2020–1. Each phase consisted of workshops, a combination of face-to-face and online depending on COVID restrictions at the time; individual coaching calls with each school team; school-based action research projects and the creation of exemplar vlogs. Overall, twenty-two schools were involved, each providing a team consisting of a school leader such as a principal or deputy, a curriculum leader and a passionate teacher.

The workshops were facilitated by an external education change consultant. In both phases, schools were given insights into the changing nature of the globalized world and the resultant changes needed for schools to adequately prepare their students for that world. The school teams were then given the opportunity to collectively unpack the PISA Global Competence Framework (2018) and explore what each of its dimensions might look like in a school context at beginning, developing, embedding and leading stages. Schools were also asked to enact an action research project targeting a specific element of the Framework relevant to their school. This cycle of development and feedback continued after the conclusion of the workshops to ensure the schools' ongoing input into the state's framework and its supporting resources, such as vlogs and professional learning programmes.

Research methods

The authors of this chapter were engaged as critical friends and researchers for the pilot programme. A mixed method approach (Creswell and Clark, 2011) including surveys (Fink, 2017), participant observations (Jones, 2013; Unler, 2012) of department planning sessions and school workshops, individual school interviews and undertaking the critical friend role with the curriculum team enabled deep and prolonged engagement (Erlandson et al, 1993, Kawulich, 2005) with the pilot as outlined in Figure 7.2.

Interpreting and contextualizing global competence

Irrespective of whether policy is generated internationally, nationally or locally, its interpretation and implementation ultimately rest with educators at school

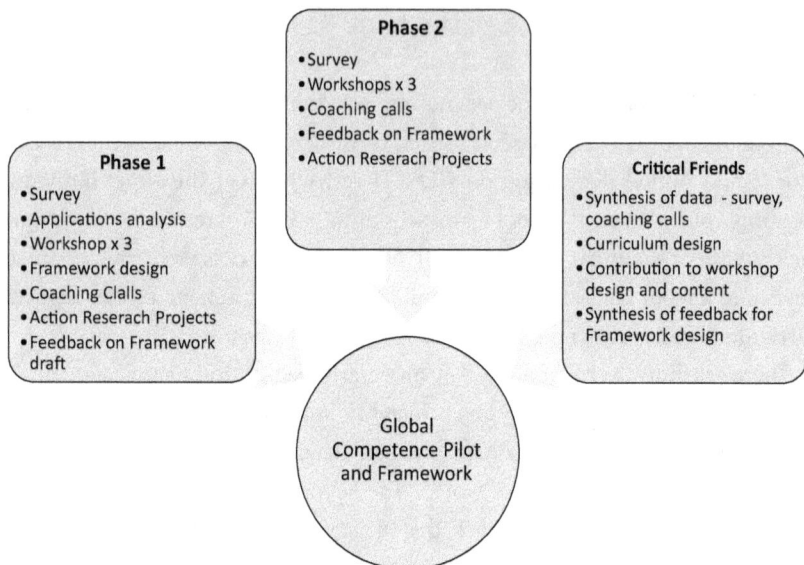

Figure 7.2 Global competence pilot data sources.

and classroom level. This in turn is dependent on the values and beliefs of these educators (Belbase, 2012, Biesta, Priestley and Robinson, 2015, Ham and Dekkers, 2019, Pantic, 2015) who use their deeply and often unconsciously held personal framework (Kelchtermans, 2009: p. 259) to guide what they consider 'good' practice. If educators deem the reform suitable in terms of their personal framework, they then consider it in the context of their situational framework (Kelchtermans, 2005; 2009; Marz and Kelchtermans, 2013) including the curriculum, assessment and resource requirements, student abilities, parent and community perception. If the educator decides that the practice is suitable according to both their personal and situational frameworks, only then will they be willing to trial it in their school or classroom.

Although the impetus for this state-based global competence pilot was the OECD PISA framework and assessment, which is considered to have a neoliberal, market orientation (Vaccari and Gardinier, 2019), the focus of the pilot, and its resultant framework, was filtered through the values and beliefs of the department personnel, the education change consultancy and the authors of this chapter in their role as critical friends. As all these people brought an equity and social justice orientation, based on their personal experiences, values and beliefs, the pilot's workshops were framed through this lens. The agenda was then further framed by the personal and situational frameworks

(Kelchtermans, 2009) of the educators from the twenty-two schools, who self-nominated to participate in the pilot, and ultimately by their colleagues and students through the school-based, action research projects. Examination of the research data gathered throughout the two-year process revealed that the application of these lenses, personal beliefs and situational frameworks resulted in a transformation of the original neoliberal global competence agenda into language and pedagogies more aligned to the UNESCO conception of global citizenship (UNESCO, 2015; 2017).

Observations from workshops

The influence of educators' beliefs about themselves and their practice was exemplified in data gathered from the planning discussions regarding similarities and differences between the first and second cohorts of pilot schools. The first cohort were approached to nominate on the basis that they were identified as schools already practising, even leading in the field. By comparison, the phase two cohort was conscious they were still developing or even just beginning their global competence journey. It was observed that, as a result of this positioning, some participants in the second cohort were more open to deep considerations of their understandings and practices around equity, social justice and intercultural competence and as a result progressed further than their predecessors.

The workshop facilitators constantly challenged both cohorts to consider the *why*: Why was it important to implement education for global competence in their context, and why had they chosen their specific action research project? Many participants found this quite difficult and thought-provoking as their tendency was to look at the problem and try to find a practical solution rather than carefully considering the root causes of the issue. Their default position was to apply rather than question or challenge existing practices (Bourn, 2022, Freire, 1980). Other participants responded positively to this constant pushback of their suggestions and ideas, reframing not only the nature of their action research project but also their mindset in approaching it, including the way they would consult with colleagues, students and the wider school community. This second group better personified Freire's vision of a democratized educational approach that creates space for dialogue and the incorporation of the living knowledge of various stakeholders (2021: p. 116).

Another key point noted in the data was the overall and individual feeling of hope and positivity in the planning sessions, workshops and the individual coaching calls. It was commented on many occasions by individual members of the team that they looked forward to the planning meetings, or 'collective genius' as they came to be called, as they offered the opportunity to engage with likeminded people and make a positive contribution to education in state schools. Similar language was used in feedback on the workshops like *'very invigorating and inspiring'* and *'thought provoking and affirming of the journey ahead'*. In the individual coaching calls one teacher tearfully explained that implementing the schools' global competence approach was the happiest he had been in his thirty years of teaching. These and other comments recorded seemed to indicate not only that the global competence work aligned strongly with the participants' belief system about education and teaching but that it gave them a sense of hope.

Framework design and consultation

The development of the department's global competence framework occurred in a cyclical fashion with department staff and the critical friends synthesizing suggestions made at the workshops, refining them, then returning the draft for feedback at the next workshop. Through this process, it was decided that the framework should be structured as a planning guide, exemplifying each dimension at beginning, developing, embedding and leading stages, so schools could identify their current position and what may be required for their next lift. Despite the use of this terminology, the educators' situational lens (Kelchtermans, 2009) was evident when their feedback revealed the criteria-like structure of the framework led them to view it as an assessment rubric rather an aspirational guide of focus and practice.

Encouraging schools to take a whole-school approach, the framework was divided into four elements with the aims: that the school community was equitable and inclusive; that there was collective agency in terms of learning and leadership; that teaching and learning were co-designed, engaging student voice; and that there was scope to connect and collaborate with both local and global communities. Although there was nervousness among the department staff as to the inclusion of social justice–oriented language and mention of pedagogies such as cultural responsive pedagogy (Ladson-Billings, 2014; Morrison et al., 2019) and 'brave spaces' (Arao and Clemens, 2013), these aspects of the framework were very well received by the pilot participants. At the time of publication, the framework was being released for wider department and community consultation, so it will be interesting to see if this pattern continues in the context of differing belief systems and competing agendas.

Action research projects

To test the framework, each pilot school identified and implemented an action research project designed to address a perceived challenge or opportunity in their context. The projects varied from incorporating the PISA dimensions in planning for a science unit to an experiential unit that put year-six students in the shoes of refugees; from developing a twenty-first-century toolkit that staff could incorporate in any key learning area to reimagining all aspects of the school's philosophy and planning through the lens of the framework. Following are three examples of the projects undertaken.

School 1: Many of the pilot projects focused on building inclusion and intercultural understanding among staff and students to ensure everyone in the school community felt safe and heard. One of the phase one primary schools, located in a suburb characterized by high numbers of immigrants and refugees, was very conscious of both the challenges and opportunities inherent in their diverse student cohort. The school had already committed to a global citizenship focus, prior to the pilot, but were concerned by the results of a recent survey that revealed only 85 per cent of students felt accepted by their peers. In response the school developed an action research project in which curriculum-based opportunities, using Project Zero's Visible Thinking Routines (Harvard Graduate School of Education, 2016), were created to allow difficult conversations about intercultural understanding,. Initially implemented through the humanities curriculum by a small group of specifically trained teachers, the pedagogy is now applied across all key learning areas and year levels.

School 2: A regional high school's commitment to building an inclusive and equitable school community started with genuine consultation with students, families and the wider school community, including the traditional owners of the land on which the school stands. An appreciative enquiry model was used to co-design charters of Global Citizenship and Reconciliation. An important part of the charters was a commitment to supporting students to lead change. One example was their Indigenous Young Leaders programme representing the 24 per cent of students of Aboriginal or Torres Strait Islander heritage. Concerned about Australia's lack of a legally binding treaty with its First Nations peoples, the group developed a school-based treaty and Imagination Declaration. Like the charters, the treaty and Imagination Declaration were signed and endorsed by the school leadership at a whole-school assembly to demonstrate the schools' commitment to '*human dignity, open-mindedness and optimism*'.

School 3: A city-based high school with an active student community, representing eighty countries of birth, was motivated to join the pilot as their Council for International Schools review had recommended that they needed a context-specific definition of global citizenship. It was decided that student voice and agency were central to this process, so design-thinking workshops were organized with students from years 7 to 12. Perspectives were also sought from staff and the wider community. The students analysed this collective feedback and deconstructed existing definitions to co-create a definition that reflected their aspirations and the school values.

> Global competence brings together the values, knowledge, and skills that shape us as members of a global community, recognising our personal and collective responsibility to understand and promote a world that respects diversity, as we advocate for social justice and environmental sustainability. (reference withheld for de-identification purposes, 2020)

Having developed a common language, a collaborative approach was used to incorporate and enhance global competence in every classroom in meaningful and manageable ways. Reflective of Freire's critical pedagogy (1980), it was decided that meaningful meant engaging and relevant to real-world issues, as well as connecting to current literacy and behaviour management strategies. To be manageable, it had to enhance what teachers were already doing and align with the existing New Art and Science of Teaching (Marzano, 2017) framework.

Lessons from the pilot

Although each pilot school contextualized the global competence framework and their action research projects to meet the needs and stage of development of their school, data gathered across the pilot revealed common themes in terms of the barriers faced and advice for schools beginning or developing a similar journey.

Barriers

Almost all schools recognized lack of time for co-design and planning as a barrier but also acknowledged it could not be an excuse as such collaboration is essential to effectively creating a whole-school approach (Hunt and King, 2015). It was evident that true collaboration needed to include time spent '*bringing the parents with them*' (Barker and Harris, 2020), as there was a perception that their children were '*missing out on learning if the teacher was not in front of the class teaching*'.

This traditional perspective of teachers as conveyors of knowledge was also reflected in staff pushback which was framed by discussions of '*teacher burnout*' and '*program overload*', indicating they saw global competence as yet another thing to 'teach'. The pilot schools reported they needed to carefully consider their language to convey global competence as a mindset and approach which enhanced existing practice. Reflecting the literature (Donnelly and Wiltshire, 2014; Dyment et al., 2013; Schulz et al., 2017), issues were also identified in terms of teachers having the confidence and capability to let go of a content focus in favour of overtly teaching skills, conceptual understanding, values and attitudes. Some teachers expressed concerns about whether it was their/the schools' role to teach values and attitudes, suggesting that this shift in pedagogical focus did not marry with the beliefs of their personal and situational frameworks (Kelchtermans, 2009).

Another identified barrier was the degree of teacher agency (Biesta, Priestley and Robinson, 2015; Fullan, 2018) at both school and system levels, with many educators explaining they often needed to work around or outside the system in order to achieve their aims. Discussion among the principals revealed that some also felt constrained by the system, whereas others managed their reporting in order to '*tick the right boxes*' and still allow their staff the freedom to implement innovative initiatives.

Interestingly, none of pilot schools saw any of the barriers they identified as insurmountable, although they did recognize that overcoming them would take time, professional learning and significant consultation.

Enablers

As part of the research for the pilot, schools were asked what advice they would give other schools who were beginning or furthering their global competence journey. Consistently their first piece of advice was to contextualize and '*start with the why*', why is global competence important for me, for my students and for my school community? This, together with the advice to '*engage hearts and minds*', clearly linked back to ensuring that the work aligned with the educators' personal and situational frameworks (Kelchtermans, 2009). It was the view of the schools that staff, students, parents and the wider school community needed to believe in the work and see its relevance to '*buy in*' and that this process takes time.

To aid the buy in, schools advised that it was firstly necessary to '*scan, assess and celebrate*' where global competence already exists in the school's vision, curriculum (both formal and informal) and extra-curricular activities. This process should also include identifying where global competence aligned with whichever pedagogical framework the school was already using. Examples from the pilot schools included New Pedagogies for Deep Learning (Fullan, 2018), the OECD Learning Compass 2030 (2019) and the New Art and Science of Teaching (Marzano, 2017). It was felt that this approach ensured that any projects aligned with the school's overall strategic direction and avoided global competence being a '*bolt on*'.

Mindful of Reimers's (2020) advice that more focus should be on how to teach it than what it is, schools still recognized the importance of '*creating a common language*' as it was felt definitional issues could derail the project. In data gathered across the pilot, participants appeared to use global competence and global citizenship interchangeably, so their advice appeared to relate not to philosophical differences between such terms (Vaccari and Gardinier, 2019) but to the importance of having a common understanding of what the terminology meant and how it was used in their individual contexts.

In terms of the practical applications of global competence, the schools advised that although the ultimate goal is a whole-school approach, it was important to '*start small*'. This could mean starting in one discipline or one year level or giving a group of passionate teachers, leaders and/or students the opportunity to trial new approaches that became exemplars for others to follow and adapt to their contexts. Most schools also stressed a need to '*be flexible*' and '*create a risk culture*' giving teachers agency and allowing them to '*fail early, fail often*'. It was the schools' perspective that you '*can't do much damage as long as you are focused on curriculum, pedagogy and learning outcomes*'.

Conclusion

Although not claiming to be a perfect example, it is argued that this case study highlights important elements of a pedagogy of hope and social justice. It recognizes that teaching is not neutral and should not be one way (Bourn, 2022; Freire, 1980; Robinson, 2011), and that all stakeholders – the department, the school leaders, the teachers, the students and the wider community – need to have agency in both dialogues about and implementation of the education of the next generation. Data gathered also reinforce the importance of understanding the core role played by educators' beliefs and situational frameworks (Kelchtermans, 2009) and how professional learning framed to inspire critical thinking and challenge those beliefs is a more positive and effective model than deficit, technician approaches (Bentall, 2020). Shifting the educators' situational framework by providing space and a mandate for agency to explore their and their students' perspectives about global competence and global citizenship also acted as a reminder that academic, definitional debates become redundant at the practical school level, as it is more important that the stakeholders in each context evolve and agree on their own common language. Although this pilot started from a neoliberal global competence agenda, evidence gathered suggests that the educators' and their students' deep personal beliefs about social justice, equity and intercultural understanding transformed it into an inspiring journey of hope for all involved.

References

ACARA (2012). 'The Shape of the Australian Curriculum: Version 4.0'. Retrieved from http://www.acara.edu.au/verve/_resources/the_shape_of_the_australian_curriculum_v4.pdf

ACARA (June 2020). 'Review of the Australian Curriculum'. Retrieved from https://www.acara.edu.au/docs/default-source/Media-Releases/20200612-media-release---review-of-the-australian-curriculum_final.pdf?sfvrsn=2

Arao, B. and K. Clemens (2013). 'From Safe Spaces to Brave Spaces: A New Way to Frame Dialogue around Diversity and Social Justice', in L. M. Landreman (ed.), *The Art of Effective Facilitation: Reflections from Social Justice Educators*, 135–50. Sterling: Stylus Publishing.

Asia Education Foundation (2021). 'About AEF'. Retrieved from https://www.asiaeducation.edu.au/about-aef

Australian Curriculum Assessment and Reporting Authority (2019). 'NAP: National Assessment Program'. Retrieved from https://www.nap.edu.au/

Australian Curriculum Assessment and Reporting Authority (2021). 'F-10 Curriculum'. Retrieved from https://www.australiancurriculum.edu.au/f-10-curriculum/

Australian Government: Department of Heritage and Environment (2005). *Educating for a Sustainable Future: A National Environmental Education Statement for Schools*. Carlton South: Curriculum Corporation.

Barker, B. and D. Harris (2020). *Parent and Family Engagement: An Implementation Guide for School Communities*. Canberra: ARACY.

Belbase, S. (2012). 'Teacher Belief, Knowledge, and Practice: A Trichotomy of Mathematics Teacher Education'. Retrieved from http://ezproxy.cqu.edu.au/login?url=http://search.ebscohost.com/login.aspx?direct=true&db=eric&AN=ED530017&site=eds-live&scope=site

Bentall, C. (2020). 'Continuing Professional Development of Teachers of Global Learning: What Works?' in D. Bourne (ed.), *The Bloomsbury Handbook of Global Education and Learning*, 356–68. London: Bloomsbury

Biesta, G., M. Priestley and S. Robinson (2015). 'The Role of Beliefs in Teacher Agency'. *Teachers and Teaching* 21(6): 624–60.

Bourn, D. (2022). *Education for Social Change*. London: Bloomsbury Academic.

Buchanan, J., N. Burridge and A. Chodkiewicz (2018). 'Maintaining Global Citizenship Education in Schools: A Challenge for Australian Educators and Schools'. *Australian Journal of Teacher Education* 43(4): 51–67.

Cobb, D. J. and D. Couch (2018). 'Teacher Education for an Uncertain Future: Implications of PISA's Global Competence', in D. Heck and A. Ambrosetti (eds), *Teacher Education in and for Uncertain Times*, 35–47. Singapore: Springer.

Creswell, J. W. and V. Clark (2011). *Designing and Conducting Mixed Methods Research*. 2nd edn. Thousand Oaks: Sage Publications.

Donnelly, K. and K. Wiltshire (2014). 'Review of the Australian Curriculum: Final Report'. Retrieved from https://docs.education.gov.au/system/files/doc/other/review_of_the_national_curriculum_final_report.pdf

Dyment, J. E., J. M. Davis, D. Nailon, S. Emery, S. Getenet, N. McCrea and A. Hill (2013). 'The Impact of Professional Development on Early Childhood Educatos' Confidence, Understanding and Knowledge of Education for Sustainability'. *Environmental Education Research* 20(5): 1–20.

Education Services Australia (2019). 'Alice Springs (Mparntwe) Education Declaration'. Retrieved from https://docs.education.gov.au/documents/alice-springs-mparntwe-education-declaration

Erlandson, D., E. Harris, B. Skipper and S. Allen (1993). *Doing Naturalistic Inquiry: A Guide to Methods*. Newbury Park: Sage Publications.

Fahey, G. (9th November 2020). 'While Our Schools Coach Kids in Social Activism, Literacy Takes a Back Seat'. *The Australian*. Retrieved from https://www.theaustralian.com.au/commentary/while-our-schools-coach-kids-in-social-activism-literacy-takes-a-back-seat/news-story/f1ad98394a2a8043cbcdabc00e41e319

Fink, A. (2017). *How to Conduct Surveys: A Step-By-Step Guide*. 6th edn. Los Angeles: Sage Publications.

Freire, P. (1980). *Pedagogy of the Oppressed*. New York: Continuum.

Freire, P. (2021). *Pedagogy of Hope: Reliving Pedagogy of the Oppressed*. London: Bloomsbury Academic.

Fullan, M., J. Quinn and J. McEachen (2018). *Deep Learning: Engage the World, Change the World*. Thousand Oaks: Corwin.

Gilbert, R. (2012). 'Review of the AusAID Global Education Program'. Retrieved from Brisbane.

Government of Pakistan (2019). 'Pakistan's Implementation of the 2030 Agenda for Sustainable Development-Voluntary National Review'. Retrieved from https://scholar.google.com/scholar?hl=en&as_sdt=0%2C5&q=Pakistan%E2%80%99s+Implementation+of+the+2030+Agenda+for+Sustainable+Development+Voluntary+National+Review&btnG

Ham, M. and J. Dekkers (2019). 'What Role do Teachers' Beliefs Play in the Implementation of Educational Reform? Nepali Teachers' Voice'. *Teaching and Teacher Education* 86: 1–9.

Harvard Graduate School of Education (2016). 'Project Zero's Thinking Routine Toolbox'. Retrieved from https://pz.harvard.edu/thinking-routines

Heffernan, A. (2018). 'How School Principals Respond to Govt Policies on NAPLAN. (Be surprised how some are resisting)'. *Education Research Matters*. Retrieved from https://www.aare.edu.au/blog/?p=3143

Heggart, K. (2015). 'Social Capital and Civics and Citizenship: Developing a Framework for Activtist Education'. *Issues in Educational Research* 25(3): 276–90.

Hunt, F. and R. P. King (2015). *Supporting Whole School Approaches to Global Learning: Focusing Learning and Mapping Impact*. London: Development Education Research Centre.

Jones, G. (2013). 'Other Research Methods', in M. Walter (ed.), *Social Research Methods*. Third edn. South Melbourne: Oxford University Press.

Kawulich, B. (2005). 'Participant Observation as a Data Collection Method'. *Forum: Qualitative Social Research* 6(2): 1–21.

Kelchtermans, G. (2005). 'Teachers' Emotions in Educational Reforms: Self-understanding, Vulnerable Commitment and Micropolitical Literacy'. *Teaching and Teacher Education* 21(8): 995–1006.

Kelchtermans, G. (2009). 'Who I am in How I Teach is the Message: Self-understanding, Vulnerability and Reflection'. *Teachers and Teaching: Theory and Practice* 15(2): 257–72.

Ladson-Billings, G. (2014). 'Culturally Relevant Pedagogy 2.0: a.k.a the Remix'. *Harvard Educational Review* 84(1): 74–84.

Marz, V. and G. Kelchtermans (2013). 'Sense-making and Structure in Teachers' Reception of Educational Reform. A Case Study on Statistics in the Mathematics Curriculum'. *Teaching and Teacher Education* 29: 13–24.

Marzano, R. J. (2017). *The New Art and Science of Teaching*. Melbourne: Hawker Brownlow Education.

Menzie-Ballantyne, K. and M. Ham (2022). 'School Strike 4 Climate: The Intersection of Education for Sustainable Development, Education for Global Citizenship and the Australian Curriculum'. *Australian Journal of Environmental Education* (Published online 23 August 2021). doi: https://www.doi.org/10.1017/aee.2021.14

Morrison, A., L.-I. Rigney, R. Hattam and A. Diplock (2019). *Toward an Australian Culturally Responsive Pedagogy: A Narrative Review of the Literature*. Adelaide: University of South Australia.

OECD (2018). *Preparing Our Youth for an Inclusive and Sustainable World: The OECD PISA Global Comptence Framework*. Paris: OECD.

Oxfam GB (2015). *Education for Global Citizenship: A Guide for Schools*. Oxford: Oxfam GB.

Pantic, N. (2015). 'A Model for Study of Teacher Agency for Social Justice'. *Teachers and Teaching* 21(6): 759–78.

Peterson, A. (2016). 'EnActing the Common Good: What does it mean for Social and Citizenship Education?' *The Social Educator* 34(2): 4–10.

Rautalin, M., P. Alasuutari and E. Vento (2019). 'Globalisation of Education Policies: Does PISA have an Effect?' *Journal of Education Policy* 34(4): 500–22.

Reimers, F. M. (2020). *Educating Students to Improve the World*. Cambridge: Springer Open.

Reimers, F. M., V. Chopra, C. K. Chung, J. Higdon and E. B. O'Donnell (2016). *Empowering Global Citizens: A World Course*. North Charleston, South Carolina: CreateSpace Independent Publishing Platform.

Reynolds, R., S. MacQueen and K. Ferguson-Patrick (2019). 'Educating for Global Citizenship: Australia as a Case Study'. *International Journal of Development Education and Global Learning* 11(1): 103–19.

Reysen, S. and I. Katzarska-Miller (2013). 'A Model of Global Citizenship: Antecedents and Outcomes'. *International Journal of Psychology* 48(5): 858–70.

Robinson, K. (2011). *Out of Our Minds: Learning to be Creative*. Chicester: Capstone Publishing Ltd.

Sant, E., I. Davies, K. Pashby and L. Shultz (2018). *Global Citizenship Education: A Critical Introduction to Key Concepts and Debates*. London: Bloomsbury Academic.

Schulz, W., J. Ainley, J. Fraillon, B. Losito, G. Agrusti and T. Friedman (2017). *Becoming Citizens in a Changing World: IEA International Civic and Citizenship Education Study 2016 International Report*. Netherlands: The International Association for the Evaluation of Educational Achievement.

Scoular, C., D. Ramalingam, D. Duckworth and J. Heard (2020). *Assessment of the General Capabilities*. Camberwell: Australian Council for Educational Research Ltd.

Sjoberg, S. (2016). 'OECD, PISA and Globalization: The Influence of the International Assessment Regime', in C. H. Tienken and C. A. Mullen (eds), *Education Policy Perils; Tackling the Tough Issues*, 102–32. New York: Routledge.

UNESCO (2015). 'Global Citizenship Education: Topics and Learning Perspectives'. Retrieved from https://leer.es/documents/235507/415170/Global+Citizenship+EDucation+UNESCO+2015/6c1bb493-db6b-464b-b95f-4e83a179d084

UNESCO (2017). 'Learning to Live Together'. Retrieved from http://www.unesco.org/new/en/social-and-human-sciences/themes/international-migration/glossary/citizenship/

United Nations (1989). 'Conventions of the Rights of the Child Treaty no. 27531'. Retrieved from https://www.ohchr.org/en/instruments-mechanisms/instruments/convention-rights-child

United Nations (2015). 'Transforming Our World: The 2030 Agenda for Sustainable Development'. Retrieved from https://sustainabledevelopment.un.org/post2015/transformingourworld

Unler, S. (2012). 'Being an Insider Researcher while Conducting Case Study Research'. *The Qualitative Report* 17: 1–14.

Vaccari, V. and M. P. Gardinier (2019). 'Towards One World or Many? A Comparative Analysis of OECD and UNESCO Global Education Policy Documents'. *International Journal of Development Education and Global Learning* 11(1): 68–86. doi: https://doi.org/10.18546/IJDEGL.11.1.05

8

How Chinese Philosophies Affect the Chinese Understanding of Global Citizenship Education

Jun Teng and Yuxuan Gong

Acknowledgements

Thanks for the constant support of Ron Liskey. We would also like to appreciate Gregory Massara and Peter Huston for comments and revisions.

Introduction

In 2019, UNESCO's Institute for Statistics (Sandoval and Miranda, 2019) drafted the definition of Global Citizenship Competencies as 'nurtures respect for all, building a sense of belonging to a common human nature and helping learners become responsible and active global citizens'. The Southeast Asia Primary Learning Metrics (SEA-PLM) states that 'Global citizens appreciate and understand the interconnectedness of all life on the planet' (UNICEF, 2020). In the Chinese context, Mansilla and Wilson (2020) defined global competence as 'The life-long process of cultivating oneself, one's human capacity and disposition to understand issues of global and cultural significance and act towards collective well-being and sustainable development' (p. 11). These definitions imply basic elements of its core meaning. When interpreting global citizenship competence in the Chinese context, there is an important question: How to cultivate oneself, become a global citizen and understand sustainable development within the Chinese context?

To answer this question, we explore how ancient Chinese philosophers understood the relationship between themselves and the world. Based on their attempts, this chapter offers an ontological 'Relational Rationality Theory' to expand the current understanding of 'global' in the context of Global Citizenship Education. We do this by offering a generalized framework for Relational Rationality Theory with five basic elements (Figure 8.1). We hope this contributes to a heuristic understanding of current global citizenship education.

There is a debate about the relationship of Global Citizenship to promoting universality while respecting particularity, such as globalization versus localization (Benavot, 2022). For the ancient Chinese, this was not viewed as a tension; rather, they utilized dualistic systems such as Yin/Yang to focus on both aspects while stressing social relations. We have found that the Chinese understanding of 天下 *Tianxia (Global)* helps integrate diverse cosmopolitanism and universal human values, in particular 'interconnectedness'. Many view Eastern and Western perspectives as opposite (e.g. individualist vs. collectivist); however, this is only a phenomenological dichotomy. In fact, core perspectives are shared by both. For example, the idea of oneness is also shared by the ancient Stoics (σύμπαν).

This chapter explores common perspectives by analysing the complex meaning of the term 天下 *Tianxia* (Global) to support international efforts towards a peaceful, sustainable and just planet. We concluded that this term cannot be removed from its Chinese context. As this chapter laid out, 天下 *Tianxia (Global)* often relates to multiple concepts, including 'cosmos', 'Tao' and, in some cases, 'human heart', 'the unity of humanity with the cosmos' and 'anthropo cosmos' (the relationship between self, society and the cosmos). Confucius (551 BC–479 BC), Lao Tzu (571 BC–unknown) and Hui Neng (638–713) considered their relationships with all things; therefore, Global Citizenship in the Chinese context must be understood as focusing on

relationships between self-self (e.g. self-cultivation), self-society (e.g. human heart) and self-cosmos (cosmos, Tao, etc.). For this reason Relational Rationality, rather than individualism, is the core philosophy used to understand global citizenship competence within Chinese society.

In this chapter, we conducted the following analysis:

1. As Figure 8.1 shows, we presented the requisite environmental factors (Benevolence, Human Heart, Equality) needed for Relational Rationality. Then we analysed the Five Basic Elements of Relational Rationality Theory: (1) Diversity, (2) Respect for All, (3) Self-cultivation, (4) Universal Compassion and (5) Interconnectedness.
2. We gave examples of how the term Global is understood in Confucianism, Buddhism and Taoism, three schools of thought that profoundly shaped Chinese culture and the attitudes of its citizens.

Figure 8.1 The five elements.

3. By interpreting the idea of 天下 *Tianxia* (*Global*) and potential forms of global citizenship advocated by these philosophies, we proposed a model of Relational Rationality Theory, and mapped its Five Basic Elements onto the teachings of ancient Chinese masters.

Relational rationality – contingent pedagogy

Economic rationality is just one possible way to be relationally rational. Relational rationality shifts a dualistic system to an integrated process. Aronsson (2002) confirmed that children use Relational Rationality. In the Lemon Car Game designed by Hofstede et al. (2019), a study including over 800 players from more than 70 countries concluded that Economic Rationality fails to fully explain players' actions. Instead, people consider interpersonal relationships in a social context. Relational Rationality is typically used when society is considered. Thus, in contrast to Economic Rationality, Relational Rationality considers the interconnectedness of all Relational rationality – contingent pedagogy.

Economic rationality is just one possible way to be relationally rational. Relational rationality shifts a dualistic system to an integrated process. Aronsson (2002) confirmed that children use Relational Rationality. In the Lemon Car Game designed by Hofstede et al. (2019), a study including over 800 players from more than 70 countries concluded that Economic Rationality fails to fully explain players' actions. Instead, people consider interpersonal relationships in a social context. Relational Rationality is typically used when society is considered. Thus, in contrast to Economic Rationality, Relational Rationality considers the interconnectedness of all relations: human, social, natural, time, continuity and change. Precisely this is the Relational Rationality decision-making process, as described in several international relations papers (Zhao, 2005; Qin and Nordin, 2019), and in sociological literature (Lin, 2001; Bian, 2010; 2013; 2019).

In this chapter, Relational Rationality refers to an adaptive approach to decision-making that focuses on relationships, including the self, society and the cosmos. This is similar to what the Stoics thought, for example, 'for a rational creature, to act according to nature and to act according to reason is one and the same' (*Marcus Aurelius, Meditations, Book 7:11*, Robin Hard translation, 2011).

Relational Rationality also applies to education. People often view student-centred learning as axiomatic and may classify all learning that is not student-centred as teacher-centred (Komatsu, Rappleye and Silova, 2021). However, Relational Rationality Education does not fit either category. It is better understood as a competency-based, situation-based and benevolence-based educational system. Core competencies must be consistently included when developing Global Citizenship Competence. Confucianism, Taoism and Buddhism shape the social-emotional skills of Chinese students. Inspired by this, we adopt a contingent pedagogy (Komatsu, Rappleye and Silova, 2021) in Relational Rationality education because of its situational and adaptive features.

Relational Rationality works as a common ontological category for the Chinese to identify confusion and challenges. Zhai (1993) analysed how a system combining Buddhism, Confucianism and Taoism works in Chinese relationship structures. There are three ways to simultaneously understand a question: *why, how, what*. The Chinese use the theory of Karma to explain 'why questions' (i.e. questions of fate 人缘). For example, 'Why am I the one going through this dilemma or having this experience?' When encountering 'how questions' (i.e.

questions of ethics 人伦), such as how to maintain perfect human relations, a question similar to 'What would Jesus do?' might be asked. 'What questions' are used to interpret feelings (人情). The Chinese use models of perfect or idealized human relationships to guide their actions. For example, the *Analects of Confucius* is often used as a guidebook of manners to inspire people to act well. However, in the Chinese context, the inner form of 'benevolence' comes first and is beyond blind obedience to customary rules and social norms. Our understanding of Karma and our goal of achieving perfect human relationships combine in each circumstance to guide us. In this way, Relational Rationality shows in the outer form of customary manners and in the inner form of 仁 (benevolence).

Relational Rationality is indispensable for understanding how the Chinese language influences East Asian societies. It is embedded in the important characters: 儒 (Confucianism) and 仁 (benevolence). The character for 儒 (Confucianism) is a combination of the characters for 人 (human) and 需 (need). This highlights the core meaning of Confucianism as a theory of human needs. Similarly, the character for 仁 (benevolence) consists of 人 *ren* (people) and 二 *er* (two). On the surface it means to be kind, but at the core it refers to all relationships. In this chapter, we will clarify Relational Rationality and its varying forms of justice in different settings. In Chinese, the term for relationships is *Guanxi*, which is often viewed as social capital in China. In several sociological studies by Bian (2010) (2013) (2019) that were aligned with Lin Nan (2001), *Guanxi* was further developed. This chapter recognizes relationships as the embodied state of cultural capital, which can be transferred into social capital. Embodied cultural capital such as behavioural styles, ways of speaking, perceptions of justice and understanding of valued cultural knowledge are the main areas of focus for Relational Rationality. Thus, Relational Rationality works in the Global (*Tianxia*) system through embodied cultural capital and has to be discussed in its rationality from human heart, and two of its most important concepts: benevolence and equality.

Benevolence, human heart, equality

In this section, we will explore how to shift a dualistic system into an integrated one incorporating a contingent pedagogical perspective by analysing the basic concepts of 'human heart', 'benevolence' and 'equality' in Confucianism and Buddhism.

A common and dualistic interpretation of *Tianxia* is 人心 *renxin* (*human heart*). In this interpretation people differentiate between right and wrong, and share common understandings of 'commiseration', 'shame and dislike', 'modesty and complaisance', and 'approval and disapproval'.[1] The well-known proverb, 'Who wins the human heart wins *Tianxia*' illustrates this idea.

There is a deeper, non-dualistic (non-mutually-exclusive) understanding of 人心 *renxin* (human heart), that includes an understanding of 人性 *renxing* (human nature) and 'pure knowing' (see this chapter). Practice based on 'human nature' should be non-judgemental. For example, Mencius stated that there is no such thing as 'bad' since human nature is like water. He pointed out that 'water indeed will flow indifferently to the east or west, but will it flow indifferently up or down? The tendency of man's nature to good is like the tendency of water to flow downwards. There are none but have this tendency to good, just as all water flows downwards' (Mencius, 6A.2).

'Human nature' as understood here is different from culturally imposed ethics or norms, and is not equivalent to having a 'good' or popular personality. Although respect for hard work and authority is strongly valued in East Asia, it is a superficial understanding of ancient philosophy. Benevolence and self-cultivation as promoted by Confucius do not refer to top-down pressure to conform to society's expectations of 'good citizenship'. Instead, they are nurtured naturally from within by the 人心 *renxin* (human heart) and 人性 *renxing* (human nature).

Wang Yang-ming (1472-1529) applied these ideas to the art of self-cultivation by using the discovery model to discover a way towards higher levels of 良知 *liangzhi* (pure knowing). According to Wang, this is similar to discovering a clean mirror that is covered by dust, or the sun when it is blocked by clouds (Chan, 1963b; Ivanhoe, 2018). Ivanhoe (2018) explained the discovery model of Wang:

> strengthening one's faith in the unerring ability of pure knowing [innate knowledge] and developing an alert awareness of one's inner thoughts and feelings; one was to constantly monitor one's moral psychological state to root out self-centeredness so that pure knowing [innate knowledge] could function unobstructed and guide one to all and only proper behavior.

To further understand how the concept of 良知 *liangzhi* (pure knowing) can be applied to daily teaching, Wang (1472–1529) pointed out:

> such things which we usually call learning and inquiry, reflection and making distinctions, will only tend to increase his pride and conscious error so that while he considers himself to be becoming more intelligent and superior, he fails to realize that he is sinking into the depths of hatred and jealousy. (translated by Ching, 1972: p. 28)

Against this backdrop, benevolence in the Chinese context refers not merely to conformity despite how it is often described in literature (Kennedy and Fairbrother, 2004; Kennedy and Brunold, 2016; Lee, 2003). Confucius understood that benevolence has two aspects, and cannot be clearly defined since it is simultaneously universal and contextual. In the Yin aspect we are admonished to 'not do to others what we would not wish done to ourselves' (*Analects, 12.2*). In the Yang aspect we are admonished 'to help others while striving to be successful ourselves' (*Analects, 6.30*).

平等 *pingdeng* (Equality) is another essential element. Buddhist master Hsing Yun (1927–2023) transcribed the Sutras into more modern language, writing that *all beings are equal*, including non-living systems such as material objects. However, this didn't mean that all beings are phenomenologically identical. Differences exist due to Karma, but in each being remains an essential Buddhahood. The Buddhist idea of the Middle Way[2] – living a life free from the duality of suffering and joy – refers to a similar concept in the Chinese *Doctrine of the Mean*.

Diversity and respect for all

Ideas of *diversity, respect for all* and *freedom* are closely related. We can find similar concepts in Taoist philosophy. In Taoism, 'Cosmos'[3] implies a global view, and whether it refers to 'Tao' or nature itself is neutral regarding human relations and morality (Zhang, 2007). Therefore, Taoist thought on 'the unity of humanity and nature' is indifferent to everyday human affairs, and advocates not destroying the Cosmos through human action.

The parable of the Happy Excursion[4] is written about the beauty of the *Kunpeng*, a huge bird which could fly 90 kilometres. For huge birds such as the *Kunpeng*, it is sometimes necessary to prepare food for 'three months in order to take a trip'. In contrast, small insects are not worried about storing food since they only fly a short distance and within this distance they can easily find food. Starting from a discussion of large and small, high and low, aggression and suppression, Chuang Tzu indicated that all such dualistic conceptions are motivated by superficial outside expectations. Therefore, regardless of our dualistic judgements, 'no self, no merit, no name' captures the meaning of true freedom. Which is to say, we must be able to 'take advantage of the righteousness of Cosmos and earth, and the change of the six energies including Yin, Yang, Wind, Rain, Dark, Bright, then we can travel indefinitely' (Chuang Tzu, Happy excursion). Here the Happy Excursion indicates freedom.

On the basis of Lao Zi's Taoism, Chuang Tzu discusses how nature surpasses humanity's spiritual realm, such as in the 'Four Points' (see p. 7). In Chuang Tzu's Theory of the Equality of All Things, he wrote, 'Cosmos and earth live side by side with me, and all things are one with me', and here 'Cosmos' refers to Nature. The combinations 'man and nature' and 'Cosmos and earth' recur, but the difference between ourselves and others, or humans and non-humans, no longer exists. His 'Butterfly Dream'[5] is a vivid expression of his realm of 'unity of man and nature'.

Self-cultivation

As various scholars (Kennedy and Fairbrother, 2004; Kennedy and Brunold, 2016; Lee, 2003;) have pointed out, notions of 'collectiveness' 'relationships (guanxi)' and 'social harmony' are at the core of the Asian Global Citizenship (GC) concept. However, these values should not be viewed as exhortations to good citizenship or some obsolete form of moral education. Benavot (2022) mentioned 'the main force in their development lies inside each individual and in individual efforts to bridge individuals together with collectiveness'. An important citizenship-related concept is 'self-cultivation'. While the idea of the 'self' in neoliberalism can have both positive and negative connotations, the notion of 'self-cultivation' has only positive connotations in the Chinese context. As discussed by Lee (2003), the Self in Chinese is related to 'liberty' and 'nature'. As seen in Figure 8.1, self-cultivation plays a critical role as the trunk of the tree. In the Chinese perspective, 'self-cultivation' is an active construction and not a one-size-fits-all process. Furthermore, self-cultivation contains a contextual perspective in different relational situations. Ultimately, self-cultivation leads towards 'No self' and 'Tao'. Self-cultivation towards morality is 'a state of conscious knowing (directionality of the mind)' as well as 'a process of conscientious acting (transforming effect of the heart)' (Tu, 1985). In this respect, global citizenship education using Relational Rationality is not imposed on 'subjects' but is meant to construct self-in-the-world (Myers, 2016).

Confucius offered his ideas and methods of personal development as a model. He mentioned that

> At fifteen I set my mind upon learning, at thirty I took my place in society, at forty I became free of doubts, at fifty I understood Cosmos's Mandate, at sixty my ear was attuned, and finally at seventy I could follow my heart's desires without transgressing the bounds. (Confucius, Analects, 2.4)

Confucius understood 'global' by using a view of his relationship with Tao, and pointed out that this is an ongoing process of lifelong learning.

Cognition, emotion and behaviour in this context are all reshaped in accordance with cultural ideals, critical conscientiousness and a reservoir of wisdom shaped by careful, conscious reasoning. For example, in modern time, Buddhist Hsing Yun (2015) explained only by purifying the three Karmas of body, speech and mind can human beings maintain the wisdom to rightly protect the environment:

> Protecting the ecosystem relies on everyone's concerted support. The preservation of the spiritual environment relies on the individual to purify the three karmas of body, speech and mind. Environmental preservation usually takes place externally, yet internally, the purity of the mind is the greatest environmental preservation because Buddhism believes the establishment of the notion of environmental preservation should start from the human mind. ... As 'Buddha Land Chapter' in Vimalakirti Sutra states, 'If one wants to be in a Pure Land, one should purify the mind. When the mind is pure, the land is pure.' ... Thus Hsing Yun promoted that 'we need to clean away the filth in our minds with tools and weapons such as right view, right faith, compassion, wisdom, tolerance, diligence, friendliness, devotion, sacrifice, shamefulness, repentance, and so on. With these tools, the mind will be clear, bright, and clean'.

Typically, self-cultivation (a purification process expressed mainly through the development of body, speech and mind) is understood to begin a sequence, which includes regulation of the family, serving the nation and finally bringing about a peaceful world. However, action at the family or global level does not need to wait until self-cultivation is complete. By working at multiple levels at once, we are able to cultivate Heart. It can be done by striving to solve overwhelming global challenges while also practising self-cultivation. This more balanced approach avoids one-sided, dualistic traps that can lead to passivity, bitterness and burnout. This non-dualistic Relational Rationality approach enables self-cultivation to function both internally and externally. Internally it serves to develop body, speech and mind, and externally by helping to maintain harmonious family relations, lead the nation and contribute to a peaceful world.

Universal compassion – interconnectedness – the oneness

Universal compassion, according to Miao Zhe (2008), 'is a fundamental concept in Buddhism' and refers to 'cultivating loving-kindness without conditions, and grounding compassion in Oneness'. This is because all beings exist equally and are interconnected through Karma. As Miao Zhe (2008) wrote on harmony through 'Oneness and Coexistence':

> Compassion means unconditional loving-kindness, undifferentiated magnanimity. As kindness, it renders happiness, and as mercy, it relieves the suffering of others. . . . The Mahaprajnaparamita Sutra says Compassion opens the path to the realization of one's Buddha-nature. . . . Celebrating the differences in people while viewing everyone through the eyes of Oneness nurtures powerful connections and make the planet interconnected and coexistent together.[6]

Compassion is more than sympathy and empathy, which are often encountered in social-emotional learning materials. Sympathy refers to caring about another's suffering, yet it may contain a sense of superiority. Empathy enables people to put themselves in another's shoes, share their feelings and understand why they have these particular feelings. Buddhism deepened the Chinese understanding of compassion. In Chinese, the word 'compassion' consists of two characters, 慈 Ci（让人欢喜）, which means to be able to integrate with others and bring them sense of peace, while 悲 Bei（拔人离苦）means to be able to help others out of trouble. Therefore, Ci Bei enables people to return to the full Buddha nature, enabling them to link with others properly, and help them to return to their full Buddhahood. Ultimately, compassion includes the wisdom to help us connect with others and relieve their sorrow. This contributes to further understanding of how to self-cultivate one's perfect virtue, and support others cultivate themselves, as well as the virtuousness of the whole Anthropo-Cosmos.[7]

The term 'Oneness' as used in Buddhism is nearly identical to the ideas of another Confucian scholar, WangYang-ming (1472–1529), who successfully merged Chinese Buddhism and Taoism. Ivanhoe translated Wang's ideas as 'Heaven, earth and the myriad creatures have always been of one body with human beings' (Ivanhoe, 2009: p. 115). Wang asks rhetorically, 'Is there any suffering or bitterness of the great masses that is not disease or pain in my own body?' (translated by Chan 1963a: p. 166).

Wang tells the story of a child falling into a well. We feel nervous when imagining the child falling. That is to say, the hearts of the child and other human beings are in Oneness. Tan (2020) indicated the Oneness human beings share with all things is metaphysical: it is premised on the 'common stock of principles, which link us and lead us to care, in varying ways and degrees, about the world' (Ivanhoe 2009: p. 114). If not in the Oneness, why would we feel nervous when we imagine the child falling into a well? A limited sense of connectedness is due to our inability to use Pure Knowing (Innate Knowledge). Under Wang's inspiration, Chinese society recognized this Oneness as a form of solidarity with the Cosmos, society, human beings and all things. From this comes a shared sense of human nature. For instance, Tan (2020) noted:

> Our shared human nature, as envisioned by Wang, is predicated on and displayed by our 'regard[ing] other people as their own persons, regard[ing] the people of other countries as their own family' and feeling the 'suffering or bitterness of the great masses' in our own bodies (translated by Chan 1963a, 166). . . . His (Wang's) metaphysical position of cosmic unity and universal love provides a moral basis for Global Citizenship Education beyond utilitarian concerns and superficial outcomes.

The idea of 'Oneness and Interconnectedness' is also found in Taoism. For example the Taoist master Zhuang Zi wrote that 'All things are one with me'. The idea of Oneness is also expressed in statements by the current president of China, Xi Jinping, who consistently advocates building a community with a shared future for all humankind.

Over 2,000 years ago, this concept also emerged among the Stoic philosophers of early Western Civilization. Marcus Aurelius (Robin Hard translation, 2011) wrote in Meditations Book 12:30:

> There is one light of the sun, even though it is interrupted by walls, and mountains, and countless obstacles besides. There is one common substance, even though it is divided into countless individual bodies, each with its own particular qualities. There is one soul, even though it is divided amongst countless natures, each with its own limitations. There is one intelligent soul, though it may appear to be divided.

We suggest that 'Oneness' can play an important role in constructing categories of ontological Relational Rationality. This might be interpreted as the reason, 'I feel what you feel. I know who you are because I know who I am.' Metaphorically, we are all part of the same tree. As John Donne wrote so compellingly, 'therefore never send to know for whom the bell tolls; it tolls for thee.'

Conclusion

The concepts of Global Competence and Global Citizenship Competence were first developed in the West, and are usually discussed from a Western perspective. However, a more peaceful, tolerant, inclusive and secure world cannot be built on these efforts without including perspectives from the Global South. In this chapter, we have analysed 'benevolence', 'equality' and 'human heart' in the Chinese context. And furthermore, 'diversity and respect for all', 'self-cultivation', 'universal compassion' and 'interconnectedness' were discussed because these constructs lay the foundation of Relational Rationality Theory.

We started from the basic concepts of diversity and respect for all, which are fundamental concepts in Taoist theory. Respect for all is the precondition of respect for diversity, and furthermore, in order to encourage cooperation in the whole society, Chinese philosophers tend to choose the road to self-cultivation in order to encourage compassion towards, and interconnectedness with, the whole world. This environment, in turn, promotes self-cultivation, and consequently helps nurture more layers of universal compassion in the circle.

Relying on the non-duality of critical consciousness, Relational Rationality advocates self-cultivation through speech, body and mind. It can encourage otherwise indifferent people to take action on large, seemingly remote global challenges. We hope this chapter provides insight and inspires dialogue on how global citizenship/global education can be contextualized in countries with widely differing societies.

Notes

1. 'The feeling of commiseration is the principle of benevolence; the feelings of shame and dislike are the principle of righteousness; the feelings of modesty and complaisance are the principle of propriety; the feelings of approving and disapproving are the principle of knowledge. Human beings have these four points just as they have their four limbs' (Mencius, 2A6.3).
2. Retrieved on 30 November 2021. Miao Guang, http://yingyu.xdf.cn/201805/10783200.html
3. 天 is typically translated as 'Heaven'; however, a more accurate translation here might be 'Cosmos'.
4. 逍遥游
5. https://en.wikipedia.org/wiki/Peng_(mythology). 'Chuang Tzu was a philosopher in ancient China who one night went to sleep and dreamed that he was a butterfly. He dreamt that he was flying around from flower to flower and while he was dreaming he felt free, blown about by the breeze hither and thither. He was quite sure that he was a butterfly. But when he awoke he realized that he had just been dreaming, and that he was really Chuang Tzu dreaming he was a butterfly. But then Chuang Tzu asked himself the following question: 'was I Chuang Tzu dreaming I was a butterfly or am I now really a butterfly dreaming that I am Chuang Tzu?' https://www.philosophy-foundation.org/enquiries/view/the-butterfly-dream.
6. Retrieved on 1 May 2022 http://www.china.org.cn/culture/2008buddha/2008-07/09/content_15982762.htm
7. 善己达人，兼济天下

References

Aronsson, K. and K. Hundeideb (2002). 'Relational Rationality and Children's Interview Responses'. *Human Development* 45: 174–85.

Aurelius, M. (2011). *Meditations*. New York: Oxford University Press (Robin Hard translation).

Benavot, A. (2022). 'Feasibility Study on Monitoring Global Citizenship Competencies'. *The Asia-Pacific Centre of Education for International Understanding (APCEIU)*. https://www.gcedclearinghouse.org/sites/default/files/resources/210059eng.pdf

Bian (2010). 关系社会学及其学科地位，西安交通大学学报（社会科学版），101.

Bian (2013). 论关系文化与关系社会资本，人文杂志，201301, 107–13.

Bian (2019). 作为中国主体话语的关系社会学，人文杂志，201909, 23–34.

Chan, W.-T. (1963a). *Instructions for Practical Living and Other Neo-Confucian Writings by Wang Yang-ming*. New York: Columbia University Press.

Chan, W.-T. (1963b). *A Source Book in Chinese Philosophy*. Princeton: Princeton University Press.

Ching, J. (1972). *The Philosophical Letters of Wang Yang-ming*. Canberra: Australian National University Press.

Chuang Tzu (2020). Translated by J. Legge, 中州古籍出版社.

Hofstede, G. J., C. M. Jonker, T. Verwaart and N. Yorke-Smith (2019). 'The Lemon Car Game across Cultures: Evidence of Relational Rationality'. *Group Decision and Negotiation* 28(5): 849–77.

Hsing Yun (2015). *Environmental and Spiritual Preservation*, trans. Miao Guang and Miao Zhe. https://www.fgsitc.org/wp-content/uploads/2023/04/B8-Environmental-and-Spiritual-Preservation-2019.pdf

Isac, S. and D. Miranda (2019). *Measurement Strategy for SDG Global Indicator 4.7.1 and Thematic Indicators 4.7.4 and 4.7.5 using International Large-Scale Assessments in Education*. UNESCO.

Ivanhoe, P. J. (2009). *Readings from the Lu-Wang School of Neo-Confucianism*. Indianapolis: Hackett Publishing Co.

Ivanhoe, P. J. (2018). 'Selfishness and Self-centeredness'. *Journal of Korean Religions* 9(2): 9–31.

Kennedy, K. J. and A. Brunold (2016). *Regional Contexts and Citizenship Education in Asia and Europe*. London: Routledge.

Kennedy, K. J. and G. P. Fairbrother (2004). 'Asian Perspectives on Citizenship Education in Review: Postcolonial Constructions or Precolonial Values?' in W. O. Lee, D. L. Grossman, K. J. Kennedy and G. P. Fairbrother (eds), *Citizenship Education in Asia and the Pacific*, 289–301. Springer Netherlands. https://doi.org/10.1007/978-1-4020-7935-1_17

Komatsu, H., J. Rappleye and I. Silova (2021). 'Student-Centered Learning and Sustainability: Solution or Problem?' *Comparative Education Review* 65(1): 6–33. https://doi.org/10.1086/711829

Laozi (2020). *Tao Te Ching*, trans. J. Legge, 中州古籍出版社.

Lee, W. O. (2003). 'Conceptualizing Citizenship and Citizenship Education in Asia Pacific'. *Asian Education* 15(2): 8–26.

Lin, N. (2001) 'Guanxi: A Conceptual Analysis', in A. So, N. Lin and D. Poston (eds), *The Chinese Triangle of Mainland China, Taiwan, and Hong Kong: Comparative Institutional Analysis*, 153–66. London: Greenwood Press.

Mansilla, V. B. and D. Wilson (2020). 'What is Global Competence, and What Might it Look Like?' *Journal of Research in International Education* 19: 3–22.

Mencius (2020). Translated by J. Legge, 中州古籍出版社

Zhe, Miao (2008). 'Harmony through Oneness and Coexistense'. http://www.china.org.cn/culture/2008buddha/2008-07/09/content_15982762.htm

Myers, J. P. (2016). 'Charting a Democratic Course for Global Citizenship Education: Research Directions and Current Challenges'. *Education Policy Analysis Archives* 24: 1–15.

Qin, Y. and A. Nordin (2019). 'Relationality and Rationality in Confucian and Western Traditions of Thought'. *Cambridge Review of International Affairs* 32(5): 601–14.

Tan, C. (2020). 'An Ethical Foundation for Global Citizenship Education: A Neo-Confucian Perspective'. *Journal of Beliefs & Values* 41(4): 446–57.

The Confucian Analects (2020). Translated by J. Legge, 中州古籍出版社.

Zhai, X. (1993).《中国人际关系的特质——本上的概念及其模式》,《社会学研究》, 4: 74–83.

Zhang (2007). 张世英：《中国古代的"天人合一"思想》,《求是》, 7: 34–7/62.

Zhao, Tingyang (2005). *Tianxia Tixi: Shijie Zhidu Zhexue Daolun* [The Tianxia system: A Philosophy for the World Institution]. Nanjing: Jiangsu Jiaoyu Chubanshe.

UNICEF (2020). *SEA-PLM 2019 Main Regional Report: Children's Learning in 6 Southeast Asian Countries*. Bangkok: UNICEF.

Decolonizing Citizenship, Becoming Planetary with Paulo Freire's Hope-in-Action in Brazilian Education

Silvia Elisabeth Moraes, Luiz Botelho Albuquerque and Diana Nara da Silva Oliveira

Introduction

As in every other country in the world, Brazil experienced a pandemic of planetary dimensions, when deaths were counted in millions, where specialists and health authorities had the sole responsibility of providing for medicines, hospitals and supplies. In an atmosphere of fear, depression, uncertainty and lack of perspectives, educators, in turn, sought adequate strategies to educate citizens respond to these challenges. The themes outlined in this chapter need to be seen within this context.

From our locus of action, the university, more specifically from the Faculty of Education (FACED) at Federal University of Ceará (UFC), we have been putting into practice a proposal that has encouraged us to exercise Paulo Freire's hope-in-action: the inclusion in the university curriculum of planetary citizenship as a transdisciplinary theme, where we radically defend all forms of life on the planet, including Indigenous peoples and Afrodescendants, with their knowledge and traditions, au pair with scientific knowledge (Moraes and Freire 2017). Planetary citizenship is being addressed as a floating signifier (Laclau, 2007, in Moraes, 2014); floating signifiers are articulated in a variety of concrete projects according to the discursive contexts in which they are inserted.

Our proposal aims to address decolonization through a form of citizenship that crosses geographic and epistemological borders. Influenced by the ideas of Paulo Freire, its goal is to educate better citizens, teachers and intellectuals, with sensitivity, care and hope.

The dream of every proposal is to be multiplied into projects. This chapter outlines how we came to develop this proposal under the theme of planetary citizenship at our university and how it is being multiplied into projects. The chapter includes reference to a number of leading Brazilian educators who have influenced our thinking, the historical and social conditions that enabled us to develop a curriculum based on hope-in-action, informed by the ideas of Paulo Freire, and the work that has been so far produced articulating the floating signifier planetary citizenship.

Citizenship in Brazil: A long, hard path

The struggle for citizenship has accompanied Brazilians since the times when it was a Portuguese colony (1500–1815). For 300 years, slaves were brought from Africa and with the Indigenous Natives provided most of the work force for the Brazilian export economy. This legacy of slavery still haunts us as the Indigenous territories are invaded, with many Indigenous people still being killed and their natural environment destroyed. In addition, the descendants of the slaves reflect the ever-present racist society, with Black people still being among the poorest in Brazil.

Citizenship in Brazil should also be understood within the historical context of political struggle. From April 1964 to March 1985, a military dictatorship existed in Brazil with the pretext of preventing the advance of communism in the country. Individual and social guarantees were restricted, and two of the basic constituents of citizenship – the right to vote and freedom of speech – were suppressed. Nationalism and authoritarian military thinking were imposed in all spheres, including in the school and university curriculum.

In May 1968,[1] a climate of contestation shook the world, and this brought us even closer to the university as a space of welcome and freedom. It meant an awareness of the possibilities of change, and this is what we experienced with our teachers. In 1988, political rights were re-established when, in the new Federal Constitution known as the 'Citizen Constitution', citizenship appeared as a fundamental principle.

Citizenship became global when, in 1992, thirty years ago, Rio de Janeiro hosted the United Nations Conference on Environment and Development, known as Eco-92, Rio-92 or Earth Summit. Participants were invited to 'think globally, act locally'. The Agenda 21, a document containing a political commitment to promote sustainable development as a new standard on a global scale, was signed. The Greenhouse effect, deforestation, ozone layer brought ecological awareness to the public debate. 'There is no Planet B', shouted youngsters on the streets of Rio de Janeiro. The developments that remained, in addition to the theme of sustainable development incorporated into the public debate, are the treaties and conferences that have emerged since 1992.

Educators who have inspired us

Underpinning the epistemological basis outlined in this chapter are the ideas of Paulo Freire. But to understand his contribution it is necessary to situate his ideas within the broader history that began in the nineteenth century with authors who put forward a Brazilian national education for the Brazilian people and made by Brazilians. As we educators do not seek isolation or solipsism in relation to the international educational community, in our search for alternatives that promote a meaningful, transformative education, Freirean epistemology helps in thinking the subject in a collective and total sense, as inhabitants of one Planet, heirs of one destiny. We also realized that our practices allowed us to pursue what Santos and Menezes (2010) defend as an epistemology of the South, which validates the knowledge born in the social struggles against oppression fundamentally produced by three forms of domination: capitalism, colonialism and patriarchalism.

Brazilian universities have long followed the modern occidental model, ignoring and excluding the African and Indigenous matrix. *This shows that underlying our social and economic inequality is an attitude of disdain and disregard for popular/traditional knowledge* (Moraes and Freire, 2017: p. 28). Santos's ecology of knowledges is based on the recognition of the plurality of heterogeneous knowledge, one of which is modern science, and in sustainable and dynamic interactions between areas, without compromising their autonomy. It implies giving visibility to cultural, epistemological experiences, made invisible by a hegemonic logic that disqualifies them. In the curriculum, the ecology of knowledges gives support to the inclusion of our indigenous and African matrices together with the Western knowledge.

To understand and situate our proposal within a Brazilian educational context, it is necessary to make reference to a number of Brazilian educators who have contributed to the idea of citizenship in Brazil, teaching us about the university and its place in our history, about culture, political structure and society: Nísia Floresta, who, in the nineteenth century, carried out the extraordinary work of creating the first school for women, designed by women, and directed by women; Machado de Assis, perhaps the greatest writer of the Portuguese language in Brazil, inaugurated a critique of colonized attitudes that still guide us today, aiming to overcome subordination in relation to metropolitan hegemony and the construction of an autonomous national thought open to dialogue; Cecilia Meireles and Anísio Teixeira, educators linked to the Modern Art Week of 1922,[2] and the Manifesto of the Pioneers of a New Education, anticipated the ideals of a secular and compulsory education of high quality for the entire population.

With Darcy Ribeiro, anthropologist, historian, sociologist, author and politician, we learned about quality in higher education, public and free to all. Ribeiro influenced several scholars of Brazilian and Latin American studies. As Minister of Education, he carried out profound reforms which led him to be invited to participate in university reforms in Chile, Peru, Venezuela, Mexico and Uruguay, after leaving Brazil due to the 1964 coup d'état.

Acknowledging the importance and influence of these educators is important because it gave us inspiration to see that different models of education are possible. What we saw as limitations were the founding characteristics of an educational institution linked to the churches, as reflected in the University of Coimbra, alma mater of our conservative theorists. The emphasis on the reproduction of knowledge of classical antiquity and on the revealed texts opposed the knowledge that emerged from the research of a university designed in Germany by Humboldt, who also opposed articulating knowledge and social life of the French University of Napoleon. We felt the difficulties, but we did not know how to ask the right questions, or who to listen to. We sought to clarify ourselves by studying conventional school knowledge, but also by dialoguing with our intellectuals, those who have nurtured our hope for a better future.

Those of us who have learned to look at universities as multi-secular institutions, whose somewhat imprecise origins are lost in the mists of the twelfth century, were delighted to meet their founders. And this led us to reflect on colonial domination, slavery and international asymmetries, in defining what is legitimate culture, what knowledge is valid, what aesthetic, epistemological, theoretical and methodological options deserve respect.

A key influence on the development of our ideas has been Milton Santos, one of the most renowned intellectuals in Brazil in the twentieth century, a master on the renewal of geography in the 1970s, especially in Third World urbanization and globalization in the 1990s, who has presented a critical position on the capitalist system and advocated another type of globalization, where indigenous philosophies and thoughts will not be suffocated by global capitalist rationalism. Another key influence has been Lelia Gonzalez, author, politician, teacher, philosopher anthropologist, a Black activist and intellectual, a pioneer in studies on Black Culture in Brazil and co-founder of the Institute for Research on Black Cultures of Rio de Janeiro (IPCN-RJ). She has denounced racism and sexism as forms of violence that subordinate Black women. These authors, as well as Boaventura de Sousa Santos (2010) and Homi Bhabha (1998), show the relevance of a Southern way of thinking, reflecting our old Machado de Assis, who, already in 1883, warned us of the damage of internalized slavery and colonization.

Sergio Miceli (2001) has opened our eyes to the magnitude of the challenge that is the education of intellectuals and the production of knowledge in the peripheries of capitalism. Understanding relationships of all kinds – personal and political, dominant, and dominated strategies; questions of the social and family origins of the agents; institutions and the market – which end up influencing academic initiatives – has simultaneously disenchanted and clarified us.

However, disenchantment is a condition for understanding. We have learned that the schools themselves cannot make the necessary structural changes, but they can prepare those who make them. On the other hand, they can reproduce the worst of a society like the Brazilian in its colonial and slave heritage, in the most complete way, and with the most devastating results, as we see happening now.

We understand, with Machado de Assis and Paulo Freire, that no educational project will transform us until we get rid of the slave colonizer we carry within us. Educating our sensitivity from the perspective of caring for others, society and nature is what prevents us from taking the whip and becoming the oppressor.

We must not forget that oppression has a crucial epistemological dimension. The classification and hierarchy of knowledge, legitimacy and cultural discretion all need to be considered in the education of a citizen with planetary aspirations. Only an interdisciplinary stance will establish a democracy in the field of disciplinary knowledge; and humility is part of the minimum skills and competence necessary to exercise this citizenship.

Our contribution is to believe that some intervention is possible through scientific knowledge combined with social, human, artistic and environmental sensitivity. We know that we were educated to become Cartesian; therefore, the difficulties of implementing effectively interdisciplinary research practices are overwhelming. But we are fascinated by the possibility of proposing knowledge in a critical, peaceful and fertile dialogical coexistence for the creation of new knowledge, which Brazilian culture can offer to the civilization of humanity as a vital contribution to the construction of a planetary citizenship.

Our enchantment knows that this is a space marked by asymmetries and hierarchies, and that it obeys epistemologies structured by gender, ethnicity, by financial, symbolic and cultural capital. Perhaps it is reasonable to say that this field is also structured by an epistemology of intolerance and prejudice.

We are all for an epistemology of the South (Santos, 2010) that is sensitive to other paradigms that derive from the experience of colonized and enslaved peoples, who had, in their education, the critical contribution of military experience, economic and cultural domination and ethnic destruction. We joyfully believe that the vitality of the culture that emerges from the slave colony is the surprising and inspiring element for a confident attitude towards the future, particularly if articulated with a national project of popular and higher education defined in the national interest.

Planetary citizenship in the curriculum is our hope-in-action

Celebrating Paulo Freire's 100 years of wisdom, compassion, care and hope, we honour him by using his pedagogy in our planetary citizenship proposal. Born on 19 September 1921, in Recife, Pernambuco, to a very poor north-eastern family, Freire has been considered one of the most outstanding figures in the history of world pedagogy, proof of which is the number of translations of his work and the changes in the school and university curriculum that incorporate his dialogical method.

Freire's life and work were marked by his clear choice in favour of the oppressed. Observing the survival difficulties of the underprivileged classes, he used his indignation against injustices to transform society through an emancipatory education. Evidence in his favour is the strong opposition to his ideas coming from dictatorial governments, as occurred during the Brazilian military coup of 1964 that caused his exile in Bolivia and Chile, and under the leadership of Bolsonaro, a government that flirted with the destruction of democratic institutions, that dreams of streets with armed troops in every corner and dared to suggest, with no success, depriving Freire from his title of Patron of Brazilian Education. Freire's emphasis on developing a critical consciousness and the centrality and necessity of dialogue as the main tool for achieving such consciousness are vital for confronting radical ideologies, opposing dogmatic versions of social reality, both left and right.

The only effective instrument for a humanizing pedagogy, says Freire (2005b), is a permanent dialogue with the students, originated in the context of a problem-posing education where society permanently questions itself. It directly opposes a *banking education* (Freire, 2005b) that regards humans as adaptable, manageable beings, uncapable of transforming the world, with teachers depositing knowledges in students' brains without any possibility of discussion or disagreement. It is what happens in a fragmented, linear and alienating curriculum.

Dialogue is an existential demand that characterizes an epistemological relationship. It is the encounter between humans mediated by the world. Engagement in dialogue is the recognition of the social and not merely the individualistic character of the process of knowing: dialogue is an indispensable component of the process of both learning and knowing for which Freire establishes the following essential elements: Love, Humility, Faith, Trust, Hope and Critical Consciousness.

For Freire (2005: p. 90), it was through love for the world and for humans that dialogue is established.[3] The pronunciation of the world, which is an act of creation and re-creation, is not possible if it is not infused with love. Love is at the same time the foundation of dialogue and dialogue itself. Love is an act of courage; it is a commitment. Humility is essential in dialogue:

> How can I dialogue if I see ignorance in the other, never in myself? How can I dialogue if I consider myself participant of a ghetto of pure human beings, and those who are outside are inferior natives? How can I dialogue if the reading of the world is a task for select people and the presence of the masses is a sign of deterioration? How can I dialogue if I close myself to others' contribution, that I never recognize and that even offends me? How can I dialogue if I fear resilience and only in thinking of it, I suffer and wither? (Freire, 2005b: p. 93)

Faith in our power to make and remake, to create and re-create, faith in our vocation to be more fully human:

> Faith in humankind is an a priori requirement for dialogue (Freire, 2005a: p. 91)

As dialogue is based on Love, Humility and Faith, Trust is an obvious consequence:

> Trust makes dialogic subjects more and more companions in the pronunciation of the world (Freire, 2005b: p. 94)

There is no dialogue if there is no Hope. Despair is a kind of silence, a refusal of the world:

> Hope is in the essence of human imperfection, leading us to an eternal search. This search cannot be performed in isolation but in communication with one another. (Freire, 2005b: pp. 94–5)

Hope in Freire requires a linguistic explanation. In Portuguese, hope represents the noun *hope* (*esperança*) and the verb *to wait* (*esperar*). It comes from Latin *sperare* which also means *to wait, to trust, to desire*. *I hope* means *I have hope* (*Eu tenho esperança*), but also *I hope* (*Eu espero, I wait for things to happen*). To escape the passivity of the term, Paulo Freire replaced *esperar* for *esperançar*, which means hope-with-action. *I move myself in hope while I fight and, if I fight with hope, eu esperanço.* Hope is therefore an ontological need that must be anchored in practice to become historical concreteness. Hope alone does not have the power to transform reality.

> Finally, true dialogue requires Critical Consciousness, which means a non-acceptance of a dichotomy between humans and world but an unbreakable solidarity between them:
>
> It is a thinking which perceives reality as process, as transformation, rather than as a static entity – a thinking which does not separate itself from action, but constantly immerses itself in temporality without fear of the risks involved. (Freire, 2005b: p. 95)

Consciousness is by definition a method:

> the external form of consciousness manifest in acts, which takes on the fundamental property of consciousness – its intentionality. (Freire, 2005a: pp. 68–9)

Our context for practising dialogue – with Love, Faith, Humility, Trust, Hope and Critical Consciousness – is the curriculum. A planetary citizenship means dedicating ourselves to practice a humanizing pedagogy, together with our students and our identity companions – Europeans, Indigenous and Africans – in an epistemological relationship, that includes coming to terms with our past of colonization and slavery, together with our responsibility in preserving life on the planet.

It is the influence of Freire's ideas that enables to develop the concept of planetary citizenship which emerges as an evolution and contextualization of global citizenship. Its nature is ontological, given that, as unfinished beings, and aware of our inconclusiveness, we seek complete humanization in a dialectical relationship between human-humans, human-world. It is epistemological because, by including the knowledge of the indigenous and Afrodescendants, it reacts to the imposition of Western knowledge as the only valid and worthy of consideration. This can be achieved through putting into practice a Freeman dialogue approach of humans-humans and humans to the world approach: *No one educates anyone, no one educates himself, men educate one another, mediated by the world* (Freire, 2005b: p. 78). It is political because it is based on *critical and liberating dialogue, which presupposes action* (Freire, 2005a: p. 75).

Freirean pedagogy in our curriculum practice

Planetary citizenship in our curriculum draws upon Paulo Freire's idea, perhaps one of the most consistent, of a perennial construction of humanity, implying the constant struggle against oppression, ignorance and the evil destruction of our Terra-Pátria. The main locus of our dialogue is the Federal University of Ceará (UFC), a public institution founded in 1954 in the Northeast of Brazil, a country immersed in a profound and long-lasting sanitary, climatological, economic, political and ethical crisis which conditions our judgement, but that, at the same time, makes us look at the future with optimism, hope and responsibility. UFC offers graduate and post-graduate courses in various areas of knowledge, and the Faculty of Education (FACED) responds for school and university teaching degrees.

In what we call Permanent Curriculum Seminar at UFC, students and professors (around twenty-five every semester) present their dissertations, thesis, publications and projects developed in their schools and universities. In the pandemic, there has been an increase in the number of institutions, areas and cities where participants come from. We also encourage the development of group projects using Paulo Freire's method that begins with *the cultural circle*, a spatial disposition of students and teachers in the classroom (virtual or face-to-face) that favours dialogue and interaction, where all are invited to talk about their lives in community, thus identifying their *generative themes*. Freire (2005a: p. 95) explains:

> I called these themes 'generative' because (however much they are understood and any action they may evoke) contain the possibility of unfolding again like many themes, which in turn require that new tasks be fulfilled.

The themes are investigated, examined within participants' specialties/areas, contextualized and consulted in various sources. In the end, their conclusions are socialized in oral presentations, articles, books, videos, and so on.

Human–world relationship that originates the generative themes can be applied to any teaching program in any area, any language and the dialogical methodology being used in the planetary citizenship project is therefore dynamic and contextualized.

Throughout the years, we have collected some generative themes that constitute the students' *thematic universe* (Freire, 2005b: p. 101), and characterize their *epochal unit* (Freire, 2005b: p. 107), a set of ideas, conceptions, values, which are recurrent at a specific time: Evolution, Energy, Biodiesel, the Universe, Ethanol, Television, Industrial Waste, Amazonia, Hunger Around the World, Water, Global Warming, Cellular Phones, Work and Consumerism, Bullying, Cultural Pluralism, Renewable Energy, Environment, Recycling, Africa, Our Ethnic Origins, North-eastern Culture, Affirmative Action, Citizenship, Origin of the Universe, Corruption, Nationalism, Prejudice, Popular Culture, Political Awareness, Military Dictatorship in Brazil, Cyberbullying, Sustainability, *Sertão do Nordeste*,[4] Environmental Awareness, The Sabiaguaba Dunes in Fortaleza, Ceará, Fake news, Covid-19, Afro-Brazilian Culture: *Maracatu*.[5]

As Bourn points out (2021: p. 70), *hope must be grounded in real issues of the time but encouraging an approach to learning that is forward-thinking, posing questions and ideas for the future.*

Projects that support the floating signifier planetary citizenship

Our project comes in a context of social movements that have denounced inequalities, fought for equal rights and representation, and pressed public authorities for compensatory policies. In 2003, a law included the mandatory teaching of Afro-Brazilian, African History and Culture in Brazilian schools. As for the Indigenous people, several Brazilian universities, in the last ten years, have created courses on their language, culture and traditional customs. Topics like ethnicity, subjectivity, gender, coloniality/decoloniality, diversity, inclusion and interculturality are part of a movement for decolonizing the curriculum.

We already have a number of projects and publications that illustrate the floating signifier planetary citizenship.

At UFC, the Kuaba Indigenous Intercultural Degree covers the history, culture and music of the original peoples of Ceará. Its aim is to educate indigenous teachers in a combination of traditional with academic/scientific knowledge.

A post-doctorate research, *Indigenous Music in Ceará in the Education of Planetary Citizens: Exploring Sounds with the Choir of PAAP – UFC*, is about five ethnic groups – their culture, craftsmanship, food, rituals, social organization – who compose songs where they honour the forest, birds, trees, dances, rituals and language.

A group of postgraduate students of UFC studied the role of Popular Healers in Ceará, women who descend from Africans or Natives, who use herbs and roots to restore physical and spiritual balance of those suffering from bronchitis, asthma, nervousness, insomnia and other ailments. Popular Healers are recognized as a Cultural Heritage of Brazil (Garcia, 2015), their healing prayers, considered an oral tradition and the memories that the elders share with their descendants, the most valuable goods of a people.

The e-book (Oliveira and Moraes, 2021) is another example of the acceptance and development of the proposal. Lopes et al. make a commitment to promote planetary citizenship in learning. Lima, C.R. calls for humanization and reconnection of knowledges. Moraes, S.E., Albuquerque, L. B. and Rogério, P. discuss how we become planetary humans.

Conclusions

The main question that the planetary citizenship educational project asks is how to materialize in the curriculum the proposal of humanization of Paulo Freire's Pedagogy of Hope and Social Justice in a country in transition from a slave colony to an independent nation, whose identity is unequally formed by Europeans, Afrodescendants and Indigenous peoples. The responsibility of the university is to establish a dialogue that results in agreements, considering the variables in the demands of each group. However, the first step in a humanization in Paulo Freire's terms is to encourage ourselves and our students to see how much of the oppressor/oppressed is in us: we are dealing with this autobiographically.

Scientific citizenship is guaranteed when scientists have space, time and resources needed for their job; for the Afrodescendants, who were uprooted from their country and brought as slaves, their demand is to have the same rights as all others, since this is their home now; for Indigenous peoples, whose territory is threatened by economic power and invaded by miners, *grileiros*[6] and the like, their right is to live in the same way and place as their ancestors, if they so desire.

Humanization is lost when humans are beaten, chained by the neck, hands, legs and sold as merchandise, or when their body characteristics – curly hair, thick lips, large hips – are associated with savagery, inferiority or low intellectual capacity. Humanization is lost when those in extreme poverty are homeless and eat from the dumpsters, or when rivers are polluted, secular trees are cut down and sold, animals are killed and the forest is burned. The emphasis on the Planet is in direct relation to its endangerment. All areas of knowledge are responsible for proving how disastrous is the path that has been trodden by the country and the world.

Notes

1. May 1968 was a political movement in France that, marked by general strikes and student occupations, became an icon of an era when the renewal of values came accompanied by the prominent strength of a young culture.
2. The Week of Modern Art, 1922 took place between 13 and 18 February 1922, at the Municipal Theater of São Paulo, and it is considered a landmark in Brazilian Modernism.
3. The original in Portuguese has *pronunciar o mundo* (pronouncing the world). Some translations bring *naming the world*.
4. *Sertão,* derived from *desertão* (great desert), the semi-arid region of north-eastern Brazil.
5. Maracatu is an Afro-Brazilian folk dance that emerged in the mid-eighteenth century, from the musical miscegenation of Portuguese, Indigenous and African cultures.
6. *Grileiros* are those who illegally occupy the land and claim the right to own and sell it.

References

Bhaba, H. K. (1998). *The Site of Culture*. Belo Horizonte: Editor of UFMG.
Bourn, D. (2021). 'Pedagogy of Hope: Global Learning and the Future of Education'. *International Journal of Development Education and Global Learning* 13(2): 65–78.
Freire, P. (1992). *Pedagogia da Esperança*. Rio de Janeiro: Paz e Terra.
Freire, P. (2005a). *Pedagogy of the Oppressed*, trans. Myra Bergman Ramos. New York: The Continuum International Publishing Group.
Freire, P. (2005b). *Pedagogia do Oprimido*. 46ª edição. Rio de Janeiro: Paz e Terra.
Garcia, J. Q. (2015). *The Prayers: Popular Culture and Historical Tradition*. 1 ed-Rio de Janeiro: Letra Capital.
Laclau, E. (2007). *Emancipation(s)*. London: Verso.

Miceli, S. (2001). *Brazilian intellectuals*. São Paulo: Companhia das Letras.

Moraes, S. E. (2014). 'Global Citizenship as a Floating Signifier: Lessons from UK Universities'. *International Journal of Development Education and Global Learning* 6(2): 27–42.

Moraes, S. E. and L. de A. Freire (2017). 'Planetary Citizenship and the Ecology of Knowledges in Brazilian Universities'. *International Journal of Development Education and Global Learning* 8(3): 2017.

Oliveira, D. N. S. and S. E. Moraes (2021). *Cidadania planetária como significante flutuante: Articulando significados na universidade e na escola*. Embu das Artes: Alexa Cultural.

Carvalho, K. E. B. and L. F. Souza (2021). 'Educação de jovens e adultos pelas lentes de Sebastião Salgado: construtores da cidadania planetária', in D. N. S. Oliveira and S. E. Moraes, *Cidadania planetária como significante flutuante: Articulando significados na universidade e na escola*. Embu das Artes: Alexa Cultural.

Carvalho, M. A. S., Y. F. Maia, P. S. V. Castro, J. A. C. Gomes and D. N. S. Oliveira (2021). 'O romance IRACEMA em sala de aula: uma proposta interdisciplinar', in D. N. S. Oliveira and S. E. Moraes, *Cidadania planetária como significante flutuante: Articulando significados na universidade e na escola*. Embu das Artes: Alexa Cultural.

Coelho, M. C. S. and F. O. Silva (2021). 'Educação em solos: proposição didático-pedagógica de ensino contextualizado', in D. N. S. Oliveira and S. E. Moraes, *Cidadania planetária como significante flutuante: Articulando significados na universidade e na escola*. Embu das Artes: Alexa Cultural.

Costa, M. F. and J. M. Rodrigues (2021). 'Colonialidade e decolonialidade no ensino da História africana e afro-brasileira: saberes e formação docente através do RPG', in D. N. S. Oliveira and S. E. Moraes, *Cidadania planetária como significante flutuante: Articulando significados na universidade e na escola*. Embu das Artes: Alexa Cultural.

Cruz, F. A. M., N. M. Sousa and M. A. T. Nascimento (2021). 'Atividade de criação artística em sala de aula: uma proposta pedagógica Francisca Antonia Marcilane Gonçalves Cruz', in D. N. S. Oliveira and S. E. Moraes, *Cidadania planetária como significante flutuante: Articulando significados na universidade e na escola*. Embu das Artes: Alexa Cultural.

Freitas, E. K. S., H. G. S. Maia, N. N. C. Silva and C. R. F. Lima (2021). 'Interdisciplinaridade e formação de professores polivalentes: didática e as múltiplas linguagens na educação infantil', in D. N. S. Oliveira and S. E. Moraes, *Cidadania planetária como significante flutuante: Articulando significados na universidade e na escola*. Embu das Artes: Alexa Cultural.

Gadelha, M. L. S. L. and A. C. Moraes (2021). 'Aprendizagem significativa e práxis pedagógica por meio de mapas mentais e da literatura de cordel', in D. N. S. Oliveira and S. E. Moraes, *Cidadania planetária como significante flutuante: Articulando significados na universidade e na escola*. Embu das Artes: Alexa Cultural.

Gondim, A. M., M. R. Bezerra and P. P. Scherre (2021). 'As frutas do meu cotidiano: proposta interdisciplinar de alfabetização mediada pelas tecnologias e Paulo

Freire', in D. N. S. Oliveira and S. E. Moraes, *Cidadania planetária como significante flutuante: Articulando significados na universidade e na escola*. Embu das Artes: Alexa Cultural.

Lima, C. R. (2021). 'Da embrutecida solidão transmissiva à um convite multidimensional, reconectador de saberes e humanização', in D. N. S. Oliveira and S. E. Moraes, *Cidadania planetária como significante flutuante: Articulando significados na universidade e na escola*. Embu das Artes: Alexa Cultural.

Lima, M. J. M., C. M. R. Silva and L. B. Albuquerque (2021). 'Educação para a paz na perspectiva interdisciplinar e transdisciplinar', in D. N. S. Oliveira and S. E. Moraes, *Cidadania planetária como significante flutuante: Articulando significados na universidade e na escola*. Embu das Artes: Alexa Cultural.

Lopes, C. E., D. C. Joaquim, F. L. A. Pereira, M. G. Rodrigues and M. J. M. Lima (2021). 'Amar e mudar as coisas me interessam muito mais', in D. N. S. Oliveira and S. E. Moraes, *Cidadania planetária como significante flutuante: Articulando significados na universidade e na escola*. Embu das Artes: Alexa Cultural.

Marcos, A. I. R. and M. S. Bastos (2021). 'Ecologia de saberes: Análise da produção audiovisual "O começo da vida 2: "lá fora"', in D. N. S. Oliveira and S. E. Moraes, *Cidadania planetária como significante flutuante: Articulando significados na universidade e na escola*. Embu das Artes: Alexa Cultural.

Miranda, R. S., A. W. T. Noronha and R. C. M. Leite (2021). 'O surgimento de pandemias e o desequilíbrio ambiental: Uma proposta transdisciplinar para a formação de cidadãos planetários', in D. N. S. Oliveira and S. E. Moraes, *Cidadania planetária como significante flutuante: Articulando significados na universidade e na escola*. Embu das Artes: Alexa Cultural.

Sampaio, P. S. L., J. A. C. Gomes and P. S. Teixeira (2021). 'O estudo dos povos pré-cabralianos para além do livro didático: uma proposta pedagógica a partir da decolonialidade e da interdisciplinaridade', in D. N. S. Oliveira and S. E. Moraes, *Cidadania planetária como significante flutuante: Articulando significados na universidade e na escola*. Embu das Artes: Alexa Cultural.

Schere, P. P., M. M. Miranda, M. A. G. Reges, M. O. Barbosa and C. R. F. Lima (2021). 'Projetos interdisciplinares na formação inicial de pedagogos: experiências, desafios, aprendizagens e reflexões', in D. N. S. Oliveira and S. E. Moraes, *Cidadania planetária como significante flutuante: Articulando significados na universidade e na escola*. Embu das Artes: Alexa Cultural.

Santos, B de S. and M. P. Meneses, eds (2010). *Southern Epistemologies*. São Paulo: Cortez.

Part III

Applying Global Social Justice

10

Transformative Social and Emotional Learning and Digital Learning for Global Citizenship Education

Limits and Possibilities

Yoko Mochizuki[1]

Introduction

With the Covid-19 pandemic accelerating urgent calls for effective and ethical use of digital technology in education and more attention to educators' and learners' emotional well-being, digital learning and Social and Emotional Learning (SEL) have gained renewed relevance and significance in the global education debates. As UNESCO's first and only Category-I research institute in the Asia-Pacific region with a global mandate on the Sustainable Development Goal (SDG) Target 4.7, the UNESCO Mahatma Gandhi Institute of Education for Peace and Sustainable Development (MGIEP) has championed SEL and digital learning in rethinking approaches to Education for Sustainable Development (ESD) and Global Citizenship Education (GCED) since the pre-pandemic days (see UNESCO MGIEP, 2019; 2020). This chapter discusses the limits and possibilities of SEL and digital learning in addressing equity, social justice and societal transformation. It unpacks MGIEP's fundamental approaches to learning against the backdrop of various concerns raised in relation to the rapid rise in interest in 'evidence-based' behaviour change interventions, in an attempt to give a broader societal and historical context in which MGIEP's approaches and initiatives are conceptualized and promoted.

Social and emotional learning and digital learning: Strange bedfellows for SDG 4.7?

On the back cover of a brochure entitled *Building Kinder Brains*,[2] UNESCO MGIEP (2021) articulates its goals as follows:

> UNESCO MGIEP focuses on achieving the UN Sustainable Development Goal 4.7 towards education for building peaceful and sustainable societies across the world by developing programmes that promote social and emotional learning, innovate digital pedagogies and empower the youth.

As the title of this brochure clearly suggests, MGIEP declares that its programmes are based on neuroscience. Statements such as 'Kindness releases dopamine, which is the brain chemical for reward and pleasure' (UNESCO MGIEP, 2021: p. 1), 'Kindness increases endorphins in the body; these are natural pain relievers which reduce pain and increase energy' (15), and 'Witnessing acts of kindness produces oxytocin, also called the love hormone' (27) give the brochure a scientific look. MGIEP champions 'evidence-based' SEL interventions to promote 'core competencies' which it defines as 'EMC²' (empathy, mindfulness, compassion, critical inquiry) (Duraiappah and Singh, 2019; UNESCO MGIEP, 2020). It aspires to scale up SEL by increasing the number of people who register for and complete digital courses on its online learning platform[3] and boosting the number of kindness stories collected as part of its global youth campaign 'Kindness Matters for the SDGs'[4] aiming to 'mobilize the world's youth to achieve the 17 SDGs through transformative acts of kindness'.

Taking inspiration from behavioural science and the neuroscientific interpretations of human behaviour that are commanding increasing attention in the policymaking circle today, MGIEP reinterprets ESD/GCED as educational efforts to intervene and modify human behaviour (personal habits, decisions and thought patterns) that is perceived as being at the heart of challenges related to peace and sustainable development. MGIEP's approaches need to be understood against the backdrop that economists and psychologists have long established a highly privileged position in policy and governance and in the historical context in which behavioural economics – a hybrid of psychology and economics – started guiding public and social policy, with strategies to 'nudge' people to make better choices that might be beneficial at both individual and collective levels. Following the establishment of a trendsetting 'Behavioural Insights Team' (BIT), or 'Nudge Unit', in the UK government in 2010, similar units have been established in governments as well as in academic institutions and businesses around the globe. The UK's BIT has partnered with the education business giant Pearson, self-designated 'world's learning company', on a report about using behavioural insights in formal education (O'Reilly et al., 2017). 'Nudge' techniques are based on a key behavioural insight that most human decision-making is habitual, unconscious, automatic and irrational (as opposed to rational, calculated self-regarding and strategizing) yet can be predictable and made amenable to being intervened and modified.

In response to the 'behavioural turn' within governments in the past decade (Feitsma, 2018: p. 388), key transnational policy actors are exploring or leveraging behavioural science in their work. The World Bank (2015) focused on behavioural science in its 2015 World Development Report. The application of behavioural science is arguably growing in the United Nations (UN), with the publication in 2021 of the UN Behavioural Science Report, in which UNESCO credits behavioural science as having contributed to the success of ESD scaling up and of the GCED competency framework (UN Innovation Network, 2021: p. 42) – although it is unclear from the text if UNESCO adequately understood what is meant by 'behavioural science'. One of the appeals of behavioural science interventions is that they tend to be low-cost – both to policymakers and to participants – and thus easy to scale up. The ubiquity of networked digital devices has made it possible to implement these interventions at a massive scale. Accompanying the Covid-related school and college closures, the use of online learning to ensure learning continuity has become a global imperative, with the UN calling for '[expanding] the definition of the right to education to include connectivity' (UN, 2020: p. 4). This signals a considerable weakening of a traditional suspicion about the overreliance on technology as leading to dehumanization, which was manifested in UNESCO's humanistic approaches to education, for example notably in the 1972 Faure report (Elfert, 2018).

Activities proposed by MGIEP as its contribution to SDG 4.7 implementation represent a fundamental shift from the conventional notion of ESD/GCED to foster 'knowledge, skills, values and attitudes' needed to shape a better world to 'evidence-based learning interventions' to promote 'pro-social behaviour'. Today UNESCO characterizes GCED as building on 'the work of Peace and Human Rights Education' and aiming to 'instil in learners the values, attitudes and behaviours that support responsible global citizenship',[5] thereby showing compatibility with the psychological language of 'pro-social behaviour'. In the field of ESD, however, 'behaviour change' tends to be associated with instrumentalist and technocratic approaches (see Vare and Scott, 2007), and behaviour change interventions have been seen as not 'transformative' enough to deserve focus or as outright ineffectual, questionable and contentious, and even 'in conflict with the goals of ESD' (UNESCO, 2011: p. 36).[6] Still, the Berlin Declaration on ESD adopted in 2021 at the UNESCO World Conference on ESD (UNESCO, 2021) refers to 'promoting individual behavioural change for sustainable development' as one of its long list of commitments, making a subtle, yet important, departure from the declarations adopted at the previous World Conferences on ESD (UNESCO, 2009; 2014), which made no mention of behaviour change. Further, the mainstreaming of ESD has encouraged researchers from different fields to scrutinize its concept and practice, leading to a critique of ESD which problematizes the insufficient attention it pays to psychological mechanisms underlying human behaviour (e.g. Ojala, 2013; 2017).

Traditionally, behavioural science interventions have been deployed in public policy to promote 'pro-social behaviour' such as eating healthy, exercising, getting regular medical check-ups, voting, paying tax on time and reducing littering (Rowson, 2011; Feitma, 2018). But the UK's BIT, which mobilizes behavioural economics expertise to undertake randomized controlled trials in key public policy areas including education, is already using the 'nudge' theory to support SEL in schools (Williamson, 2021). Furthermore, in recent years, a convergence between behavioural science and data science has enabled novel forms of 'persuasive computing' and 'hypernudge' techniques seeking to shape learner behaviour towards predefined aims (Yeung, 2017, as cited in Knox, Williamson and Bayne, 2019: p. 2). This raises a fundamental question of whether ESD/GCED can or should be reduced to interventions to promote 'pro-social' and 'pro-environmental' behaviour through digital pedagogies, as advocated by MGIEP. As, so far, there has been limited scholarly investigation of MGIEP's deployment of 'digital SEL' as a strategy for SDG 4.7 implementation (see Bryan 2022 and Vickers 2022 for the initial attempts to critically examine MGIEP's approaches), the next section delves into the context in which policy interest in SEL has taken hold, and new sources of knowledge and expertise have been sought as 'objective' and 'scientific' – as opposed to 'ideological' or 'normative' – justifications for ESD/GCED.

Is well-being a skill?

While it certainly seems reasonable that theories of human nature inform what the UN and governments do to support individual and collective well-being, it is important to reflect on the implications of adopting behaviour change interventions as a strategy for fostering global citizenship. MGIEP's interventions fundamentally rest on a view that 'well-being is a skill' (Davidson, 2016; 2018; 2019; Ricard, 2006). There is no shortage of 'evidence' to demonstrate that what is known as mindfulness, meditation or contemplative practices, empathy and compassion trainings, or other SEL interventions 'work' to improve objectively measurable skills for well-being (see UNESCO MGIEP, 2020, for a recent review). As a powerful SEL campaigning organization in the United States, the Collaborative for Academic, Social, and Emotional Learning (CASEL) commissioned two highly cited 'meta-analyses' of the research evidence on SEL (Durlak et al., 2011; Taylor et al., 2017). The aim of this chapter is not to challenge these zealously produced pieces of 'evidence' per se (see, for example, Humphrey, 2013 for discussion of challenges related to this including confirmation bias) but to critically examine the logic underpinning the production and use of such 'evidence'. From philosophical and sociological viewpoints, I problematize the foundational claim 'well-being is a skill' as an ideological basis for ESD/GCED, using the lenses of 'learnification' (Biesta, 2005; 2006), 'datafication' (Williamson, 2019) and 'happinisation' (Zembylas, 2020) of education.

First, the idea that one can learn well-being as a 'skill' can be firmly located within what philosopher Gert Biesta (2005) calls 'learnification' or re-ordering of the education sector and its key activities around the concept of 'learning' in the twenty-first century. With the concept of 'learnification', Biesta has critiqued various trends such as the marginalization of teacher expertise and the casting of learners as consumers. Significantly, 'learnification' is accompanied by the emphasis on measurement of learning and the pivotal importance quantitative data on learning outcomes occupy in education policymaking today. It can be argued that advocacy for 'evidence-based' SEL is based on what Biesta (2015: p. 13) characterizes as 'technological conception of education' which treats 'the main role for research as that of discovering knowledge about the connections between inputs and outcomes, and with the ambition that education itself can ultimately be transformed into a predictable technology'. Leading SEL researchers have built 'evidence' to further the SEL agenda, but in such research that focuses on 'what works', education is essentially conceived like a 'machinery' where there are inputs, mediating variables and outcomes. Drawing on insights from systems theory and complexity theory, Biesta (2015: p. 16) posits that cause–effect relationships occur in systems that are 'closed' (no interaction with the context in which the system works) and 'mechanistic' (internal connections between the parts of the system operate in a pre-determined way). This means that turning education systems into a 'predictable technology' requires having 'total control over processes of meaning making and interpretation and . . . the thinking and judging of the actors [teachers and students] in the process' (2015: p. 16). Clearly such education systems would be a far cry from education that is participatory, dialogic and transformative.

The second phenomenon essential for understanding the idea that social and emotional skills are malleable and measurable – most notably exemplified by the OECD Survey on Social and Emotional Skills[7] – is 'datafication' of education. 'Datafication' involves the development of infrastructures of policies, people, money (including venture capital and philanthropic funding), metrics and technologies, and, in particular for SEL, encompasses the monitoring of students' emotions and behaviours through, albeit still in extreme cases, the use of wearable biometric devices (Knox, Williamson and Bayne, 2019; Williamson, 2021). There is 'a substantial interest in new education technology development . . . directed towards "bodily" and "emotional" data, as a source of supposedly new accuracy and authenticity in understanding human learning' (Knox, Williamson and Bayne, 2019: p. 12). EdTech businesses, philanthropies and venture capitalists are putting significant resources into technologies of 'datafication', which is facilitated by policies and so-called 'innovative' funding schemes. In the United States, for example, the 2015 Every Student Succeeds Act (ESSA) – which obliges states to report a 'nonacademic measure' for accountability purposes – has directed investors' attention to SEL programs by providing a federal support to 'social impact bond' schemes (SIBS) or 'pay for success', which offers funders returns on investment as repayments and bonuses if the metrics are met or surpassed. By privileging approaches that generate hard, numerical evidence of 'what works', SIBS incentivizes for-profit philanthropies, venture capital firms and investment banks to invest in SEL measurement as a lucrative path to profit (Williamson, 2021). Another crucial consideration for the entanglement between 'learnification' and 'datafication' of education is 'the (re)turn to behaviourism' – the kind of '*radical* behaviourism' associated with the work of B. F. Skinner – which co-articulates with the resurgence of empiricism enabled by the 'data revolution' (Knox, Williamson and Bayne, 2019: p. 5, emphasis in original).

Third, the idea 'well-being is a skill' needs to be understood in the context of the 'happinisation' of education or the foregrounding of the individualized notion of happiness as an educational goal, which has serious implications for social justice education as it diverts attention from structural injustice in education and broader society (Zembylas, 2020). While the idea that 'well-being is a skill' has been put forward to communicate a positive message that anybody can learn to be happy, framing happiness as a skill one needs to cultivate leads to the framing of 'unhappiness' as an individual deficit. Individualizing and depoliticising (un)happiness, such framing implies turning a blind eye to systemic oppression and discouraging us from challenging the status quo. Alarmed by the happinisation of education, Zemblylas (2020: p. 26) highlights the importance for activists, educators and policymakers 'to identify, address and transform the structural inequalities and oppression' in their effort to address social justice. With the heightened awareness of systemic oppression as exemplified by the #MeToo and #BlackLivesMatter movements in recent years, to tackle the perception that SEL fails to address structural inequalities, SEL advocates themselves have started engaging in what can be termed a 'reformist' SEL advocacy and practice, linking SEL explicitly with social justice (Ancess and Rogers, 2015; CASEL, 2020) as well as with ethics (Center for Contemplative Science and Compassion-based Ethics, n.d.). For example, during the Covid-19 pandemic, CASEL organized a webinar series on racial injustice, characterizing SEL as a 'lever for equity and social justice' (CASEL, 2020). However, this will unlikely loosen the entanglement of 'learnificaiton', 'datafication' and 'happinisation' of education underpinning SEL, as discussed in the next section.

The entanglement of 'learnification', 'datafication' and 'happinisation': Deadly resonance with the neoliberal agenda

Underpinning the policy traction of SEL is the idea that social and emotional skills can be improved – ultimately *to what end* could be debatable, as discussed herein – through 'evidence-based' interventions ('what works'). However, looking into the entanglement of 'learnification', 'datafication' and 'happinisation' of education underpinning policy interest in SEL clearly shows that reliance on new sources of expertise itself is neither apolitical nor neutral. SEL has attracted influential philanthropies seeking leverage to 'reform' public education, which often means accelerating the digital transformation of the education sector. Not only does the application of behavioural insights (including the collection of data through, for example, randomized controlled trials, wearable biometric devices and neuroimaging technologies) appeal to policymakers and funders as informed by 'objective' and 'scientific' knowledge, it also supports a neoliberal agenda to marketize the education sector and usher in an extraordinary return on investment (including through 'innovative' financing schemes). Among twelve 'foundations partners' listed on CASEL's website[8] are the Bill and Melinda

Gates Foundation, established in 2000 by Microsoft founder Bill Gates, the Chan-Zuckerberg Initiative, founded in 2015 as a 'for-profit' philanthropy by Facebook founder Mark Zuckerberg, the Patrick J. McGovern Foundation,[9] which is 'a global philanthropy bridging the frontiers of artificial intelligence, data science, and social impact', and New Profit,[10] 'a national venture philanthropy organization created by and for social entrepreneurs'.

In addition to the increasing role of 'new' philanthropies in shaping national and global educational policy and delivery (see Verger, Fontdevila and Zancajo, 2016), it is important to consider the rise of the global measurement industry which is now interested in measuring not only 'cognitive' but also 'non-cognitive' skills. For example, Educational Testing Service (ETS), the world's largest private non-profit educational testing and assessment organization, was one of the organizations that supported the 'Salzburg Statement for SEL' that came out in 2019, which states: 'Every education system should explicitly include SEL in their pedagogical, curriculum and assessment practices across all ages from early childhood through adolescence to adulthood' (Salzburg Global Seminar, 2019). In 2014, OECD commissioned Pearson to develop the PISA 2018 frameworks (Steiner-Khamsi, Appleton and Vellani, 2018: p. 198), which included a framework for the measurement of 'global competence'.[11] This fact is not negligible, given that OECD's 'global competence' has been closely associated with GCED. While often self-positioned as diametrically opposed to education focused on testing of cognitive skills, much SEL advocacy pushes for including social and emotional skills in assessment rather than questioning the culture of testing and competition altogether. Not surprisingly, Pearson in 2017 released a digital product called Social Skills Improvement System (SSIS™) SEL Edition: 'A comprehensive, evidence-based, social-emotional learning system that also assesses key academic skills.'[12]

Furthermore, the 'learnification'–'datafication'–'happinisation' entanglement resonates with a neoliberal agenda that seeks to 'responsibilize' learners, citizens and workers to change their behaviour, rather than transforming the material and economic conditions that affect their 'well-being' or 'success' (measured in terms of educational outcomes, employment, physical and mental health, etc.). Framing happiness or well-being as an individual responsibility and achievement is convenient for the public and private sectors, as the former cuts down on equity measures and safety nets and the latter makes profits in the newly developed markets related to SEL and mindfulness or in the so-called 'happiness industry' or 'feel-good industry' (Ahmed, 2010: p. 3). But the issue here is not simply the state withdrawal from its responsibility for education or the 'greed' of the private sector. Not only does this entanglement contribute to the further marketization and commodification of education and undermine the possibilities of education as a social equalizer and a common good, it also appears to weaken the foundations of a democratic society by reinforcing control and surveillance of populations at the expense of fundamental human freedoms and human rights, including privacy. As Knox, Williamson and Bayn (2019: p. 2) argue writing about the convergence between behavioural science and data science, 'human learning appears susceptible to heightened forms of governance as digital environments become ever more connected, and education becomes subsumed into broader political agendas of behavioural governance'. As they elaborate, 'learning itself is reconceptualised in terms of psychologically quantifiable affective characteristics which are both detectable as autonomic bodily signals and amenable to being changed and modified in line with particular theories about what constitutes the "correct", "preferable", or "desirable" behaviours for learning' (11). Ironically, such reconceptualization seems to be fundamentally at odds with the kind of learner-driven, participatory approaches often championed by organizations in the business of transforming education.

Rather than taking SEL at its face value as a benign movement to foster social and emotional skills to enhance individual and collective flourishing, Williamson (2021) argues that underpinning the ascending policy attention to the development and measurement of SEL is the need to foster human capacities – with a particular emphasis on 'emotional intelligence' – to be coupled with 'artificial intelligence' (AI), to maximize the productivity potential of the digital economy. An illustrative case can be provided by the World Economic Forum's (WEF) call for 'human-centric skills', including 'cooperation, empathy, social awareness and global citizenship' (WEF, 2020: p. 6), which it predicts will provide humans with 'a distinct advantage over machines in the workplace' (10). Here, we seem to have reached an extremely grim conclusion. As the inequalities within and across nations and exclusivist nationalisms leave us ever more divided and a looming environmental crisis poses an existential threat to humanity, education is being reimagined to prioritize SEL – to the ultimate end of ensuring the political management of populations through psychological interventions and the safeguarding of 'human capital' in an AI-driven future. Such reimagining appears to have little to do with fundamentally addressing the human and planetary predicament, while much to do with ever strengthening the entanglement of learnification, datafication and happinisation. Is there still hope for transformative SEL and digital learning for fostering global citizenship?

Revisiting a pedagogy of hope: Towards transformative SEL and digital learning

Paulo Freire developed a powerful critique of what he called the 'banking' model of education – a unidirectional and top-down pedagogy whereby information is deposited by the teacher in the student's minds. Freire's (1994) *Pedagogy of Hope* called for overcoming the banking model of education through 'hope', engaging in and with the world to transform structural inequalities and oppressions and expanding possibilities for social justice. Freire (1994: p. 30) argued that hopelessness is intensified in the absence of a 'critical knowledge of reality'. If we are to embrace the SDGs and global citizenship seriously, we must critically examine the structural factors that led to the interconnected global crises that necessitated the SDGs in the first place.

Writing decades before the kind of neoliberal penetration of the education sector we are witnessing today, Freire was already cautioning against the capture of 'hope' by 'neoliberal ideals, of individualism, self-improvement and "private notions of getting ahead"'(Freire and Shor, 1987: p. 110 as cited by Bourn, 2021: p. 69). In the third decade into the twenty-first century, SEL seems to represent a spectacular manifestation of 'hope' caught by the neoliberalist ideals, embraced at platforms like WEF, WISE (World Innovation Summit for Education)[13] and TED.[14] The now-familiar neoliberal discourse, policy and practice normalize inequalities by dismantling public institutions and depriving people, while giving immense authority and opportunities to big businesses and philanthropies and creating a culture of 'winners take all' in which the ruling groups engage in a 'charade of changing the world' (Giridharadas, 2019). Today the challenge is not simply the state's withdrawal from its responsibility of ensuring inclusive and equitable education or even the 'swindles of innovative educational finance' (Saltman, 2018), but the highly sophisticated, seductive and spectacular arrangements of technology, money and people – from billionaires and superstar academics to mindfulness gurus and influential politicians – that support the research and development of what can be termed 'predictive technology of happiness'.

In the immediate context of a post–Cold War world, Freire (1994) challenged a neoliberal overshadowing of the continued existence of class struggles by reasserting them as a major force in the struggle for social change. He remained optimistic that the continued existence of social classes in the post–Cold War world provides educators with an opening to seek 'the socialist dream, purified of its authoritarian distortions' (Freire, 1994: p. 96). Thirty years on from the original publication of *Pedagogy of Hope* in 1992, in the third year into the Covid-19 pandemic, in the 'post-truth' age, what dream can we draw? What will allow us to be optimistic?

Clearly, the answer is neither refining techniques to 'nudge' people to be happy nor producing more and better 'evidence' to mainstream SEL – even though that is where money will likely be. 'No matter what we learn and know about human nature', to borrow Rowson's (2011: p. 5) words in a report cautioning against 'neuromania' and 'nudges', 'the question of how we should live and what we should care about remains a value judgment and a matter for collective deliberation'.

What we need is the kind of education that can support us counter the amplification of the tendencies that are leading us to a dystopian future. In order for SEL and digital learning to be transformative, then, they must be able to support us disentangle the deleterious entanglement of 'learnification', 'datafication' and 'happinisation' of education, helping us liberate ourselves from the 'tyranny of merit' (Sandel, 2020), 'tyranny of metrics' (Muller, 2019) and the culture of 'winners take all' (Giridharadas, 2019). What such transformative SEL and digital learning should and could look like in concrete terms is an open question that requires a rich diversity of expertise and collective deliberation to answer. For one, we need an open and transparent platform – digital and otherwise – not hijacked by corporate or political agendas. A 'pedagogy of hope' in the twenty-first century should rest in cultivating the uniquely human capacity to override our biological and genetic drives by way of learning to think more deliberately, collectively and critically and joining forces to co-create a world that is based on universal values of justice, equality and freedom. The hope comes from collectives with a vision and commitment that social change is possible, not from atomized individuals in despair – or even individuals who have become the best versions of themselves thanks to SEL, if it simply means becoming better able to cope with the world as it exists today.

Notes

1 The findings, interpretations and conclusions expressed in this chapter are entirely those of the author and should not be attributed in any manner to UNESCO or UNESCO MGIEP. All UNESCO and UNESCO MGIEP publications are available at UNESCO's digital library (https://unesdoc.unesco.org/).

2   Although secondary to arguments put forward in this chapter, it is nonetheless useful to point out a fallacy of MGIEP's brain-centred approach. As this title 'Building Kinder Brains' indicates, MGIEP's approach commits a 'mereological fallacy' of ascribing to parts (in this case the brain) that which is the function of the whole (the person in context) (Rowson, 2011; Gabriel, 2017). It is not the brain that is 'kind', but the person. As Rowson (2011: p. 6) puts it: 'Neuroscience is often misused to provide a pseudo-objective basis for theories of the self, which in fact often amounts to ascribing personal properties to impersonal neural matter.' Concurring with Raymond Tallis (2011), Rowson (2011: p. 5) highlights the 'need to guard against "neuromania" i.e. the complete identification of persons with their brains and the misconceived hope that an improved understanding of the brain will tell us how to live well'.
3   https://framerspace.com/
4   https://mgiep.unesco.org/kindness-stories
5   https://en.unesco.org/themes/education-sustainable-development
6   Following excerpts from UNESCO's expert review of ESD literature show the extent to which 'behaviour change' is seen in a negative light in the field of ESD: 'Participatory and democratic learning approaches are especially important, given concerns that ESD could be co-opted as a social engineering process that would in fact limit freedom through efforts to manipulate behavior' (UNESCO 2011: p. 36); 'As has been shown in studies of behaviour change in ESD (and on related issues such as habit formation), efforts to manipulate behaviour based on a negative framework that identifies certain actions as problematic do not tend to succeed and are in conflict with the goals of ESD' (p. 36); 'the language of "behaviour change" is contentious . . . and the effectiveness of simplistic strategies aimed at changing behaviour is questioned by some ESD literature' (p. 58).
7   https://www.oecd.org/education/ceri/social-emotional-skills-study
8   https://casel.org/about-us/supporters/
9   https://www.mcgovern.org/
10 https://www.newprofit.org/
11 https://www.oecd.org/pisa/innovation/global-competence/
12 https://pearsonclinical.in/solutions/ssis-social-emotional-learning-edition-ssis-sel
13 https://www.wise-qatar.org/
14 https://www.ted.com/

References

Ahmed, S. (2010). *The Promise of Happiness*. Durham: Duke University Press.

Ancess, J. and B. Rogers (2015). *Social Emotional Learning and Social Justice Learning at El Puente Academy for Peace and Justice*. Stanford: Stanford Center for Opportunity

Policy in Education. Available online: https://edpolicy.stanford.edu/sites/default/files/publications/scope-pub-elpuente-case-report.pdf (accessed 15 January 2022).

Biesta, G. (2005). 'Against Learning. Reclaiming a Language for Education in an Age of Learning'. *Nordisk Pedagogik* 25(1): 54–66.

Biesta, G. (2006). *Beyond Learning: Democratic Education for a Human Future*. London: Routledge.

Biesta, G. (2015). 'On the Two Cultures of Educational Research and How We Might Move Ahead: Reconsidering the Ontology, Axiology and Praxeology of Education'. *European Educational Research Journal* 14(1): 11–22.

Bourn, D. (2021). 'Pedagogy of Hope: Global Learning and the Future of Education'. *International Journal of Development Education and Global Learning* 13(2): 65–78.

Bryan, A. (2022). 'From "the Conscience of Humanity" to the Conscious Human Brain: UNESCO's Embrace of Social-emotional Learning as a Flag of Convenience'. *Compare: A Journal of Comparative and International Education,* https://doi.org/10.1080/03057925.2022.2129956 [online first].

CASEL (2020). 'SEL as a Lever for Equity and Social Justice. CASEL Cares Initiative'. The Collaborative for Academic, Social and Emotional Learning (CASEL). Available online: https://casel.org/events/sel-as-a-lever-for-equity-and-social-justice/ (accessed 15 January 2022).

Center for Contemplative Science and Compassion-based Ethics, Emory University (n.d.). 'Social, Emotional, and Ethical Learning — SEE Learning'. Available online: https://compassion.emory.edu/see-learning/index.html (accessed 15 January 2022).

Davidson, R. (2016). 'The Four Keys to Well-Being'. Available online: https://greatergood.berkeley.edu/article/item/the_four_keys_to_well_being (accessed 15 January 2022).

Davidson, R. (2018). 'Well-being is a Skill. Eighth Distinguished Lecture of UNESCO MGIEP (Complete Video)'. Available online: https://www.youtube.com/watch?v=lggEMJdk07U (accessed 15 January 2022).

Davidson, R. (2019). 'Well-being is a Skill'. Available online: http://www.globart.at/wp-content/uploads/2019/02/Richard-Davidson-Wien-Vortrag-Transkribtion-English.pdf (accessed 15 January 2022).

Duraiappah, A. and N. C. Singh (2019). 'The Science of Social and Emotional Learning'. *Teacher* 13(4): 4–6.

Durlak, J. A., R. P. Weissberg, A. B. Dymnicki, R. D. Taylor and K. B. Schellinger (2011). 'The Impact of Enhancing Students' Social and Emotional Learning: A Meta-analysis of School-Based Universal Interventions'. *Child Development* 82(1): 405–32.

Elfert, M. (2018). *UNESCO's Utopia of Lifelong Learning: An Intellectual History*. New York: Routledge.

Feitsma, J. N. P. (2018). 'The Behavioural State: Critical Observations on Technocracy and Psychocracy'. *Policy Sciences* 51: 387–410.

Freire, P. (1994). *Pedagogy of Hope: Reliving Pedagogy of the Oppressed*. New York: Continuum Publishing Company.

Freire, P. and I. Shor (1987). *A Pedagogy for Liberation*. Basingstoke: Macmillan.

Gabriel, M. (2017). *I am Not a Brain: Philosophy of Mind for the 21st Century*. Cambridge: Polity.

Giridharadas, A. (2019). *Winners Take All: The Elite Charade of Changing the World*. New York: Vintage.

Humphrey, N. (2013). *Social and Emotional Learning: A Critical Appraisal*. Thousand Oaks: SAGE Publications.

Knox, J., B. Williamson and S. Bayne (2019). 'Machine Behaviourism: Future Visions of "Learnification" and "Datafication" across Humans and Digital Technologies'. *Media and Technology* 45(1): 1–15.

Muller, J. Z. (2019). *The Tyranny of Metrics*. Princeton: Princeton University Press.

Ojala, M. (2013). 'Emotional Awareness: On the Importance of Including Emotional Aspects in Education for Sustainable Development (ESD)'. *Journal of Education for Sustainable Development* 7(2): 167–82.

Ojala, M. (2017). 'Hope and Anticipation in Education for a Sustainable Future'. *Futures: The Journal of Policy, Planning and Futures Studies* 94: 76–84.

O'Reilly, F., R. Chande, B. Groot, M. Sanders and Z. Soon (2017). *Behavioural Insights for Education: A Practical Guide for Parents, Teachers and School Leaders*. London: Pearson.

Ricard, M. (2006). *Happiness, A Guide to Developing Life's Most Important Skill*. New York City: Little Brown.

Rowson, J. (2011). *Transforming Behaviour Change: Beyond Nudge and Neuromania*. London: Royal Society of Arts.

Saltman, K. J. (2018). *The Swindle of Innovative Educational Finance*. Minneapolis: University of Minnesota Press.

Salzburg Global Seminar (2019). 'The Salzburg Statement for Social and Emotional Learning'. Available online: https://www.salzburgglobal.org/fileadmin/user_upload/Documents/2010-2019/2018/Session_603/SalzburgGlobal_Statement_SEL_01.pdf (accessed 15 January 2022).

Sandel, M. J. (2020). *The Tyranny of Merit: What's Become of the Common Good?*. New York: Farrar, Straus and Giroux.

Steiner-Khamsi, G., M. Appleton and S. Vellani (2018). 'Understanding Business Interests in International Large-scale Student Assessments: A Media Analysis of the Economist, Financial Times, and Wall Street Journal'. *Oxford Review of Education* 44(9): 190–203.

Tallis, R. (2011). *Aping Mankind: Neuromania, Darwinitis and the Misrepresentation of Humanity*. Durham: Acumen Publishing.

Taylor, R. D., E. Oberle, J. A. Durlak and R. Weissberg (2017). 'Promoting Positive Youth Development Through School-Based Social and Emotional Learning Interventions: A Meta-Analysis of Follow-Up Effects'. *Child Development* 88(4): 1156–71.

UN (2020). 'Policy Brief: Education during COVID-19 and Beyond'. Available online: https://www.un.org/development/desa/dspd/wp-content/uploads/sites/22/2020/08

/sg_policy_brief_covid-19_and_education_august_2020.pdf (accessed 15 January 2022).

UN Innovation Network (2021). 'United Nations Behavioral Science Report'. Available online: https://www.uninnovation.network/assets/BeSci/UN_Behavioural_Science_Report_2021.pdf (accessed 15 January 2022).

UNESCO (2009). 'Bonn Declaration'. UNESCO World Conference on Education for Sustainable Development, Bonn, Germany.

UNESCO (2011). *Education for Sustainable Development: An Expert Review of Processes and Learning*. Paris: UNESCO.

UNESCO (2014). 'Aichi-Nagoya Declaration on Education for Sustainable Development'. UNESCO World Conference on Education for Sustainable Development, Aichi-Nagoya, Japan.

UNESCO (2021). 'Berlin Declaration on Education for Sustainable Development'. UNESCO World Conference on Education for Sustainable Development: Learn for Our Planet, Act for Sustainability.

UNESCO MGIEP (2019). *Rethinking Pedagogy: Exploring the Potential of Digital Technology in Achieving Quality Education*. New Delhi: UNESCO Mahatma Gandhi Institute of Education for Peace and Sustainable Development (MGIEP).

UNESCO MGIEP (2020). *Rethinking Learning: A Review of Social and Emotional Learning for Education Systems*. New Delhi: UNESCO MGIEP.

UNESCO MGIEP (2021). *Building Kinder Brains*. New Delhi: UNESCO MGIEP.

Vare, P. and W. A. H. Scott (2007). 'Learning for a Change: Exploring the Relationship between Education and Sustainable Development'. *Journal of Education for Sustainable Development* 1(2): 191–8.

Verger, A., C. Fontdevila and A. Zancajo (2016). *The Privatization of Education: A Political Economy of Global Education Reform*. New York: Teachers College Press.

Vickers, E. (2022). ' Rebranding Gandhi for the 21st century: Science, Ideology and Politics at UNESCO's Mahatma Gandhi Institute (MGIEP)'. *Compare: A Journal of Comparative and International Education*, https://doi.org/10.1080/03057925.2022.2108374 [online first].

WEF (2020). 'Schools of the Future: Defining New Models of Education for the Fourth Industrial Revolution'. Available online: https://www3.weforum.org/docs/WEF_Schools_of_the_Future_Report_2019.pdf (accessed 15 January 2022).

Williamson, B. (2019). 'Datafication of Education: A Critical Approach to Emerging Analytics Technologies and Practices', in H. Beetham and R. Sharpe (eds), *Rethinking Pedagogy for a Digital Age: Principles and Practices of Design*, 212–26. New York: Routledge.

Williamson, B. (2021). 'Psychodata: Disassembling the Psychological, Economic, and Statistical Infrastructure of "Social-emotional Learning"'. *Journal of Education Policy* 36(1): 129–54.

World Bank (2015). *World Development Report 2015: Mind, Society and Behavior*. Washington D.C.: World Bank.

Yeung, K. (2017). '"Hypernudge": Big Data as a Mode of Regulation by Design'. *Information, Communication & Society* 20(1): 118–36.

Zembylas, M. (2020). '(Un)happiness and Social Justice Education: Ethical, Political and Pedagogic Lessons'. *Ethics and Education* 15(1): 18–32.

11

The Evolving Development Education in Ghana

Implications for Social Justice Education and Pedagogies of Hope

John Kwame Boateng, Ellen M. Osei-Tutu, Olivia Adwoa Tiwaah Kwapong

Introduction

In line with Paulo Freire's concept of pedagogy of hope, our chapter aims to discuss the emerging development education at the Department of Adult Education and Human Resource Studies of the University of Ghana, where the tenets of pedagogy of hope and social justice have been factored into the design and development of the curriculum and have been given the role of pedagogy of hope to provide valuable approaches to learning about local content and the ways these have been impacted by globalization issues in different parts of the world. The objectives of the chapter are as follows:

- To review and reflect upon the shift to development education as a pedagogy of hope at the University of Ghana
- To discuss global issues like the Covid-19 pandemic, increasing youth population, mass unemployment, rise in artificial intelligence, climate change and technological advancements that have necessitated the shift to development education
- To discuss the role of development education as a pedagogical approach in response to the challenges and inequalities in Ghana brought about by global events

Shift to development education as pedagogy of hope at the University of Ghana

Development education (DE), according to Monteiro (2021), emerged in the 1960s as a strategy to increase public awareness, understanding and support for international aid and development from developed countries (DCs) to less-developed countries (LDCs). As new challenges and questions, which were not limited to LDCs, emerged in the field of development, DE evolved to attempt to help solve these varied development challenges from identity and culture to politics and power (Andreotti, 2006; Mesa, 2011). Thus, Regan and Sinclair hinted:

'There has been a general movement from seeing development education as a matter of information, to make up an information deficit in the "West", to seeing education as the very fuel for the engine of development both in the "West" and in the "Third World"' (Regan and Sinclair, 2006: p. 109).

According to Bourn (2021), global events, including the Covid-19 pandemic, the climate emergency campaigns and the Black Lives Matter movements, have brought in their wake challenges for educationalists about their role, especially when it comes to projecting positive visions of the future. Furthermore, Bourn (2021) noted that development education and global learning could make major contributions to these agendas, especially when it draws from the practices and the ideas of Paulo Freire and his concept of the pedagogy of hope. Torres-Olave (2021) observes that pedagogy of hope is relevant as an invitation to build from change that begins as a collective, rather than an individualizing, sense. Freire (1992) argues that no human being can be without others; therefore, a change both in the ways people relate and build knowledge with others instead of about others is to be treasured. Although hope is often viewed as an idealistic and utopian term, if it is grounded in real-life issues and challenges, it can provide a valuable approach to learning about global issues (Bourn, 2021). Freire (1992) endorsed students' ability to think critically about their education situation which allowed them to build and recognize connections between their individual problems and experiences and the social contexts in which they are placed.

According to Freire (1970), the banking model of education treats students as empty vessels to be filled with knowledge, like a piggybank. Freire criticized the banking model of education, and in pedagogy of hope, invites the world to 'overcome this model through hope, in a non-idealistic but ontological manner, acting in the world to transform oppressive conditions and expanding possibilities for social justice. One key to achieving this is democratic dialogue aimed at "opening up to the thinking of others'" (Freire, 1992: p. 110). The powerful messages of pedagogy of hope have significantly influenced academics in the University of Ghana, chiefly those in Adult Education to work with their students and others to further develop the importance of democratic dialogue in education, informed by ideals of love and community as essentials for an emancipatory praxis. The result is the design and development of five courses in development education. These are all tailored to meet the needs of twenty-first-century learners.

The programmes in development education have been designed to train scientific researchers and practitioners to influence policy and practice in the areas of development education, human resource studies and sustainable development.

Generally, students will be equipped with higher-level research competencies to conduct scientific enquiry into individual, organizational, institutional, national and global processes and programmes aimed at dealing with inequalities, social injustice and communal empowerment for inclusive socio-economic development. The programmes are interdisciplinary in nature. By this focus, the programmes expose students to principles, concepts and theories of sustainable development, development education, adult education and human resource and development.

Global issues necessitating a shift in focus to development education

There have been calls for the incorporation of a critical global pedagogy into citizenship education in African countries since they result in the building of competencies, skills and critical thinking (Simonneaux, Tutiaux-Guillon and Legardez, 2012; Eten, 2015). Foaleng (2015) has bemoaned the scarcity of adequately qualified trainers as a major encumbrance to the successful incorporation of critical global pedagogy in Africa. Additionally, Lauwerier (2018) also gathered that the typical large class sizes and teacher-dominated teaching techniques that stress reciting and memorizing make it difficult to engage students in complicated activities, and so the traditional teaching methods that focus solely on 'knowledge transfer' are insufficient for an impactful DE programme.

Belle (2019) observes that the notion of social justice pedagogy has assumed importance in education, particularly in urban communities with a history of oppression through education. The art and practice of social justice teaching and learning ensure that students are recognized for who they really are and from where they originate. Freire (1970) wrote about praxis, involving theory and practice, reflection and action as activism. In his sense, Freire's action is not just an activity for the sake of doing something but an activity that is purposeful, social justice–oriented and relevant to a changing society. Freire (1992) argues that hope is an ontological need, an existential concrete imperative, which demands anchoring in practice.

According to Freire (1992), hope is necessary but not enough. Just hoping for the sake of hope is to hope in vain. He wrote about critical hope: the way a fish needs unpolluted water, the same way our world needs a kind of education in hope. To Freire, the education we need is that kind of education that will rid the world and our nation of hopelessness and despair that have become the order of the day and are both the consequences and the cause of inaction or immobilism (Freire, 1992).

The powerful messages of pedagogy of hope have significantly influenced academics to develop the importance of democratic dialogue in education, informed by ideals of love and community as essentials for emancipatory praxis (Torres, 2020). The following global events have influenced the decisions of academics in Adult Education to shift focus to development education in the light of promoting global citizenship education and empowering both adults and youth, men and women. Waghid (2014) argued that education for social justice is an encounter, as it invokes both the capacities and cultural stock of individuals and groups. Since social justice is interconnected to issues of need, access and equality, it can be claimed that development education for social justice should be responsive to the demands of need, equality and access. Waghid (2014) observes that social justice seems to manifest in instances, such as sustainable development (SD), economic development and equity (not at the expense of equality, but rather as a shift in focus from striving towards equity in an equal manner). Drawing from the works of Bell (1997), hooks (2003) and Hackman (2005), nurturing equal participation through deliberation, self-reflexivity and openness will contest dominance and privilege, and would help develop critical understanding and awareness to bring about education for social justice in and beyond the university classroom.

The Covid-19 effect on pedagogies of social justice and hope

In Ghana, Covid-19 pandemic and the ensuing economic crisis precipitated reactions among educational workers through strikes in calling for better conditions of service from government. Globally, massive acts of peaceful demonstrations such as that of 'Black Lives Matter' have moved the inequality and injustice argument in public debates. In Ghana, as in other countries, such as the United Kingdom, the United States, Canada, Australia and Europe, these local and global events have provided an opportunity for change; an opportunity that must be seized and taken advantage of. At the recent virtual International Summit on the Teaching Profession with Education Ministers organized with the OECD, inequalities were high on the agenda. It was noted, among others, that Covid-19 has produced a disproportionate impact on vulnerable students (Hopgood, 2020).

Apart from the digital divide that has disadvantaged many students in the sub-Saharan African space during distance learning, there are many other factors. Even prior to the incidence of the Covid-19 pandemic, there were many inequalities already present; Covid-19 incidence and its associated events made teaching conditions worse. There is the need for governments in Ghana and sister African countries and teacher associations and bodies as well as educational leaders to come together and carry out equity audits in schools and universities to identify those students and teachers who were most affected, evaluate their needs and provide them with the appropriate support services.

Hopgood (2020) noted that the Covid-19 pandemic and its economic consequences have helped to create greater awareness of inequalities of gender, national origin and status, ethnicity, persons with disabilities, indigenous peoples (who have suffered enormously) and many others and observed that the time to act is now, to right the wrongs and level the playing fields.

Hicks (2016) noted that hope is needed to promote in education, a sense of what the future brings about. Hicks (2016) also observed that building the right skills and capacities in learners to help them develop their own sense of agency so that they will be ready to contribute appropriate action for change when the future comes is equally essential. Likewise, Kool (2017) has stressed that future thinking cannot be overemphasized. He shows that understanding the past, confronting the present and envisioning the future is the way to go when he predicted that the future will bring threatening dangers to societies around the globe, impacting severely the diversity of life on earth, and warned of the need to come up with ways of imagining the future(s) the children of today will want to live in, grounded in the realities of the present times (Kool, 2017: p. 141).

During the Covid-19 pandemic, social justice education and pedagogies of hope pointed to diversity of ways of approaching alternative teaching modes. Teaching at the Department of Adult Education and Human Resource Studies,

University of Ghana, was undertaken through applications associated with the use of computers and the Internet. Providing the enabling environment and infrastructure such as the constant supply of electricity, adequate bandwidth and internet connectivity would enable students living in deprived communities to have access to radio or television and the internet. Even in the big cities, there are families who do not have a radio or television and teachers, who might not have easy access to computer materials and the Internet. Building an enabling environment is crucial to the successful promotion of social justice education and pedagogies of hope.

The polarization and hate politics identified in African politics do not create the environment for hearty discussions, civilized debate and consensus building. Meanwhile, social justice education can help build a better future. It will help young people understand that their humanity is shared with everybody else. It will help them develop critical thinking skills and become active citizens shaping their own lives rather than being determined by others. As was shown in the 'black lives matter demonstrations' with Black, white, Asian and other ethnic groups coming together to fight for 'Justice for all', the tenets of social justice education must catch up with young people of Ghana, Africa and around the globe to articulate the human values around which decent societies are built.

Students and their needs are the core tenets of good social justice education. It develops not just the competencies, but the confidence to make Ghana, Africa and the world a better place. Social justice education gives the hope that motivated, committed young people need to build their skills and develop their capacities, to make their contribution as part of a special, valued and essential profession. For this to happen, lessons of the pandemic must be learned well and understood that human life is more precious than profits. Having healthy communities in Ghana, Africa and the world is more important than cutting deals or collecting dividends. In the words of Hopgood (2020), identity should be defined by what one is for and not what one is against. And for that, an integrated Ghana needs rules, massive solidarity, credible institutions and efficient public services.

Taking it all together, there is a call for a greater public investment, including social justice education. The United Nations Sustainable Development Goals and particularly goal number four have more important roles to offer after the pandemic. This means that workers and their trade unions, including education unions, matter and should be respected and be involved to make their significant contributions to democracy and social progress. Their arguments and agitations should not only focus on negotiating wages, work hours, working conditions and better conditions of service but also enact and build policies that will serve the public interest and secure social justice education. The post-Covid-19 pandemic demands for social justice education need better responses with renewed mission inside and beyond the school and university communities. This is the basis for transforming hopes into accomplishments and creating a better tomorrow out of the chaotic era brought on by the Covid-19 pandemic.

Teaming youth populations in Ghana and the rest of Africa

The African Union's (AU) African Youth Charter notes that the growing youth population in Africa is the continent's biggest resource, and it offers enormous potential if harnessed properly. According to the charter, development in health and education on the continent puts the African youth in a more advantageous position in comparison to generations before. This is in line with the African Institute for Development Policy, which prioritized spending on health and education coupled with an environment that facilitates jobs and investment which are enablers for fulfilling the dividends from the huge youth population (*The Guardian*, 2021).

The potential of young people is the driving force for Africa's collective prosperity. The youth population of Africa is projected to represent over 40 per cent of the world's young people, in less than three generations. By 2050, the teeming numbers of young Africans are forecast to form over a quarter of the world's labour force, and there is a growing consensus that Africa's youthfulness will continue to grow for the next fifty years while the other continents are ageing. The analysis suggests that young people must be meaningfully involved in the implementation and tracking of the Sustainable Development Goals and the African Union Agenda 2063 (UNECA, 2017).

Engaging the youth of Africa in meaningful education and meeting the expectations for a more inclusive future development requires a better understanding of their needs, interests, challenges, potential as well as their diversity. That assertion is the basis and inspiration for Africa's youth and prospects for inclusive development (UNECA, 2017)

A team of researchers led by Parfait M. Eloundou-Enyegue, a development sociologist, is researching into a range of policies and pedagogies of social justice and hope to facilitate the socio-economic integration of this generation, using 5,000 high school seniors in the sub-Saharan setting. The team is examining difficulties students face as they move into adulthood, with particular emphasis on economic integration and social integration, and identity. A key research hypothesis of the team is that integration is not only about jobs but also about the social integration of youth in rapidly changing societies which are marked by a breakdown of families, rapid urbanization, growing inequality, consumerism and globalization (Cornell Research, 2021).

This approach by the research team at Cornell has been a wakeup call to academics in the School of Continuing and Distance Education at the University of Ghana, African Union, African governments and institutions of higher learning, and organizations in both public and private sectors should also take up the challenge and upscale social justice education and pedagogies of hope interventions to take advantage of the opportunities in the huge numbers of the African youth (Kwapong, Boateng and Addae, 2022).

Mass youth and graduate unemployment

ILO (2015a) noted that the young people in developing countries continue to be plagued by working poverty stemming from the irregularity of work and the lack of formal employment and social protection. Pierre Frank Laporte further observed that the future of youth employment policy planning should not only address youth unemployment but should also build the human capital needed to sustain Ghana's economy (Fosu, 2021).

Furthermore, social justice education and pedagogies of hope demand the integration of pre-employment support activities into our development education programmes and the education system of the entire country to better prepare young people for the transition to work. The promotion of social inclusion initiatives will ensure that no one is left behind. Designing social justice education and pedagogies of hope also emphasizes the need for greater collaboration among different stakeholders to reduce duplication and fragmentation of youth employment programming.

While strong industry links in a booming economy are crucial, social justice education has a clear focus on identifying and meeting the needs of disadvantaged youth. Social service education serves the dual purpose of building a relationship with the community and developing a better understanding of the individual context of the learner. In social justice education, technical skills development is complemented by non-cognitive (soft) skills and sector-specific language training. Students learn from facilitators as well as industry guest lecturers and through interactions with peers, content and facilitators on online platforms.

A growing body of evidence-based research indicates that education and training, when supported at the macro level, are important means of enhancing youth employability (World Youth Report, 2019). Ghanaian youth, like their counterparts in Africa, need relevant skills, knowledge, competencies and aptitudes to help them obtain jobs and establish career paths. With the demand for skilled labour going up as a result of globalization, technological advancements and the changes in the ways in which work is organized around the globe and in Ghana as well, quality education and appropriate training are key to addressing youth employment challenges. Social justice education does provide present and future generations of youth with the tools they need to successfully navigate the school-to-work transition and secure decent work.

Work is the fulcrum on which economic stability and prosperity are built. According to the World Youth Report (2019), putting the skills and talents of young people to productive use promotes economic prosperity for entire populations and helps to reduce economic inequality and poverty alleviation. Support for social justice education, training and employment lies at the front of national and international efforts to improve economic outcomes and to strengthen prosperity and security among the nations of the global community. The alignment of education and skills with the needs of the labour market enhances opportunities for decent work for the teeming youth populations in Ghana and Africa. This dynamic relationship between education and employment constitutes a key component of the 2030 Agenda.

Making education quality and relevant to supplying needed skills

Social justice education must provide the basic skills that are relevant to the world of work. Basic skills include functional literacy and numeracy, which are typically learned in school. While some level of technical skills is often required even for entry-level jobs, the vast majority of technical learning takes place on the job. Social justice education should ensure that the right partnerships are established between educational institutions and industry so that students who pick entry-level jobs will hit the ground running and increase their chances of finding jobs and reducing unemployment.

Information and communications technology (ICT) skills are a subset of technical skills that are gaining recognition as increasingly essential and cross-cutting across industries because of the rapid pace of technological change.

Behavioural or soft skills including interpersonal skills intrapersonal skills such as time management, problem-solving and creativity; and workplace cultural skills, which include understanding and navigating norms in the workplace, are identified as essential to promote employment of school leavers (Burnett and Jayaram, 2012).

Advances in technological development, particularly artificial intelligence and digitalization, have key implications for labour markets. Assessing the impacts of artificial intelligence is crucial for developing policies including education that promote efficient labour markets for the benefit of workers, employers and societies at large. According to Autor, Levy and Murnane (2003) technology can replace human labour in routine tasks, whether manual or cognitive, but cannot replace human labour in non-routine tasks. Other researchers such as Goos and Manning (2007) have argued that the impact of technology leads to rising relative demand in well-paid skilled jobs, which typically require non-routine cognitive skills, and rising relative demand in low-paid, least-skilled jobs, which typically require non-routine manual skills.

Designing social justice education and pedagogies of hope requires planning and implementation of modalities and policies that will help accommodate new technology possibilities. Education and training programmes should be carefully redesigned so that they provide the right qualifications for graduates to interact and work efficiently alongside machines and boost relevant digital skills. If this is done well, it might help to reduce potential displacement concerns as jobs typically consist of several distinct, but interrelated, tasks. To ensure effective interaction between humans and machines and to encourage responsible environmental and climate change stewardship, it is important to prepare human labour through pedagogies that prioritize social justice and hope. This involves instilling values and skills in individuals that enable them to engage with technology in a way that aligns with ethical principles and to act towards protecting the environment through a pedagogy of hope.

Climate change and the pedagogies of hope

The uncertainty surrounding climate change makes it a complex issue to teach to students. However, it presents an interesting opportunity for teaching it to the youth in the social justice education and pedagogies of hope context. This includes teaching the realities of climate change and the levels of uncertainty and debates associated with this topic in the community. Latour (2004) mentions that to properly teach climate change, critique must be encouraged and to question the certainty of information provided. Shackely and Wynne, (1996), however, observe that scientists themselves do not agree on the level of uncertainty of current data and findings in this area. The goal of covering climate change brings to bear a despairing problem vital for the very existence of humans and to develop critical thinking skills coupled with scientific literacy.

Scientific literacy is a key component to the youth taking action to address socio-scientific issues for social and environmental justice. According to Hodson (2008), the constituents of scientific literacy as applied to social and environmental justice do entail a commitment to critically understand contemporary socio-scientific issues. The youth must feel a personal sense of investment in an issue before acting authentically on that issue. An empowered youth can take required action necessary to achieve befitting goals by combining knowledge and skills with motivation, attitudes, hope and visions.

Role of development education as a pedagogical approach

Boggs (1991) and Quigley (2000) invite development educators to reflect on how a social action focus might be renewed in adult education if it has indeed been eroded. They queried in what ways might educators be encouraged to think imaginatively, hopefully and critically about the ways in which social action focus might be renewed in the practice of educating adults. And how might the culture and politics of institutions transform to focus on a social action–oriented practice? This section does attempt to link and bring together themes from previous sections and show how development education as a pedagogical approach can bring about a focus on a social action–oriented practice in the promotion of social justice education and the realization of hope for the masses in need.

Development education is much more than learning about development; it is a pedagogy for the globalized societies of the twenty-first century that incorporates discourses from critical pedagogy and postcolonialism, and a mechanism for ensuring that different perspectives are reflected within education, particularly those from developing countries. Learning about development and global issues is now part of the school curriculum in several countries, and terms such as 'global citizenship', 'sustainable development' and 'cultural understanding' are commonplace in many educational contexts (Bourn, 2021).

This has been possible because pedagogical practices have also evolved with the changing world. The demand for quality education is at an all-time high today. So, effective pedagogical approaches are of critical importance in providing quality education.

Employing effective pedagogical approaches helps students achieve learning outcomes and realize their full educational potential.

Societies of the world today are confronted by many troubles and crises, which are cultural, economic, ecological and health related. According to Burningham and Beck (1997), the crises of the world challenge the organization of societies and social practices, imparting a sense of risk and urgency predominating over the affairs of nations. There is a need for action to avoid the worse consequences of the world's crises. However, Agyeman, Bullard and Evans (2003) and Walker (2012) show that social inequalities and environmental issues intertwine in an intricate web causing difficult and complicated challenges and producing uncertainties and disagreements about what must be done to save the situation. What makes things more difficult is that the outcomes and implications of these crises differ for different groups of people.

Development education has major contributions to make within these agendas, particularly when it brings into practice the ideas of Paulo Freire and his concept of the pedagogy of hope. Not just hope for the sake of hoping but hope that is firmly anchored in the issues of real life and challenges that are real and border on livelihoods, environment, the economy and society to provide true pathways of learning about national and global matters. To address the challenges arising from the Covid-19 pandemic, climate change emergencies, and the ongoing conflict between Russia and Ukraine, it may be helpful to draw on examples and best practices from around the world to effect meaningful change. By learning from successful approaches in other contexts, we can develop more effective strategies to address these complex and pressing issues on a global scale. Education that employs a range of pedagogical techniques to promote the comprehension of the complexities of the environment, the economy and society is what the world needs to address complex challenges and crisis situations. An evolving field in Ghana, development education has the primary goal of harnessing the power of education to advance environmental and health literacy and civic engagement that prepare students for jobs that contribute to a more equitable, socially just and sustainable future.

A thoughtfully developed pedagogy embracing development education concepts improves the quality of teaching and promotes hope and social justice. It makes the student more receptive during learning sessions. Consequently, this improves the student's level of participation in the teaching and learning process. An appropriate pedagogy helps impart education to students with different learning styles and abilities. Students develop a deeper understanding of the subject matter. Subsequently, this ensures the achievement of the learning outcomes of a programme. Development education as a pedagogical approach does make provision for students with special needs, students from disadvantaged groups, females and minorities. Also, it encourages them to be a part of the mainstream learning community. On the other hand, knowledge, comprehension and application are lower-order cognitive skills in Bloom's Taxonomy. Finally, development education teaching pedagogy enhances the effective assessment of students' performance and ensures that assessment is appropriately an essential part of the learning experience. Development education as a pedagogical approach helps to ensure the effective grading of papers while being fair to all students.

Conclusion

Drawing from Freire's views on education, the authors have examined and discussed the need for a curriculum emanating from development education to respond to the sources of contemporary despairs that are disturbing social changes and deep ethical concerns that arise from outbreaks of pandemics such as Covid-19, consumerism, globalization, scientific and technological innovations, and the interests of the rich and powerful. Curriculum developers in the development education field are called upon to address such contemporary issues as climate change and exploding youth populations and youth unemployment.

The authors have called for the development education classroom to become an area of creativity, enquiry, discussion, debate, agreement, disagreement, consensus building, dialogue and a place that promotes learning and builds capacities to solve real-world problems, challenges and despairs. Just as Freire's views on education bring to focus issues of our common humanity and consider this as a powerful tool for social transformation and promoting social justice, the authors have supported the call for social justice education and pedagogies of hope to permeate our world today of chaos and extreme challenges in ways that promote dialogue and reflection alongside actions for a liberating education.

The idea of despair-solving education or rather problem-solving education creates critical thinkers in its wake, among the teaming youth populations and the ageing adults in Africa in contrast to huge populations of docile learners with near-empty mental acumen to be filled by the expert teacher. This is a powerful way to achieve the Africa that we want, the vision of African Union's (AU) Agenda 2063 and subsequently a globalized world that we desire.

Future studies may review and reflect on the role of global citizenship education in providing visions of hope for social change. Future studies could also explore the challenges for global learning and global citizenship education post-Covid-19. Also, other areas could focus on lessons from research in schools or other settings on effective ways to engage learners in playing positive roles in shaping a just and sustainable world. In addition, future studies may also explore the role of civil society organizations in equipping students or youth with knowledge, skills and values to act on social justice and sustainability issues.

Acknowledgement

We express sincere appreciation to Mr Madumetja Jayson Ledwaba for providing research assistantship support.

References

Agyeman, J., R. D. Bullard and B. Evans, eds (2003). *Just Sustainabilities: Development in an Unequal World*. New York: Earthscan Publications.

Andreotti, V. (2006). 'Soft versus Critical Global Citizenship Education'. *Policy and Practice: A Development Education Review* 3: 40–51.

Autor, D., F. Levy and R. J. Murnane (2003). 'The Skill Content of Recent Technological Change: An Empirical Exploration'. *Quarterly Journal of Economics* 118(4): 1279–333. http://www.jstor.org/stable/pdf/25053940.pdf

Bell, L. A. (1997). 'Theoretical Foundations for Social Justice Education', in M. Adams, L. Bell and P. Griffin (eds), *Teaching for Diversity and Social Justice: A Sourcebook*, 3–15. New York: Routledge.

Belle, C. (2019). 'What Is Social Justice Education Anyway?' *Education Week* 38(19): 18–19. Available: https://www.edweek.org/teaching-learning/opinion-what-is-social-justice-education-anyway/2019/01

Boggs, D. L. (1991). *Adult Civic Education*. Springfield: Thomas Books.

Bourn, D. (2021). 'Pedagogy of Hope: Global Learning and the Future of Education'. *International Journal of Development Education and Global Learning* 13(2): 65–78. doi: https://doi.org/10.14324/ IJDEGL.13.2.01

Burnett, N. and S. Jayaram (2012). 'Innovative Secondary Education for Skills Enhancement for Employability in Africa and Asia', in *ISESE Skills Synthesis Paper*. Washington D.C.: Results for Development Institute.

Burningham, K. and U. Beck (1997). 'Ecological Politics in an Age of Risk'. *The British Journal of Sociology* 48: 149.

Cornell Research (2021). 'The Exploding Youth Population in Sub-Saharan Africa'. Available: https://research.cornell.edu/research/exploding-youth-population-sub-saharan-africa

Eten, S. (2015). 'The Prospects of Development Education in African Countries: Building a Critical Mass of Citizenry for Civic Engagement'. *Policy and Practice: A Development Education Review* 20: 136–51.

Foaleng, M. (2015). 'Education for Global Citizenship in a Post Colony: Lessons from Cameroon'. *DVV International* 82: 18–23.

Fosu, K. (2021). 'Addressing Youth Unemployment in Ghana Needs Urgent Action'. World Bank Report. Press Release No: 2021/045/AFR. Available: https://www.worldbank.org/en/news/press-release/2020/09/29/addressing-youth-unemployment-in-ghana-needs-urgent-action

Freire, P. (1970). *Pedagogy of the Oppressed*. New York: Continuum.

Freire, P. (1992). *Pedagogy of Hope: Reliving Pedagogy of the Oppressed (original version)*. London and New York: Bloomsbury Publishing.

Goos, M. and A. Manning (2007). 'Lousy and Lovely Jobs: The Rising Polarization of Work in Britain'. *The Review of Economics and Statistics* 89(1): 118–33.

The Guardian (2021, June). 'Building Young and Socially Conscious Business Leaders in Africa'. https://guardian.ng/features/building-young-and-socially-conscious-business-leaders-in-africa/ (Retrieved 24 June 2022).

Hackman, H. (2005). 'Five Essential Components for Social Justice Education'. *Equity & Excellence in Education* 38(2): 103–9.

Hicks, D. (2016). 'New Stories of Change'. *Primary Geography* 91: 10–11.

Hodson, D. (2008). *Towards Scientific Literacy: A Teacher's Guide to the History, Philosophy, and Sociology of Science*. Rotterdam: Sense Publishers.

hooks, b. (2003). *Teaching Community: A Pedagogy of Hope*. New York: Routledge.

Hopgood, S. (2020). 'COVID-19, the Struggle for Social Justice, and the Future of Education. Home / Blog Perspectives'. https://www.ctf-fce.ca/blog-perspectives/covid-19-the-struggle-for-social-justice-and-the-future-of-education/ (Retrieved 24 June 2022).

Kool, R. (2017). 'If the Past is a Foreign Country, What is the Future? The Necessity of Understanding the Past, Confronting the Present, and Envisioning the Future', in P. Corcoran, J. P. Weakland and A. Wals (eds), *Envisioning Futures for Environmental and Sustainability Education*, 141–50. Wageningen: Wageningen Academic Publishers.

The International Labour Organization (2015a). *The Global Employment Trends for Youth 2015: Scaling up Investments in Decent Jobs for Youth*. Geneva.

International Labour Organisation (ILO) (2015b). 'Global Employment for Youth'. https://www.ilo.org/wcmsp5/groups/public/---dgreports/---dcomm/---publ/documents/publication/wcms_412015.pdf (Retrieved 30 June 2022).

Kwapong, O. A. T. F., J. K. Boateng and D. Addae (2015). 'Conclusion: The Futurity of Development Education in Africa'. *Reimagining Development Education in Africa*, 247. Cham: Springer.

Latour, B. (2004). 'Why Has Critique Run Out of Steam? From Matters of Fact to Matters of Concern'. *Critical Inquiry* 30: 225–48.

Lauwerier, T. (2018). 'Global Citizenship Education in West Africa: A Promising Concept?' in *Global Citizenship Education*, 99–109. Cham: Springer.

Marouli, C. (2021). 'Sustainability Education for the Future? Challenges and Implications for Education and Pedagogy in the 21st Century'. *Sustainability* 13: 2901. https://doi.org/10.3390/su13052901

Mesa, M. (2011). 'Evolución y futuro desafíos de la educación para el Desarrollo (Evolution and Future challenges of Development Education)'. *Educación Global Research: Revista Internacional sobre Investigación en Educación Global y para el Desarrollo* (0): 122–40.

Monteiro, C. (2020). 'Learning to Change the World: An analysis of the Discourse and Power Inequalities within the Portuguese National Strategy for Development Education'. https://www.researchgate.net/publication/345329322_Learning_to_Change_the_World_An_analysis_of_the_Discourse_and_Power_Inequalities_within_the_Portuguese_National_Strategy_for_Development_Education

Monteiro, F. (2021). 'Development Education and Social Justice: A Critical Review'. *Globalisation, Societies and Education* 19(2): 181–96. https://doi.org/10.1080/14767724.2020.1864314

Quigley, B. A. (2000). 'Adult Education and Democracy: Reclaiming Our Voice through Social Policy', in A. L. Wilson and E. R. Hayes (eds), *Handbook of Adult and Continuing Education*. San Francisco: Jossey-Bass.

Regan, C. and S. Sinclair (2006). 'Engaging Development Learning for a Better Future? The World View of Development Education', in C. Regan (ed.), *Development in an Unequal World*, 107–20. Dublin: 80:20 Educating and Acting for a Better World.

Shackley, S. and B. Wynne (1996). 'Representing Uncertainty in Global Climate Change Science and Policy: Boundary-Ordering Devices and Authority'. *Science, Technology, & Human Values* 21(3): 275–302.

Simonneaux, J., N. Tutiaux-Guillon and A. Legardez (2012). 'Éditorial: éducations à . . . et sciences sociales, perspectives des recherches francophones'. *JSSE-Journal of Social Science Education* 11(4): 2–18.

Southern Oregon University (2022). 'Sustainability Education'. Viewed the Southern Oregon University website on 26 June 2022. https://online.sou.edu/degrees/education/msed/curriculum-and-instruction-stem/what-is-sustainability-edu/

Torres, C. A. (2020). *Globalizations and Education: Collected Essays on Class, Race, Gender, and the State*. Routledge is New York, USA.

Torres-Olave, B. (2021). 'Pedagogy of Hope: Reliving Pedagogy of the Oppressed'. *Educational Review* 73(1): 128. https://doi.org/10.1080/00131911.2020.1766207

United Nations Economic Commission for Africa (UNECA) (2017). 'Africa's Youth and Prospects for Inclusive Development'. Regional situation analysis report. https://www.ohchr.org/sites/default/files/Documents/Issues/Youth/UNEconomicCommissionAfrica.pdf (Retrieved 24 June 2022).

Waghid, Y. (2014). *Education and the Challenge of Development: Perspectives from Higher Education in South Africa*. Palgrave Macmillan is New York, USA.

Walker, G. (2012). *Environmental Justice: Concepts, Evidence and Politics*. New York: Routledge.

World Bank (2013). 'Enterprise Surveys: Kenya'. http://www.enterprisesurveys.org (Retrieved 24 June 2022).

World Youth Report (2019). 'Youth and the 2030 Agenda for Sustainable Development'. https://www.un.org/development/desa/youth/wp-content/uploads/sites/21/2019/02/chapter4-wyr-2030agenda.pdf (Retrieved 24 June 2022).

12

Global Education for Teachers

Online Continuing Professional Development as a Source of Hope in Challenging Times

Frances Hunt and Nicole Blum

Introduction

Research on teacher education and global education suggests that teachers in different country contexts and school settings often have limited opportunities to engage in professional development related to global education and related terms, such as global learning, global citizenship education and education for sustainable development, particularly in the Global South (Bourn, Hunt and Bamber, 2017). Recent literature has also begun to pay greater attention to the ways in which global topics are, or could be, integrated within teacher education and professional development (cf. Estellés and Fischman, 2021; Bamber, 2020; Schugurensky and Wolhuter, 2020; Ekanayake et al., 2020; O'Meara, Huber and Sanmiguel, 2018). Both academics and key international organizations such as UNESCO have also produced a wide range of resources aimed at supporting teachers with these efforts (cf. UNESCO, 2018; UNESCO, 2016; Pashby and Sund, 2019; Andreotti and De Souza, 2006). The overall lack of access to training in global education and related areas (UNESCO, 2021), however, continues to be of concern.

This is even more significant given the importance of these educational approaches to the UN Sustainable Development Goals and particularly Goal 4.7 which requires:

> By 2030, ensure that all learners acquire the knowledge and skills needed to promote sustainable development, including, among others, through education for sustainable development and sustainable lifestyles, human rights, gender

equality, promotion of a culture of peace and non-violence, global citizenship and appreciation of cultural diversity and of culture's contribution to sustainable development.

It is also clear that teachers across the world themselves have a strong interest in preparing their students for their global futures (UNESCO, 2021). They want to make sure their pupils are ready to take on global challenges and to be able to positively engage with people across cultural and geographical contexts (cf. Ferguson, Roofe and Cook, 2021; Bruce, North and FitzPatrick, 2019; Howard-Jones et al., 2021). The passion for preparing teachers to introduce global citizenship in schools can also be seen in the numbers of schools involved in global learning initiatives and engagement with online movements such as #TeachSDGs. However, teachers can be hampered from engaging in global education in practice if a combination of motivational factors, skills and opportunities are found to be missing (UNESCO, 2021). Indeed, research suggests teacher education is key – and that providing teachers with relevant professional development opportunities related to global education could play a significant role in supporting them to address pressing social and environmental challenges within their practice (cf. Murphy et al., 2021; Roemhild and Gaudelli, 2021; Tarozzi and Mallon, 2019; Bourn, 2016), which in turn should support pupils' global citizenship attributes.

It is within this context that we explore in this chapter data generated from teachers as part of an online continuing professional development (CPD) course. While the literature base is increasing (Bourn, Hunt and Bamber, 2017), there remains a dearth of evidence on global education teacher education globally and who is able to access it. Given the current international focus on the UN Sustainable Development Goals, and especially Goal 4.7, understanding more about the extent to which teachers are able to engage with global themes within their practice is crucial.

We therefore used the opportunity provided by the online course to explore areas of interest around teachers' access to global education teacher education, their motivation to engage and their experiences with global education in practice. We wanted to explore whether the format of the online CPD course could attract teachers not able to access training by other means. And through it all we also explore the notion of hope. Within the current complex global situation, can global education CPD nurture ideas of hope – either through the educator participants, their hopes for their students or through the nature of the course itself? In this chapter we respond to the following research questions:

- Who is engaging in the course?
- How do course participants experience and engage with global education in their current practice?
- How are ideas of hope evident within and through the course?

We look first at the course itself and locate the study within the wider academic literature. We then provide a methodological overview and present our findings in line with the research questions. Finally, we make some concluding remarks.

About the course

The Global Education for Teachers (GET) course was developed as a MOOC (Massive Online Open Course) by the authors in 2020 and is hosted on the FutureLearn[1] platform. The three-week course aims to provide online CPD in global education, which is accessible to teachers across the world. It is especially aimed at those without easy access to opportunities for training and professional development.

The course includes an introduction to key concepts and ideas related to global education and related terms, an exploration of approaches to global education teaching and pedagogy, and practical ideas and support for teachers who want to introduce global education into their practice (including lesson planning, guides, resources and further readings). It also provides opportunities for teachers around the world to actively engage in peer learning, support and knowledge exchange, and to share diverse perspectives and experiences – a key principle of any global education programme. The structure and teaching approach is organized around a mixture of inputs (videos, short texts), online discussions/posts, polls, a self-assessment framework, a final reflection and peer assessment activity, and a range of further resources and readings.

To date, almost 6,000 teachers and other educators from around the world have enrolled on the course, and it has received five-star reviews. Through the design of the course, we aimed to provoke discussion and exchange of ideas in 'bite-sized' pieces that would be accessible to all teachers, whether they have previous experience or knowledge of global education or not, and also to provide additional resources for those with experience who want to stretch their thinking.

Literature

Teachers, teacher education and global education

Research on teacher education and global education suggests that teachers in different country contexts and school settings often have limited opportunities to engage in initial teacher education and continuing professional development related to global education particularly in the Global South. Research from Bourn, Hunt and Bamber (2017) suggests that while there is some evidence of increased engagement with global themes in teacher education in some countries, its inclusion still often tends to be the result of individual interests of teacher trainers, school leaders or teachers in schools. They also note that 'unless there is a national drive or external input for GCED and ESD in teacher education, then provision by teacher educators tends to be ad-hoc and limited' (Bourn, Hunt and Bamber, 2017: p. 55). Research (Bentall and Hunt, 2022; Hunt, 2017) also notes the important role a vibrant non-governmental sector can play in bridging gaps in teacher education.

Unfortunately, despite calls for more research on the availability of teacher training and education related to global education (Bourn, Hunt and Bamber, 2017), the existing literature tends to focus more on how GCE, global education or ESD are conceptualized within teacher education or systematic reviews of research (e.g. Estelles and Fischman, 2022; Yemini, Tibbitts and Goren 2019; Fischer et al., 2022). That said, a recent study from UNESCO (2021) with 58,000 teachers gives some insight into the scale of engagement in professional development, although issues with sampling[2] suggest caution. The data suggest between 50 and 70 per cent of respondents had received some previous training input(s) on aspects of global education and a similar percentage identified availability of CPD opportunities. In a question on barriers to teaching global education–related themes, between a quarter and a third of respondents highlighted a lack of relevant professional development training. While there are caveats with the research, the study indicates more can still be done in terms of teacher education in global education.

Globalizing access to global education training via MOOCs

The Global Education for Teachers online course was developed as a MOOC with the hope of increasing access to global education teacher education. MOOCs are designed to provide accessible online learning for free (or at very low cost) on a large scale. Their design allows for unlimited enrolment and as a result are more widely accessible than formal higher education or training programmes and can reach much larger audiences. The field has grown rapidly in popularity in recent years, and especially as a result of the Covid pandemic, with worldwide MOOC enrolment numbers exceeding an estimated 180 million by 2020 and continuing to grow (Shah, 2020).

Although MOOCs were initially envisioned as a way to provide learning for those without access to higher education, particularly in the Global South, more recent evidence suggests that MOOCs are most frequently used by professionals looking to further develop their skills or advance their careers. It also suggests that teachers are one of the key groups accessing these opportunities (Bragg, Walsh and Heyeres, 2021; Ho et al., 2015). Certainly, the potential benefits of online professional development courses for teachers are significant. Most importantly for this chapter, this includes the potential to reach teachers who may otherwise have limited access to professional development and training (Laurillard, Kennedy and Wang, 2018). However, further research is needed to better understand how MOOCs can reach and serve particular groups of learners (cf. Schmid et al., 2015).

Ideas of hope in global education

The theme of hope has long been present in global education and sustainable development-related disciplines (Hicks, 2014; Bourn, 2021), but we would suggest hope is increasingly important given recent research highlighting ideas of eco-anxiety (Panu, 2020, Coffey et al., 2021), the impacts of the Covid pandemic (cf. Selby and Kagawa, 2020), as well as evidence of the rise of nationalism around the world.

There are different ways in which hope is positioned within the global education literature in relation to teachers and teaching. This includes the importance of teachers' retaining a sense of hope as they navigate institutions, systems and their own positionality in their pursuit of global education (Kavanagh, Waldron and Mallon, 2021). Here hope is positioned as a critical part of teachers' repertoire needed to fight oppression and guard against potential despair. Bourn (2021) describes global learning as a pedagogy of hope in and of itself. He highlights the important role that teachers play in encouraging the idea that: 'change and progress are possible through a greater understanding of the issues and having the skills and belief in taking social action' (2021: p. 67). Swanson and Gamal

(2021) explore the potential of global citizenship (if reappropriated) to nurture ideas of radical hope in educating for alternative (more hopeful) futures. They proffer an approach which supports critical consciousness and reflexivity to reach beyond and challenge the status quo.

With these in mind we explore hope in relation to the online course, its participants, as well as how the course participants articulate their own ideas of hope and global education.

Methodology

Given the relative lack of research on global education training and professional development around the world, we felt it was important to include a research strand within the course design. Therefore, in addition to the course data generated by participants, we embedded an anonymous, voluntary online survey into week three of the course. The survey gathers qualitative and quantitative data about the cohort, their experiences and engagement with global education in their current practice, and their views on why and how global education is important. And it is this survey that forms the focus of the data in this chapter, albeit with our views being informed and influenced by our engagement with learners on the wider course.

An online survey was chosen as the best means to collect data as participants were located across the world and the survey offered the potential for a large number of responses. We also wanted to be able to match up demographic data to information on their experiences and perceptions, something that FutureLearn's learner profiles do not allow for, but that an additional data collection tool could offer.

Participants on the course were already online, and the survey was embedded within the course, along with ethical information which emphasized that participation was voluntary and responses anonymous. However, this approach created a narrow sampling framework that potentially limits the scope of the study. The participants in this survey were self-selecting as they had signed up to the online course; stayed with the online course until week 3 and agreed to take part in the survey. It indicates teachers involved in the survey were actively interested in global education and saw the benefit of this kind of research.

We received 293 responses to the online survey over four course runs between October 2020 and January 2022. These 293 responses reflect 38 per cent of active learners (i.e. defined as those who mark at least one step as complete within the week) within the participants remaining in week 3 (combined total 779 active learners in week 3). Although the sample was self-selecting and may not be representative of the overall course cohort, the data nevertheless provides a useful glimpse of who engages in the course.

Analysis was conducted using both the SPSS Statistics package and thematic analysis of open-ended survey questions. We produced descriptive quantitative analysis through SPSS which provides useful detail on the nature of the cohort and their experience and engagement with global education. The open-ended free-text responses give a qualitative glimpse into participants' further thoughts and reflections on themes related to the research questions. Thus qualitative responses are used to illustrate participants' engagements with global education and how participants view global education as a source of hope within their practice. In presenting the data we retain a number of the quotes, not only to demonstrate their richness but also to illustrate the scope of teacher engagement from across the world.

Ethical approval for the study was granted by the UCL IOE Research Ethics Committee.

Findings

In the following sections, we explore the findings from survey data in terms of: the nature of the course cohort, their experiences and engagement with global education in their current practice, and their views on why and how global education is important.

Who are the course participants?

Table 12.1 provides an overview profile of course participants who took the survey.

It shows that respondents to the survey were predominantly female (71%) and the majority were teachers (72%) or school leaders (12%), working in schools as their educational settings.

Over 50 per cent of respondents had over ten years of teaching experience, with less than 10 per cent in their initial year of teaching. In terms of the age of students' participants worked with, about a third were working in primary schools and a third secondary schools. Ten per cent of respondents worked with adults only.

Table 12.1 Overview of Course Participants Who Took the Survey

	Characteristic	Number	Percentage
Gender	Female	206	71
	Male	76	26
	Others (combined)	8	4
Job	Teacher	211	72
	School leader	34	12
	Others (combined)	47	16
Experience (length of time teaching)	Under one year	25	9
	1–5 years	64	22
	5–10 years	44	15
	Over 10 years	159	55
School type	state	115	40
	Independent	64	22
	international	43	15
	Other (combined)	68	23
Age of pupils	Primary age (up to 11 years)	89	31
	Secondary age (11–18 years)	90	31
	Mixed age (primary and secondary)	40	14
	Adults	32	11
	Other (combined)	39	14
Subject specialism	Languages	77	27
	Literacy (reading, writing, literature)	39	14
	Humanities	42	15
	Science	31	11
	All/combination	29	10
	Others (combined)	69	24

Around 40 per cent of respondents worked in state schools, with independent and international schools also ranking highly. This differed by nationality with, for example, half of the respondents from the UK and 70 per cent from South Africa working in state schools; compared to almost 90 per cent of respondents from India working in independent schools.

Over 25 per cent identified languages as their main subject specialism, with around 15 per cent humanities teachers. In other UK-based studies, humanities teachers (particularly geography) tend to be the highest cohort engaging in global learning initiatives (Hunt and Cara, 2015), so this focus on languages is interesting. It might partly be an indication of who can access online international courses in English.

We had respondents coming from sixty-five countries (as per their nationality), which includes just less than a third of countries in the world. Not surprisingly, because this is where we are based, UK teachers made up the largest cohort (23 per cent). There were also strong cohorts from India (9 per cent), South Africa (6 per cent), Nigeria (5 per cent) and China (4 per cent), which suggests a relatively diverse range of participants. This is compared to FutureLearn's own estimation that most of the platform's overall learners are located in the United Kingdom, the United States, India, Egypt, Australia, Saudi Arabia, China, Japan, Ukraine and Spain.[3]

Interestingly also almost 30 per cent of respondents lived in a different country to that of their nationality, which suggests quite a mobile cohort.

Overall, this data indicates that the MOOC attracts an international profile of English-speaking (mobile) educators engaged in school-based teaching, with a particular interest in global learning approaches.

Teachers' experiences and engagement with global education

In terms of experience, almost half of the course participants indicate that they have had no previous training on global education (47 per cent), with 20 per cent having one training experience and 26 per cent more than one. This suggests the course attracted both interested participants with limited or no previous access to training and those with an informed and active interest in global education.

Figure 12.1 goes into more detail on how respondents engage with global education within their current practice. It shows responses to a set of statements, with participants asked to note whether they think they are at a beginner, early, developing or experienced stage within their global education journey against various categories related to practice and experience. It shows many respondents marking themselves at developing or experienced levels in many categories already. Those categories with weaker responses tend to be more about global learning in practice, including integrating global themes into their teaching, adopting appropriate pedagogical approaches and linking with external communities locally and internationally on a global theme. This is not surprising as research on global education indicates a lag between knowledge, confidence to teach and practice (Hunt and Cara, 2015).

This is also a bit odd in terms of formatting/ flow. The paragraph should link to the quotes below, but these are preceeded by the table. Can the table be moved earlier or later so that this is not an issue?

Global Education for Teachers 201

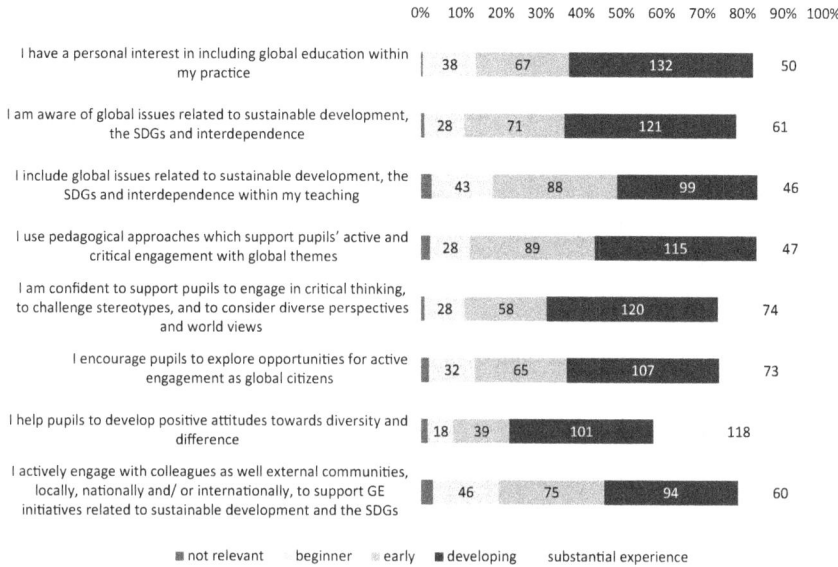

Figure 12.1 Teachers' experience, knowledge and confidence with global education.

Similarly, qualitative responses suggest that many teachers feel the need to develop more supporting knowledge and confidence through training, before including it in their teaching practice:

> I would like to become more knowledgeable and confident myself in dealing with all global issues and have regular access to discussion and information on current issues relating to GCE. (Irish secondary school teacher, government school, Ireland)

> I am aware of what global education is, and have had some experience teaching global citizenship as a subject in 6th grade.... Really grasping what is it and means for me personally, then committing and afterwards, leading my students. I need to feel confident first. (Mexican primary school teacher, independent school, Mexico)

> Deeper understanding of GCE so I can effectively put this into practice. (Filipino secondary school teacher, international school, Vietnam)

This highlights the importance of both CPD opportunities such as this and support for teachers more generally are much needed in order to develop knowledge, understanding and confidence to teach. It indicates that although around half of the respondents have experience in global education, many are only beginning to include it within their practice.

Exploring ideas of hope

In this section we explore ideas of hope which we identified through the survey responses and also our own engagement in the course. Key themes which emerged from our analysis included hope through global education itself, through access to online teacher education, through teachers and teaching, and through the children and young people they teach.

Hope through global education

Not surprisingly given the cohort and the focus of the course there was strong support for global education across the course cohort. Ideas about the importance of global education were a feature of discussions across all of the course runs, where participants frequently expressed enthusiasm and hope for the role of global education in promoting peace, understanding and change for the future. This sense of hope through global education was strikingly summarized by one survey respondent, who pointed specifically to the need for global education in our current, challenging times:

> Global Education is vital. This pandemic feels like a turning point in so much of our thinking. It feels like an opportunity to shape discussions and learning in such a way that we break with the traditions of the past, move away from colonial mindsets and begin to see education institutions as places where dialogue, creativity, open-mindedness, cooperation and empathy are favoured. (Canadian secondary school teacher, international school, Malaysia)

Hope through online teacher education

We argue here that our online Global Education for Teachers professional development course offers hope for teachers in two main ways.

First, as discussed previously the course reaches educators with little or no levels of previous training and experience (47 per cent of the respondents) and low or limited access to training provision (34 per cent). The online, free provision, while not without restrictions (e.g. due to language, access to time and technology), is seemingly able to fill a gap. Respondents noted:

> The professional development I have had this past year has been undertaken privately, not through my school. There has been no professional development related to GCE offered in my school. (Canadian secondary school teacher, international school, Malaysia)

> I didn't really [get] involved in real classroom teachings or handling the pupils because I was a teacher trainer.... And right now in this current situation, I don't have any opportunities to attend professional development courses at all, except through FutureLearn, edX etc. those MOOCs. (Malaysian teacher educator, Malaysia)

Second, the nature of the MOOC provides within it a space for interaction and engagement between teachers from across the world. Here they find commonalities across geographical barriers, while engaging critically with subject matter. This is something that participants spoke about in their responses:

> I've really enjoyed speaking with and listening to teachers from around the world share their thoughts, experiences and practices! The MOOC has helped me to view GCE from a wider perspective. (British primary school teacher, government school, Scotland)

> I enjoyed learning about global education and connecting with other teachers from around the globe. (South African primary school teacher, international school, Qatar)

Hope through teachers and teaching

When asked about their future plans for global education practice, responses were understandably varied, with some participants identifying specific targets such as finding new resources, sharing their learning with colleagues or identifying appropriate strategies for relevant curricular areas. Underpinning many responses, however, was a desire to incorporate more global education within teaching practice, with many noting the direct influence of the course. For some it was the beginning of their global education journey and they spoke about the newness of the field. Others spoke in more detail of changes they wished to make to current practice, with the course seemingly acting as a catalyst for action, adaptation and expansion:

> Develop my global perspectives department to be the best in the school with cutting edge practice, online training and teachers involved in diverse activities relating to improving the community. (British headteacher, international school, Egypt).

> Embedding meaningful changes in the sustainability practices at the school so we are role models for the children and their families. (British arts teacher, international school, Thailand)

We also take it as a sign of hope that the majority of the survey respondents (80 per cent) already see themselves as 'global educators'. While it is difficult to know whether the responses are evidence of actual teaching practice or are more aspirational in tone, it nevertheless suggests that participants see engagement with global education as positive. Teachers also spoke in some detail about their own role, not necessarily as activists or agents of change, but as learners – and the continuing need for them to access training to better support their students.

Overall, we suggest there are signs of hope both for teachers and within their teaching practice.

Hope through children and young people

Many survey responses highlighted a view of hope that focuses on children, their futures and the futures of the world. In this regard global education is a key part of supporting young people and subsequently in some cases a more hopeful global future, with the focus tending to be on young people as global citizens in the making rather than global citizens now.

If we look in more depth at this though as per Table 12.2, we see a range of respondents' accounts that relate to global education, young people and hope, with some more evidence-based than others. Can Table 12.2 be moved to directly under this para? Otherwise the quotes which follow the paras below are split up again.

Respondents were asked to complete the sentence 'global education is . . .'. and varied responses can be seen below. Many of the responses directly relate to young people, their development as global citizens and their role in the future.

A number of responses relate to developing children and young people as global citizens, whereby global education interventions increase learners' knowledge, skills and competences to develop as global citizens. For these respondents, global education is

Table 12.2 Typology of Hope

Through global education children and young people develop knowledge, skills, values to develop as global citizens	Through global education children and young people more globally informed and aware	Through global education children and young people either now or in the future (as adults) take informed action on a global issue	Through global education as adults, these children and young people, solve global problems, make the world better.
Evidence-based		Less evidence	Little or no evidence

> a process whereby students develop critical thinking skills, global values, and an awareness of the world and people around them, which together contribute to them becoming a global citizen. (British teacher, international school, China)
>
> preparing students with the essential knowledge and skills to be global citizens and become active members in the rapidly changing world. (British primary school teacher, government school, England)

Through the global education process, many respondents also saw children and young people becoming more globally informed, confident and able to engage with global issues. In these cases, global education is

> the active engagement of children in developing their knowledge, understanding and skills of the world and where they fit in. (South African secondary school teacher, international school, Qatar)
>
> learning about the world around us, issues we may face and learning to feel confident tackling issues. (British primary school teacher, government school, UK)

There is a growing evidence base that global education supports the development of children's global citizen attributes (cf. O'Flaherty and Liddy, 2018; Ahmed and Mohammed, 2021; Hunt, 2017; Hunt and Cara, 2015), but less on how this contributes to action. That said, global education in schooling often includes opportunities for young people to take part in and experience an 'active' citizenship element. Respondents therefore also noted how global education supports young people either now or in the future (as adults) to develop a sense of their role within the world, the interconnections between people and experience informed action on (a) global issue(s). For example, global education is

> essential for children who are hearing about significant problems in the world around them and who need to understand them and develop a sense that they can act on them rather than being helpless. (Australian secondary school teacher, government school, Australia)
>
> about facilitating learners to become more aware of their role on this earth and to see how their actions and behaviours can influence others. It is also about developing tolerance and understanding of the value of diversity and equality. (British secondary school teacher, government school, England)
>
> a way to exchange thoughts, to bridge cultures, to be more inclusive and to shape the world into a better world. (Chinese secondary school teacher (15-18), independent school, China)
>
> important for pupils as they will begin to take care of the Earth where they live. (Armenian primary school teacher, government school, Armenia)

There were also a large number of responses where global education was seen as a vehicle to support young people to solve major global problems in the future. While this approach is definitely hopeful, there is thus far limited longitudinal research which tracks the impact of global education into adulthood, so whether this hope is realistic, is not certain. Moreover, this kind of focus tends to put the onus of change on young people in the future and not the adults of today. Responses that support this include: Global education is

> of key importance to ensure life in the planet earth on the long term. (Brazilian teacher trainee, Brazil)
>
> foundational to giving students the mindset necessary for them to solve the problems of the world. (American teacher trainee, USA)
>
> very important to make the global citizens with the knowledge, values, skills and actions so that they would solve the global problems in future. (Bangladeshi primary school teacher, government school, Bangladesh)

Hope for and via young people emerge from these accounts and dovetail clearly with discussions about the aims of global education, as well as related areas such as global learning, global citizenship education, and education for sustainable development, throughout the academic literature (cf. Bourn, 2021, Davies et al., 2018). They also run parallel to current international policy statements, and especially the UN Sustainable Development Goals, which argue for the central role of education in achieving a more just and sustainable world in the future. They possibly link more readily to the concept of hope as advocated by Bourn (2021) whereby teachers develop skills and knowledge to foster the hope that change and progress is possible; but perhaps less obvious support for more radical versions of hope as advocated by Swanson and Gamal (2021).

Concluding thoughts

Literature in global education and related areas has often highlighted the need for global education pedagogies as an important source of hope, particularly in the context of increasing global inequality, climate change and, more recently, the global pandemic (cf. Friere, 2004; Bourn, 2021; Selby and Kagawa, 2020; Hicks, 2014). Alongside this, however, is also a long-standing recognition of the lack of support for teachers (and educators more generally) who would like to integrate these approaches into their educational practice.

So, while the news continues to be full of the challenges of climate change, the global pandemic and armed conflict, we found in this course evidence of hope on a range of levels. First, in terms of the participants' own expressions of hope, their current practice and engagement, their plans for continued engagement and their hope for their pupils. Second, for us as educators, the course gave us hope for making global education accessible to new cohorts and bringing together teachers to speak to and engage with diverse peers around the world, to share practice, and to learn from one another. As Bourn notes, such educational initiatives are important because:

> People and communities need not only to be kept informed about these global issues, but also to have the opportunities to develop their skills within a framework of a values base built on social justice to ensure that change is long lasting and meaningful. (Bourn, 2021: p. 67)

While the long-term impacts of the course are difficult to assess, we believe that online courses like this one have a potentially important contribution to make in addressing the ongoing gap in teacher professional development related to global education around the world. Certainly, if SDG 4.7 is to be achieved, it will require not just attention to policy and curricula, but also much greater investment in the professional development of teachers.

Notes

1. The course can be found on https://www.futurelearn.com/courses/global-education-for-teachers.
2. Ninety per cent of their respondents came from two countries only (Mexico and Ukraine); there is little information about school type. Respondents were self-selecting.
3. https://www.futurelearn.com/info/blog/ten-million-learners

References

Ahmed, E. I. and A. Mohammed (2021). 'Evaluating the Impact of Global Citizenship Education Programmes: A Synthesis of the Research'. *Education, Citizenship and Social Justice* 1–19. doi: 10.1177/17461979211000039

Andreotti, V. and L. M. T. M. de Souza (2008). *Learning to Read the World through Other Eyes*. Derby: Global Education, Derby.

Bamber, P., ed. (2020). *Teacher Education for Sustainable Development and Global Citizenship: Critical Perspectives on Values, Curriculum and Assessment*. Abingdon, Oxon: Routledge.

Bentall, C. and F. Hunt (2022). 'The Value of Third Sector Organisations' Provision of Global Learning CPD in English Schools'. *Professional Development in Education*. doi: 10.1080/19415257.2022.2038656

Bourn, D. (2016). 'Teachers as Agents of Social Change'. *International Journal of Development Education and Global Learning* 7(3): 63–77. doi: 10.18546/IJDEGL.07.3.05

Bourn, D. (2021). 'Pedagogy of Hope: Global Learning and the Future of Education'. *International Journal of Development Education and Global Learning* 13(2): 65–78. doi: 10.14324/IJDEGL.13.2.01

Bourn D., F. Hunt and P. Bamber (2017). 'A Review of Education for Sustainable Development and Global Citizenship Education in Teacher Education', in *GEM Background Paper*. Paris: UNESCO.

Bragg, L. A., C. Walsh and M. Heyeres (2021). 'Successful Design and Delivery of Online Professional Development for Teachers: A Systematic Review of the Literature'. *Computers and Education* 166(February): 104158. doi: 10.1016/j.compedu.2021.104158

Bruce, J., C. North and J. FitzPatrick (2019). 'Preservice Teachers' Views of Global Citizenship and Implications for Global Citizenship Education'. *Globalisation, Societies and Education* 17(2): 161–76. doi: 10.1080/14767724.2018.1558049

Coffey, Y., N. Bhullar, J. Durkin, M. S. Islam and K. Usher. (2021) 'Understanding Eco-anxiety: A Systematic Scoping Review of Current Literature and Identified Knowledge Gaps'. *The Journal of Climate Change and Health* 3: 100047. doi: 10.1016/j.joclim.2021.100047

Davies, I., L. C. Ho, D. Kiwan, C. L. Peck, A. Peterson, E. Sant and Y. Waghid, eds (2018) *The Palgrave Handbook of Global Citizenship and Education*. London: Palgrave Macmillan UK. doi: 10.1057/978-1-137-59733-5

Ekanayake, K., M. Shukri, A. Khatibi and S. M. F. Azam (2020). 'Global Citizenship Education Practices and Teacher Education: A Review of Literature'. *Journal of Education, Society and Behavioural Science* 33(6): 36–47. doi: 10.9734/jesbs/2020/v33i630234

Estellés, M. and G. E. Fischman (2021). 'Who Needs Global Citizenship Education? A Review of the Literature on Teacher Education'. *Journal of Teacher Education* 72(2): 223–36.

Ferguson, T., C. Roofe and L. D. Cook (2021) 'Teachers' Perspectives on Sustainable Development: The Implications for Education for Sustainable Development'. *Environmental Education Research* 27(9): 1343–59. doi: 10.1080/13504622.2021.1921113

Fischer, D., J. King, M. Rieckmann, M. Barth, A. Büssing, I. Hemmer and D. Lindau-Banket (2022). 'Teacher Education for Sustainable Development: A Review of an Emerging Research Field'. *Journal of Teacher Education*, online: 1–16. doi: 10.1177/00224871221105784

Freire, P. (2004). *Pedagogy of Hope*. New York: Continuum.

Hicks, D. (2014). 'A Geography of Hope'. *Geography* 99(1): 5–12.
Ho, A. D., I. Chuang, J. Reich, C. A. Coleman, J. Whitehill, C. G. Northcutt, J. J. Williams, J.D. Hansen, G. Lopez and R. Petersen (2015). 'HarvardX and MITx: Two Years of Open Online Courses Fall 2012–Summer 2014'. *SSRN Electronic Journal* 10: 1–37. doi: 10.2139/ssrn.2586847
Howard-Jones, P., D. Sands, J. Dillon and F. Fenton-Jones (2021). 'The Views of Teachers in England on an Action-Oriented Climate Change Curriculum'. *Environmental Education Research* 27(11): 1660–80. doi: 10.1080/13504622.2021.1937576
Hunt, F. (2017). 'Schools for Future Youth Evaluation Report: Developing Young People as Active Global Citizens', in *DERC Research Paper no. 17*. London: IOE.
Hunt, F. and O. Cara (2015). 'Global Learning in England: Baseline analysis of the Global Learning Programme Whole School Audit 2013–14', in *DERC Research Paper no. 15*. London: IOE.
Kavanagh, A. M., F. Waldron and B. Mallon (2021). *Teaching for Social Justice and Sustainable Development across the Primary Curriculum: An Introduction*. Abingdon, Oxon: Routledge.
Laurillard, D., E. Kennedy and T. Wang (2018). 'How could Digital Learning at Scale Address the Issue of Equity in Education?'. Available at: http://dl4d.org/wp-content/uploads/2018/05/Learning-at-Scale-for-the-Global-South-Main-Paper.pdf
Murphy, C., B. Mallon, G. Smith, O. Kelly, V. Pitsia and G. Martinez Sainz (2021). 'The Influence of a Teachers' Professional Development Programme on Primary School Pupils' Understanding of and Attitudes towards Sustainability'. *Environmental Education Research* 27(7): 1011–36. doi: 10.1080/13504622.2021.1889470
O'Flaherty, J. and M. Liddy (2018). 'The Impact of Development Education and Education for Sustainable Development Interventions: A Synthesis of the Research'. *Environmental Education Research* 24(7): 1031–49. doi: 10.1080/13504622.2017.1392484
O'Meara, J. G., T. Huber and E. R. Sanmiguel (2018). 'The Role of Teacher Educators in Developing and Disseminating Global Citizenship Education Strategies in and beyond US Learning Environments'. *Journal of Education for Teaching* 44(5): 556–73. doi: 10.1080/02607476.2018.1516347
Panu, P. (2020). 'Anxiety and the Ecological Crisis: An Analysis of Eco-Anxiety and Climate Anxiety'. *Sustainability* 12(19): 7836. doi: 10.3390/su12197836
Pashby, K. and L. Sund (2019). *Teaching for Sustainable Development through Ethical Global Issues Pedagogy: A Resource for Secondary Teachers*. Manchester Metropolitan University. https://www.mmu.ac.uk/research/research-centres/esri/projects/teaching-sustainable-development
Roemhild, R. and W. Gaudelli (2021). 'Climate Change as Quality Education', in R. Iyengar and C. T. Kwauk (eds), *Curriculum and Learning for Climate Action*, 104–19. Brill. doi: 10.1163/9789004471818_007

Schmid, L., K. Manturuk, I. Simpkins, M. Goldwasser and K. E. Whitfield (2015). 'Fulfilling the Promise: Do MOOCs Reach the Educationally Underserved?'. *Educational Media International* 52(2): 116–28. doi: 10.1080/09523987.2015.1053288

Schugurensky, D. and C. Wolhuter (2020). *Global Citizenship Education in Teacher Education: Theoretical and Practical Issues*. New York: Routledge.

Selby, D. and F. Kagawa (2020). 'Climate Change and Coronavirus: A Confluence of Two Emergencies as Learning and Teaching Challenge'. *Policy & Practice: A Development Education Review* 30: 104–14. Available at: https://www.development educationreview.com/issue/issue-30/climate-change-and-coronavirus-confluence-two-emergencies-learning-and-teaching

Shah, D. (2020). 'By the Numbers: MOOCs in 2020 - Boosted by the Pandemic, MOOCs Crossed 180 Million Learners in their Ninth Year'. *The Report by Class Central*. https://www.classcentral.com/report/mooc-stats-2020/

Swanson, D. M. and M. Gamal (2021). 'Global Citizenship Education / Learning for Sustainability: Tensions, "flaws", and Contradictions as Critical Moments of Possibility and Radical Hope in Educating for Alternative Futures'. *Globalisation, Societies and Education* 19(4): 456–69.

Tarozzi, M. and B. Mallon (2019). 'Educating Teachers towards Global Citizenship: A Comparative Study in Four European Countries'. *London Review of Education* 17(2): 112–25. doi: 10.18546/LRE.17.2.02

UNESCO (2016). *Schools in Action, Global Citizens for Sustainable Development: A Guide for Teachers*. Paris: UNESCO. https://unesdoc.unesco.org/ark:/48223/pf0000246888.locale=en

UNESCO (2018). *Preparing Teachers for Global Citizenship Education: A Template*. Bangkok: UNESCO Office Bangkok and Regional Bureau for Education in Asia and the Pacific. https://unesdoc.unesco.org/ark:/48223/pf0000265452

UNESCO (2021). *Teachers have their Say: Motivation, Skills and Opportunities to Teach Education for Sustainable Development and Global Citizenship*. Paris: UNESCO. https://unesdoc.unesco.org/ark:/48223/pf0000379914

Yemini, M., F. Tibbitts and H. Goren (2019). 'Trends and Caveats: Review of Literature on Global Citizenship Education in Teacher Training'. *Teaching and Teacher Education* 77: 77–89. doi: 10.1016/j.tate.2018.09.014

13

Gender Equality – The Key Role of a Pedagogy of Critical Hope and Global Social Justice

Lisa Ferro and Sandra Saúde

Introduction

The modern, neoliberal, capitalist society is set on societal paradoxes which can jeopardize the sustainability of the world itself. Gender inequality continues to be one of those. Assuming education as a structuring path capable of helping to free us from the dominant ideology (Freire and Shor, 1987), this chapter is based on the results of a research developed in Portugal and reflects on how a pedagogy of critical hope and global social justice – which seeks to transform consciousness, engagement, responsibility, and the capacity to build different futures – different questions; different answers (Freire, 1994; Andreotti, 2006; Bozalek et al., 2014) – constitutes a powerful educational framework to structurally promote gender equality.

Based on a heteronormative understanding of citizenship, gender inequality is at the heart of the current unequal world of social injustice in which the status of women is both a result and a predictor of the prevailing levels of *misdistribution*, *misrecognition*, and *misrepresentation* (Fraser, 2007). The promotion of gender equality implies commitment and action to question and transform structural barriers which have been socially and culturally legitimated and depoliticized over time and which prevent half of the world's population from having access to equal opportunities and full participation in society.

The territorialization of public policies for gender equality, promoted in Portugal since 2007, placed local governments at the centre of action, establishing their responsibility in this field and stating their fundamental role in mobilizing civil society. Local counsellors for equality were defined and the integration of gender mainstreaming in every action, namely through the adoption of local plans for equality, became an obligation of the municipalities.

In order to understand the social representations shared by stakeholders – with direct responsibility for the local implementation of public policies – on the existing practices and dynamics to promote gender equality in four municipalities of Portugal (in the Baixo Alentejo region), a qualitative study was carried out, having as participants a member of the Portuguese Government, one mayor and three councillors, four municipal counsellors for equality and one coordinator in the field of gender equality in a Non-Governmental Organization for Development.

The results reveal limited visions and lack of full commitment and critical analysis, making evident how crucial it is 'to empower individuals to reflect critically on the legacies and processes of their cultures' (Andreotti, 2006: p. 48) as an effective change demands a profound analysis and transformation of our traditional representations and action codes.

Pedagogy of critical hope and global social justice as a framework to respond to the world's challenges and social inequalities

'We can struggle to become free precisely because we can know we are not free! That is why we can think of transformation' (Freire and Shor, 1987: p. 13). The first, political (and cognitive) set of restrictions to shed light on and fight to transform is the general narrowing of the space for articulation of political, social and economic alternatives in the context of modern nation states. The destructiveness and restrictiveness of this cognitive imperialism have been described by authors such as Vandana Shiva (1993) in her analysis of 'monocultures of the mind', by Boaventura de Sousa Santos (2007) in his writings on 'abyssal thinking' and by Henry Giroux (2015), who highlights how 'profit making is the essence of democracy and consuming is the only operable form of citizenship' (Harper, 2014: p. 1078). The political side of this narrowing of imaginative space, especially in terms of institutionalized, formalized political debate, is also captured in the work of Roberto Unger (1998). He points out that, nowadays, when someone dares to think and talk differently, all programmatic proposals seem either utopian (in the sense of unrealizable and unrealistic) or trivial.

Faced with such entrenched standardized ways of thinking, being and acting, it is urgent to create and work for change and, above all, to believe in it. Without hope, even in the direst of times, there is no possibility for resistance, dissent and struggle (Giroux, 2015).

> As a species, we are at the point in our collective history where we have the greatest access ever to knowledge and to tools that enable us to collaborate. The potential for engaging humanity in creating better futures together has never been greater. (UNESCO, 2021: p. 6)

So, we have reasons to have hope. We just need to make good choices and dare to break new ground using the valuable resources and capabilities we have. Education plays a fundamental role in achieving this. It is crucial to ensure that capable people are willing to 'imagine something beyond their own self-interest and well-being, to serve the public good, to take risks, and to struggle for a substantive democracy' (Giroux, 2016). That implies asking students and educators to radically analyse their feelings, thoughts and knowledge about the society they live in and, additionally, to provoke them to go beyond simple observation and to proceed to ethical, political and knowledge-based participation in community struggles with concrete actions that combat discrimination, oppression, suffering and exploitation (Zembylas, 2014).

It is vital to work on a 'transformative approach' [in the words of Fraser (2007)] sustained on a critical ontology of one's collective self that questions what we have become and refuses to submit to normalized pre-categories and norms of superiority according to which one should think and judge one's self and others (sustaining dichotomies between 'me' and 'them'; between citizens and non-citizens, particularly natives and migrants; between 'his' and 'her' roles in society) (Bozalek et al., 2014).

Pedagogies of critical hope and social justice combine 'the affective, the ethical, and the political through actions and practices that stress the contextual nature of issues, yet they systematically link the individual with a collective sense of transformation' (Zembylas, 2014: p. 16). It is not simply about identifying and critiquing one's affective attachments to certain politics and ethics but finding ways to move beyond these attachments and establish new affective connections that are empowering for change.

It is crucial to apply the pedagogy of discomfort to deconstruct the empire of the cogito 'I think, therefore I am' (Descartes) and to centre action on being, feeling and acting (Webb, 2017). Therefore, 'learning environments' (not only classrooms) must be spaces to develop 'persistence, resourcefulness, generosity, determination, responsibility, discipline, compassion, courage, patience, accountability, humility, collaboration, attentiveness, and flexibility'

(Hytten, 2010: p. 161), where hope and action act like fuel and sustain real social transformation (Jacobs, 2005; Bozalek et al., 2014).

Central to the Freirean view of education is that 'besides being an act of knowing, education is also a political act' (Freire and Shor, 1987: p. 13). Education should not be based on mere techniques for gaining literacy or expertise for critical thinking. Rather, it should be a process based on liberating and dialogical methods, which privilege the personal experience and lived histories, critically and constructively explore the intimacy of the society – the raison d'être of every object of study – and design new possible futures (Freire and Shor, 1987). The future is a space for possibility and (social and political) change. After all, 'despair and cynicism only help those in dominance' (Apple, 2014: p. xvi).

Gender equality – Still a challenge on the path to social justice

> Any study of women and development . . . cannot start from the viewpoint that the problem is women, but rather men and women, and more specifically the socially constituted relations between them. (Ann Whitehead, 1979, quoted by Cornwall and Rivas, 2015: p. 402)

However, even though the United Nations claims that 'the perceptions, interests, needs and priorities of both women and men must be taken into consideration not only as a matter of social justice but because they are necessary to enrich development processes' (OSAGI, 2001), highlighting that gender equality is not a women's issue but should concern and fully engage men as well, the body of evidences that underline the benefits of equality between men and women still tend to portray the women's virtues as part of the narrative that presents them as a good 'investment', 'making women work for development, rather than making development work for their equality and empowerment' (Cornwall and Rivas, 2015: p. 398).

When development narratives describe women as 'more hardworking, more caring, more responsible, and more mindful of the environment than men' (Cornwall and Rivas, 2015: p. 399) and emphasize gender equality as 'an accelerator – or a catalytic policy intervention – that triggers positive multiplier effects across the spectrum of development' (Dugarova, 2018: p. 9) rather than an enshrined human right itself, the recognition of the underlying structural connections and the relations of power that produce situations of inequality and discrimination may be lost and its association with agency, accountability and human rights, consequently, remains at the level of rhetoric (Cornwall and Rivas, 2015).

An adequate theory of justice for our time must be, according to Nancy Fraser (2007), three-dimensional: encompassing *redistribution*, *recognition* and *representation*. But the fact is that the latest United Nations (UN) report on the Sustainable Development Goals (United Nations, 2020) reveals that

- globally, women are just 13% of agricultural land holders;
- in 39 countries, daughters and sons do not have equal inheritance rights;
- in 2019, women only held 28% of managerial positions worldwide; and
- women representation in national parliaments at 23.7 per cent is still far from parity.

Despite gender equality 'has come to be viewed: as not only about righting the wrongs of patriarchy by realigning opportunities, resources and positional power for women, but also about containing, reforming and reorienting men-in-general away from the potential harms that they present to women' (Cornwall and Rivas, 2015):

- in 18 countries husbands can legally prevent their wives from working and 49 lack laws protecting women from domestic violence;
- only 52% of women that are married or live in a union freely make their own decisions about sexual relations, contraceptive use, and health care;
- women spend about three times as many hours in unpaid domestic and care work as men;
- globally, 750 million women and girls were married before the age of 18; and
- at least 200 million women and girls in 30 countries have undergone female genital mutilation (United Nations, 2020).

For that reason, 'overcoming injustice means dismantling institutionalized obstacles that prevent some people from participating on a par with others, as full partners in social interaction' (Fraser, 2007: p. 20). However,

> inclusiveness is not only about giving people chances to have a say, it is also about creating the conditions of mutual respect in which people can not only give voice but also be heard. It is not only about inserting women into spaces created by others, be they patriarchal parliamentary institutions or the equally patriarchal institutions of religion, media, civil society, and business. It is also about making the men in those spaces the objects of attention: making their exclusionary practices visible and unacceptable. (Cornwall and Rivas, 2015: p. 409)

It deeply implies 'to reflect a lasting change in the power and choices women have over their own lives, rather than just an (often temporary) increase in opportunities' (Woodroffe and Smee, 2012, quoted by Cornwall and Rivas, 2015: p. 399). The promotion of gender equality is not just about guaranteeing equal rights and duties for men and women, but it is rather a question of economy, of politics and of social constructions of identities, roles and relationships (Dillon, 2019).

The typification of household activities as feminine, the wage gap between men and women, the high rates of abuse and domestic violence against women (intensified by the Covid-19 pandemic) prove the perpetuation of a binary worldview [according to Bourdieu (1998), a male order that perpetuates itself, as a heavy trend, without the need for justification]. Above all, this constructs a social order that is legitimated in the acceptance and incorporation of a hierarchy of rights, discrimination of powers and consolidation of discourse and action, based on the separation of 'I and the other' or of 'us and them', particularly if different from myself.

To work in benefit of gender equality is far more than just 'including women', 'women's issues' or 'a woman's touch' in questions or actions. It is far more than approving a parity law to ensure a minimum representation of the under-represented gender on electoral lists. It implies going beyond and deeply transforming the roots of social, economic and cultural inequality. It implies working through the discomfort of realizing that the worldview and the status quo that build the 'house of modernity' (Andreotti, 2014) and our current world undermine the possibilities of our survival, as they sustain themselves in exploitation, in discrimination and in unfair imbalances of power and wealth. It also implies nurturing and consolidating hope and determination to provoke change and to build, in each historical, social and cultural context, the right bases to guarantee pluralism and the full exercise of citizenship, working towards the elimination of barriers that are at the root of the institutionalization of discriminatory processes and their cultural replication.

Gender equality, social representations and existing practices – evidence from an exploratory study in four municipalities of Portugal (in the Baixo Alentejo region)

The process of territorializing public policies for gender equality placed local governments at the centre of action and established their direct responsibility in applying gender mainstreaming and mobilizing civil society.

However, a study about social representations on the existing practices and dynamics on gender equality (Ferro, 2021), carried out in four inland municipalities of Portugal (in the Baixo Alentejo region), characterized by rurality, high population ageing and population density between 8.6 and 18 people per km^2 (INE, 2020), reveals the long way still to go in order to minimize the structural factors that sustain the cultural replication of gender-based discrimination, suggesting that local territories might not be up to the challenge.

The exploratory case study with a qualitative and interpretative frame developed aimed to explore and characterize the social representations shared by local key actors, from the political and intervention field. Through ten (10) in-depth interviews, applied to a member of the Portuguese Government (female), one mayor (male) and three councillors (female), four municipal counsellors for equality (female) and one coordinator in the field of gender equality in a non-governmental organization for development (female), it was possible to identify the structuring dimensions of the social representations shared on the main problems and practices in this matter.

Most local stakeholders who are responsible for promoting gender equality interviewed reveal:

- a limited understanding of the theme of gender equality;
- stereotyped conceptions about the roles of men and women;
- flaws in the process of identifying gender inequalities;
- the acceptance of the patriarchal culture as an insuperable barrier, excusing its influence on domestic violence, dating violence and female unemployment rates, identified as the main problems in this field;
  It is the man who earns, it is the man who takes the money home, they (the women) are dependent. . . . . It is evident that it is not only domestic violence that happens, but they are also dependent on them. . . . . And this mentality is very male chauvinist here. (interviewee 8)

There is recognition of the need for an ongoing intervention along with the identification of activities that makes it possible to experience the inequality as a more effective way of changing behaviours:

Work real situations in the classroom, I mean. . . . . It's not watching a movie but real situations that change behaviours. (interviewee 8)

But it does not seem to find any echo when it comes to planning strategies to ensure a correct interpretation of the concept of gender equality and its assumptions:

> Well, with awareness-raising actions, with awareness-raising on the street or done in a way that we know that the information actually reaches people. (interviewee 9)

The lack of commitment to the effective promotion of gender equality also emerges from the local stakeholders' narratives, as they understate their full responsibilities in this process, fail to understand and adopt gender mainstreaming and point to the cultural matrix as an insurmountable barrier, which leads them to accepting discriminatory practices and gender inequalities rather than investing in strategies with real transformative impact:

> We try to alert and raise awareness. We cannot do more because we cannot compel people to have a Plan. But we try, at least, to sensitize them. (interviewee 10)

The position of the local stakeholders contradicts the perspective of the member of the Portuguese government, who emphasizes the need 'to be proactive' (interviewee 1) and claims 'greater production of knowledge, greater accountability of the different partners, of the different stakeholders, greater scientific knowledge on the part of people, both in public administration and in different sectors' (interviewee 1). In fact, the limited visions and the lack of full commitment and critical analysis have contributed to incomplete approaches and to the definition of an ineffective strategy which is poorly oriented towards minimizing the identified problems or their roots.

By not embracing a disruptive path, the local territories seem to have neglected the privileged position which they have to fight discrimination and promote gender equality, making evident how crucial it is 'to empower individuals to reflect critically on the legacies and processes of their cultures' (Andreotti, 2006: p. 48). Effective change demands a profound analysis and transformation of our traditional representations and action codes.

Promoting gender equality through education – key assumptions

Gender equality is inexorably an education issue. Not just because access to school is not equally available to men and women, but mainly because it is the space where inequality and the ethical, political and symbolic matrices that build the dominant power relations are projected, being replicated by established social relations.

Multiple researches – about textbooks (Blumberg, 2007; 2015; Islam and Asadullah, 2018), pedagogical practices at different levels of education (from pre-school to higher education) and/or representations shared by teachers and students (Jones, 2020, among others) – conclude that there is a prevalence of discourses and practices in the educational context that reproduce stereotyped models of women and men. There is a prevalence of the binary discourse of 'me and the other', the interpretive softening of gender stereotypes based on the patriarchal cultural tradition and/or the defence that the greater number of women with a higher education degree is evidence of the existence of gender equality. The developed exploratory study about social representations on the existing practices and dynamics in four inland municipalities of Portugal (Ferro, 2021) additionally reveals the prevalence of stereotyped political visions as well as the adoption of action plans that fail to question the structural causes of gender inequality, missing the purpose of contributing to its effective change. These are indicators of the long path that remains to be walked to achieve a sustainable transformation in the field of equality and social justice.

So, the key questions are: *How can change be effectively achieved?* Since it is evident the need to change practices and the way in which, from an educational point of view, gender equality should be worked on, *how can education be effectively made the pillar of effective transformation in the field of gender equality? What pedagogical strategies and tools should be implemented?*

To empower individuals 'to imagine different futures and to take responsibility for different decisions and actions' (Andreotti, 2006: p. 48) implies engagement rather than only raising awareness. To really engage people to act in the development of a sustainable, inclusive and fair society which is free of gender-based discrimination, it is fundamental to explore all the main domains of global citizenship education (GCE): cognitive, socio-emotional, behavioural change and an ethical relationship to difference, addressing complexity and power relations (Andreotti, 2006).

> Cognitive: To acquire knowledge, understanding and critical thinking about global, regional, national, and local issues and the interconnectedness and interdependency of the world. Socio-emotional: To have a sense of belonging to a common world and humanity, sharing values and responsibilities, empathy, solidarity and respect for differences and diversity. Behavioural: To act effectively and responsibly at local, national, and global levels for a more peaceful and sustainable world. (UNESCO, 2019: p. 15)

In the educational space, teachers are decisive elements in implementing GCE work: they should gain the mastery of knowledge, competencies and attitudes through effective, continuous and real, transformative professional development training to act as examples and, at the same time, true promoters of change (Darling-Hammond, Hyler and Gardner, 2017). As implementing a true pedagogy for GCE is difficult and deeply challenges the status quo, it is important to spend time uncovering prejudices and uncritical biases in teacher education (Sensoy and DiAngelo, 2017), making it a priority within the sphere of critical hope and social justice (UNESCO, 2019).

Schools, the learning environments, and the classrooms themselves should be exemplary spaces of action based on equity, respect for difference and social justice. It is thus essential to rethink the methodologies, practices, established relationship dynamics and the language itself.

The educational space is a space of socio-affective and power relations, shaped by the ethical, political and cultural matrix of the context. It is therefore a *locus* where the prejudices and obscurantism that conditions ways of observing must be worked on, deconstructed, criticized and exposed. More than cognitive questioning – which will always remain largely in the domain of knowledge and rationality – it is necessary to guarantee questioning from the experiential, social-emotional side that mobilizes the questioning of the ethical, moral and political foundations of action and that invokes the urgency of action for change. Thus, it will be important to ensure the active involvement of trainees in the identification and construction of the training path to be developed, based on their expectations, interests, life experiences and sociocultural and affective matrix – the interest and impact will be enhanced if the training process is truly meaningful and inspiring for all. In this sense, 'it is crucial to engage ethical self-reflection (i.e., a critical contemplation on the very terms by which we give an account of ourselves and others) through creative pedagogies' that can offer 'exciting possibilities for navigating through the discomforts of gender transformative work' (Keddie, 2021: p. 412). If training starts from the matrix of experiences of each one and guarantees contact and questioning with real facts and situations of their contexts, the process will be more transformative and make a greater impression.

> Impact comes not in the short-term, but in the longer term. (. . .) it's not with a one-off initiative that you will change a situation, there has to be a coherent approach (at a higher level). (. . .) if there is no strategy in place and if the institutional preconditions are not fulfilled (. . .) then the training will not make a difference. (UN Women Training Centre, 2016: p. 18)

For education to effectively contribute to the transformation of people and the world, it is essential for the change to be structural and not just cyclical; it implies changing mindsets, questions and practices; a change that takes on discomfort; a change that takes into account the imperialism of the current worldview and way of life and how difficult it is to change them; a change built on the hope of believing and on the capacity and resilience of action towards a more dignified, fair, ethical and truly sustainable ecosystem, where everyone can and must participate equally.

Final considerations

'When students and their teachers can examine the diversity within themselves and their communities, they can start to uncover and deconstruct the prejudices they carry' (Carroll, 2021: p. 16). Going beyond and thinking otherwise call for a critical and hopeful education that empowers them to understand their role in dismantling systematic inequalities. Education is not responsible for ending inequalities, as they are structural, but rather contributing to their dismantling based on a full understanding of their roots, consequences and the unsustainability of inaction.

When half of the world's population is prevented from having access to equal opportunities and full participation in society, as a result of the prevailing levels of *misdistribution*, *misrecognition* and *misrepresentation*, the fight for gender equality must not be driven by the good 'investment' it means for development but by the fact that it is a human right itself. Equality between men and women is a matter of social justice. Promoting it implies recognition of underlying structural connections and power relations as well as commitment and action to question and transform the barriers which have been socially and culturally legitimated and depoliticized over time.

Combating gender inequalities should not be centred only on the education system without considering its relationship with the society that creates, maintains and needs it. A pedagogy of critical hope and global social justice urges teachers and learners 'to identify cracks in dominant social structures and ideologies' (Webb, 2017: p. 555), encourages them to create 'a substantive utopian vision' (Webb, 2017: p. 562) and promotes the creation of a new basis for affective, ethical and political commitment.

The study developed in four municipalities of Portugal, about social representations on practices and dynamics to promote gender equality, reveals that the limited visions of the local stakeholders and their lack of commitment and critical analysis have contributed to incomplete approaches and to the maintenance of discriminatory practices, incapable of challenging the status quo. As the analysed studies also demonstrate the prevalence of discourses and practices in the educational context that reproduce stereotyped models of women and men, it is important to spend time uncovering prejudices and uncritical biases in teacher-education (Sensoy and DiAngelo, 2017), making it a priority within the sphere of critical hope and social justice (UNESCO, 2019).

As defended by Machado de Oliveira (2021), while we privilege a pedagogy of intellectually comfortable recipes, addicted to finding quick and merely palliative solutions to the current problems (immortalized by the modern, unsustainable and unfair way of life), we cannot aspire to hope for change. Eliminating injustice implies getting rid of the modern interpretive vices and requires the adoption of a pedagogy that really expands our capacity to 'dig deeper and interpret critically wider' to the real structural roots of the social injustice and the current worldwide unsustainability.

That is exactly the conceptual and methodological framework of global education, supported by a pedagogy of critical hope and social justice that stresses the contextual nature of issues but systematically links the individual with a collective sense of transformation (Zembylas, 2014). Embracing it is the key to ensuring that educative contexts embody the ethical and societal imperative of the urgency of building a more just and sustainable world, as well as strategies that develop the capacity for analysis and critical and constructive action of students and teachers.

References

Andreotti, V. (2006). 'Soft versus Critical Global Citizenship Education'. *Policy and Practice: A Development Education Review* 3(Autumn): 40–51.

Andreotti, V. (2014). 'Critical Literacy: Theories and Practices in Development Education'. *Policy and Practice: A Development Education Review* 14(Autumn): 12–32.

Apple, M. (2014). 'Foreword', in V. Bozalek, B. Leibowitz, R. Carolissen and M. Boler (eds), *Discerning Critical Hope in Educational Practices*, xii–xxii. New York: Routledge.

Blumberg, R. L. (2007). *Gender Bias in Textbooks: A Hidden Obstacle on the Road to Gender Equality in Education*. Background paper prepared for the Education for All Global Monitoring Report 2008. UNESCO.

Blumberg, R. L. (2015). *Eliminating Gender Bias in Textbooks: Pushing for Policy Reforms that Promote Gender Equity in Education*. Background paper prepared for the Education for All Global Monitoring Report 2015. UNESCO.

Bourdieu, P. (1998). *La domination masculine*. Paris: Éditions du Seuil.
Bozalek, V., R. Carolissen, B. Leibowitz and M. Boler, eds (2014). *Discerning Critical Hope in Educational Practices*. New York: Routledge.
Carroll, S. M. (2021). 'Anti-Oppressive Global Citizenship Education Theory and Practice in Pre-Service Teacher Education'. *Policy and Practice: A Development Education Review* 33(Autumn): 7–27.
Cornwall, A. and A.-M. Rivas (2015). 'From "gender equality" and "women's empowerment" to Global Justice: Reclaiming a Transformative Agenda for Gender and Development'. *Third World Quarterly* 36(2): 396–415. https://doi.org/10.1080/01436597.2015.101334
Darling-Hammond, L., M. E. Hyler and M. Gardner (2017). *Effective Teacher Professional Development*. Palo Alto: Learning Policy Institute.
Dillon, E. (2019). 'Connecting the Personal and the Political: Feminist Perspectives on Development Education'. *Policy and Practice: A Development Education Review* 29(Autumn): 11–30.
Dugarova, E. (2018). *Gender Equality as an Accelerator for Achieving the Sustainable Development Goals*. Nova Iorque: United Nations Development Programme.
Ferro, L. (2021). 'Igualdade de género – Representações sociais de actores-chave sobre as práticas e dinâmicas existentes em quatro municípios do Baixo Alentejo' (master thesis). Instituto Politécnico de Beja, Beja.
Fraser, N. (2007). 'Re-framing Justice in a Globalizing World', in T. Lovell (ed.), *(Mis) Recognition, Social Inequality and Social Justice. Nancy Fraser and Pierre Bourdieu*, 17–35. London and New York: Routledge.
Freire, P. (1994). *Pedagogy of Hope*. New York: Continuum.
Freire, P. and I. Shor (1987). *A Pedagogy for Liberation: Dialogues on Transforming Education*. Santa Barbara: Bergin-Garvey/Greenwood.
Giroux, H. (2015). *Dangerous Thinking in the Age of the New Authoritarianism*. London: Routledge.
Giroux, H. (2016). 'Beyond Pedagogies of Repression'. *Monthly Review*. https://monthlyreview.org/2016/03/01/beyond-pedagogies-of-repression/
Harper, V. (2014). 'Neoliberalism, Democracy and the University as a Public Sphere: An Interview with Henry A. Giroux'. *Policy Futures in Education* 12(8): 1078–83.
Hytten, K. (2010). 'AESA 2009 Presidential Address Cultivating Hope and Building Community: Reflections on Social Justice Activism in Educational Studies'. *Educational Studies* 46(2): 151–67.
INE (2020). 'Densidade populacional (N.º/ km²) por Local de residência (NUTS-2013); Annual'. Retrieved from: https://www.ine.pt/xportal/xmain?xpid=INE&xpgid=ine_indicadores&indOcorrCod=0008337&contexto=bd&selTab=tab2
Islam, K. and M. N. Asadullah (2018). 'Gender Stereotypes and Education: A Comparative Content Analysis of Malaysian, Indonesian, Pakistani and Bangladeshi School Textbooks'. *PloS one* 13(1). https://doi.org/10.1371/journal.pone.0190807

Jacobs, D. (2005). 'What's Hope Got to Do With It? Toward a Theory of Hope and Pedagogy'. *JAC* 25(4): 783–802.

Jones, K. (2020). *Challenging Gender Stereotypes in Education*. Thousand Oaks: SAGE Publications Ltd.

Keddie, A. (2021). 'Engaging Boys in Gender Transformative Pedagogy: Navigating Discomfort, Vulnerability and Empathy'. *Pedagogy, Culture & Society* 30(3): 401–14. doi: 10.1080/14681366.2021.1977980.

Machado de Oliveira, V. (2021). *Hospicing Modernity. Facing Humanity's Wrongs and the Implications for Social Activism*. Berkeley: North Atlantic Books. E-Book.

Office of the Special Adviser to the Secretary-General on Gender Issues and Advancement of Women (OSAGI) (2001). 'Important Concepts Underlying Gender Mainstreaming'. Retrieved from: https://www.un.org/womenwatch/osagi/pdf/factsheet2.pdf

Sensoy, O. and R. DiAngelo (2017). *Is Everyone Really Equal? An Introduction to Key Concepts in Social Justice Education*. New York: Teachers College Press.

Shiva, V. (1993). *Monocultures of the Mind: Perspectives on Biodiversity and Biotechnology*. London: Zed Books.

Sousa Santos, B. de (2007). 'Beyond Abyssal Thinking: From Global Lines to Ecologies of Knowledges'. *Binghamton University Review* 30(1): 45–89.

Unger, R. M. (1998). *Democracy Realized. The Progressive Alternative*. London: Verso.

UN Women Training Centre (2016). *Compendium of Good Practices in Training for Gender Equality*. Santo Domingo, Dominican Republic: UN Women Training Centre.

United Nations (2020). 'Goal 5: Achieve Gender Equality and Empower All Women and Girls'. Retrieved from: https://www.un.org/sustainabledevelopment/gender-equality/

United Nations Educational, Scientific and Cultural Organization (UNESCO) (2019). *Global Citizenship Education Actively Engaged Citizenship through Political Education with a Global Perspective in Nonformal and Informal Fields*. Berne: Swiss Commission for UNESCO.

United Nations Educational, Scientific and Cultural Organization (UNESCO) (2021). *Reimagining Our Futures Together. A New Social Contract for Act for Education*. Report from the International Commission on the Futures of Education. Paris: UNESCO.

Webb, D. (2017). 'Educational Archaeology and the Practice of Utopian Pedagogy'. *Pedagogy, Culture & Society* 25(4): 551–66.

Zembylas, M. (2014). 'Affective, Political and Ethical Sensibilities in Pedagogies of Critical Hope. Exploring the Notion of "critical emotional praxis"', in V. Bozalek, B. Leibowitz, R. Carolissen and M. Boler (eds), *Discerning Critical Hope in Educational Practices*, 11–25. New York: Routledge.

14

Social Justice and Hope

Teachers' Continuing Professional Development in South Africa

Joyce Raanhuis

Introduction

Teachers play an essential role within and outside their classrooms. They can be positive role models and can convey values and attitudes through their curriculum (Barrett, 2007; Sayed et al., 2017). Continuing professional development (CPD) programmes have the potential to empower teachers as agents of social justice and cohesion (see Horner et al., 2015; Mogliacci, Raanhuis and Howell, 2016; Raanhuis, 2021). However, teachers' abilities to bring social change are often influenced by their individual and collective agency, affecting their motivations, understandings, autonomy and reflexivity (Pantić, 2015). This chapter focuses on the experiences of teachers who participated in three different CPD programmes, aimed at social cohesion in post-apartheid South Africa. The chapter is guided by the following research questions:

- How do teachers experience the implementation of CPD programmes aimed at social justice and cohesion?
- How do CPD programmes contribute towards social justice and hope?

The chapter is structured as follows. It begins with an overview of the provision of education in South Africa and efforts towards social justice, followed by a discussion on CPD and the need for hope. The findings examine teachers' experiences of their CPD implementation in relation to their personal, classroom and school levels. Finally, the chapter provides a discussion and concluding thoughts on teachers' CPD experiences and their contribution towards social justice and hope.

Education in South Africa and efforts towards social justice

The quality of education during apartheid was highly influenced by racial and ethnical separation of schools, impacting how student teachers were trained (Booyse et al., 2011). The neo-Calvinist education was guided by racial and paternalistic values, which enabled teachers to uphold negative prejudices and stereotypes through their curriculum and pedagogy (Chisholm, 2019).

Since the democratic transition of 1994, policy initiatives were developed to erode racial privilege and inequality in and through education. In an attempt to create social justice, non-racism, democracy and equality, the government stressed the role of social cohesion and nation building (Abrahams, 2016). In relation to education, the Education Department formulated the concept of social cohesion through multiple dimensions, encompassing social trust, social and cultural capital, social inclusion, local history and heritage, and democratic governance and citizenship (DBE, 2011 in FHI360 and UNICEF, 2015). The pursuit of social cohesion is closely associated with efforts of social justice in education, including that access to quality schooling needs to be inclusive, democratic, and learning outcomes need to be meaningful for all learners (Tikly and Barrett, 2011).

South Africa is currently one of the most unequal countries in the world. Findings from the country's latest reconciliation barometer report show that the apartheid legacy still influences the lives of its citizens, relating to mistrust, inequality and racial division (Moosa, 2021). Despite the governments' efforts to redistribute funds for public schools, the current infrastructure and resources significantly influence the quality of education (Hatch, Buck and Omoeva, 2017; Spaull, 2019). Due to its historical legacy, teachers in South Africa are trained differently and are unequally prepared and supported to build socially just and cohesive classrooms through their pedagogical practices (Sayed et al., 2017). Therefore, CPD becomes essential to adequately support this agenda.

Continuing professional development: The need for hope

Continuing professional development plays an important role in the ongoing development of teachers. However, there is no consensus on the definition. Day (1999: p. 4) defines CPD as

All natural learning experiences and those conscious and planned activities which are intended to be of direct or indirect benefit to the individual, group or school, which contribute, through these, to the quality of education in the classroom.

This definition furthermore views CPD as an ongoing process by which teachers, review, renew and extend their commitment as change agents to the moral purpose of teaching (Day, 1999: p. 4). Traditional approaches to CPD often focus on the knowledge, skills and attitudes of teachers, to enhance teachers' beliefs, classroom practices and students' learning (see Day, 1999; Desimone, 2009). However, other interpretations of CPD criticize the limited emphasis on teachers' individual characters, needs, competencies participation and prior knowledge (see Sancar, Atal and Deryakulu, 2021).

Hope is a necessary condition for the permanent struggle for transformation that characterizes the process of humanization and thus also democratization, as it is an ontological need that motivates and orients this struggle (Freire, 2014; Morrow and Torres, 2002; Tiainen, Leiviskä and Brunila, 2019: p. 644). Although stressing its necessity, hope alone is not enough (Freire, 2014). Hope is connected to envisioning the future, as well as enabling learners with skills for social change (Bourn, 2021). Such an envisaged society unites people by a shared commitment to principles of diversity, equality and justice (Chipkin and Ngqulunga, 2008). Therefore, in this study, a sense of hope is to arrive at a cohesive society, partially fostered through participating in CPD programmes.

The participation in CPD programmes can potentially provide teachers with adequate knowledge, skills, attitudes and dispositions, which may contribute to social justice and hope (Dover et al., 2018; Kohli et al., 2015; Bourn, Hunt and Bamber, 2017). Such CPD needs to be context-specific, focusing on active learning, modelling, coaching and collaboration (Darling-Hammond, Hyler and Gardner, 2017). The programmes also need to be transformative (Mezirow, 2000), and provided over a sustained duration to allow teachers with time to internalize their new CPD learnings (Darling-Hammond, Hyler and Gardner, 2017). Teachers need to become aware of multiple knowledge systems, power dynamics, structural dynamics and decolonial perspectives (Abdi, Shultz and Pillay, 2015; Andreotti, 2011; Raanhuis, 2021). It is also essential that teachers critically reflect on their beliefs and behaviours to become reflexive practitioners (Mogliacci, Raanhuis and Howell, 2016; Pantić, 2015). Self-reflection could disrupt teachers' existing beliefs and assumptions (Charalambous, Zembylas and Charalambous, 2020; Walker and Palacios, 2016; Tibbitts and Weldon,

2017). Such CPD programmes provide spaces for teachers to confront and engage with their emotions and traumas of their past (Tibbitts and Weldon, 2017; Charalambous, Zembylas and Charalambous, 2020; Raanhuis, 2021). Engaging with emotions and traumas is important, considering that teachers can carry 'difficult knowledge' from their traumatic past (Britzman, 1998 as cited in Zembylas and Bekerman, 2018; Jansen, 2009), which impacts critical education. In South Africa, such difficult knowledge often refers to the legacy of apartheid, as teachers' lived experiences are significantly influenced by the structural violence originating from the segregated education system and the current structural inequalities (see Raanhuis, 2023; Spaull, 2019; Sayed et al., 2017; Tibbitts and Weldon, 2017).

Pedagogical approaches to hope, influenced by Freire, include that learners should be encouraged to take increasing responsibilities and freedom for their own learning (Waghid, 2008). Teachers do not impose knowledge on others, but work jointly on constructing it in an environment of mutual respect, whereby both teachers and learners are viewed as co-learners (Waghid, 2008: p. 747). Furthermore, pedagogies of hope promote a sense that change *is* possible, locate challenges in real-world experiences and go beyond superficial or quick-fix solutions to understand complex global problems (Bourn, 2021: p. 77). Such pedagogies actively engage in the process of change towards social justice and sustainability and recognize and directly address relationships of hope and hopelessness and go beyond emotional responses to issues (Bourn, 2021: p. 77).

Furthermore, teachers play a key role in promoting hope to learners, and their role can be understood as twofold. They can act as agents of change and as agents of conflict (Horner et al., 2015). Through their curriculum and pedagogy, teachers can perpetuate inequalities and violence between groups, but can also promote harmony and instil positive values (Horner et al., 2015). Their agency of change is not limited to their classroom and can extend to influencing social change within their school, their wider community and society (Bourn, 2016). Furthermore, teachers' agency for social justice and hope is influenced by their purpose, competences, autonomy and reflexivity (Pantić, 2015).

Despite policy provisions indicating the need for teachers to be equipped for social justice and cohesion, there is no overarching body which regulates CPD aimed at social justice and cohesion in South Africa (Raanhuis, 2023; Sayed et al., 2017). CPD in South Africa is provided by teachers' unions, universities, (I)NGOs and governments (SACE, 2013), whereby teachers' unions have historically played an important role in the professionalism of teachers (see Govender, 2015). However, over the past decades, CPD programmes were largely donor-funded by NGOs (Taylor, 2019). Similarly, CPD programmes relevant to social justice and hope are often designed and facilitated within the NGO sector (see Bourn, Hunt and Bamber, 2017). Tarozzi (2022: p. 90) argues that NGOs, civil society organizations and grassroots movements play a significant role in decision-making, by including critical and independent voices, new ideas, and innovative approaches into the national policy sphere. This is especially relevant for CPD programmes to social justice and hope, as it enables external voices, sensitive to the Global South to be included in national policy developments and potentially within schools (Tarozzi, 2022).

An understanding of the role of CPD providers is essential, as they can design CPD programmes based on their own interpretation of social cohesion, which may differ from the definition proposed by the government (Sayed et al., 2017). The absence of a unified framework or understanding of social cohesion can potentially have an adverse effect on teachers, leading to the disempowering of teachers in their pursuit of building social justice and hope.

Description of CPD programmes

The CPD programmes of focus in this research emphasize components of social cohesion, aiming to contribute to social justice and hope (see Raanhuis, 2023). The programmes were facilitated by the government, a teachers' union and an NGO in 2017. An overview of the three CPD programmes is provided in Table 14.1. CPD

Table 14.1 Overview of CPD Programmes and Objectives

CPD	CPD provider	Programme objectives
1.	Government	Providing teachers with a framework and strategies to identify, respond, and evaluate interventions aimed at improving school safety, to create safe school environments (Anon., 2016: p. 55).
2.	Teachers' union	Providing teachers with spaces for journaling and reflection, a set of learner-centred pedagogies, and aimed to create an awareness of individual differences, beliefs and values of teachers, and existing hegemonic school traditions (Anon., 2017a; Raanhuis, 2021).
3.	NGO	Providing teachers with practical classroom methodologies to reflect and learn about their identity and practices, the impact that implicit bias has on teachers and how their identity and biases can play out in diverse schooling contexts (Anon., 2017b).

programme 1 (Government) focused on school violence prevention. Reducing violence is essential for creating greater social cohesion (Pickett and Wilkinson, 2011). The programme was mandated by the government to be implemented nationwide, unlike programmes 2 and 3. Programmes 2 and 3 (Teachers' union and NGO) focused on elements of social cohesion, such as social relationships, values and equity – in relation to the teachers, their institutions and the community (Fonseca, Lukosch and Brazier, 2019).

Methods

This study formed part of doctoral research, which drew upon the reflections of high school teachers (n=30) who participated in three CPD programmes in Cape Town, South Africa, in 2017. All the teachers were South African nationals and racially identified themselves as black African (n=5), coloured (n=11), white (n=10), I Choose not to respond (n=3), other: African (n=1).[1] Twenty teachers were female and ten were male. Their ages ranged between twenty-six and sixty years old. They taught a wide range of subjects: history, life orientation, Afrikaans, English, IsiXhosa, accounting, life sciences, economics, business studies, physical sciences, mathematics and creative art. Subjects such as history, life orientation and languages are often perceived as carrier subjects for social cohesion (Sayed et al., 2017). However, this study included teachers who taught a range of subjects, as creating classrooms of social justice and hope requires individual and collective social action of all teachers, regardless of the subjects they teach (Navarro, 2018; Kohli et al., 2015; Raanhuis, 2021).

The teachers worked in seven different schools, one independent school and six government schools. Three government schools and one independent school were located in historically affluent communities, and three government schools in historically disadvantaged communities. The teachers took part in this research three to seven months after their CPD participation, as internalizing and implementing newly acquired CPD learnings requires time (see Darling-Hammond, Hyler and Gardner, 2017).

The ethics approvals were obtained from the university and the Education Department. To ensure anonymity and confidentiality, the names of the CPD programmes and participants were anonymized.

Qualitative methods, such as semi-structured interviews with teachers and a CPD programme manager/facilitator, field notes of classroom observations and CPD materials were used to understand the teachers' experiences of their CPD implementation. The interviews were transcribed, and the data were analysed using a discourse analysis (Gee, 2014).

Findings and discussion

Significant educational change consists of shifts in beliefs, teaching style and materials, which can come about *only* through a process of personal development in a social context (Fullan, 2007: p. 139). Considering that transformative processes towards hope are influenced at different levels, the following findings about teachers' CPD experiences will be discussed on the levels of the personal, classroom and school.

Personal level

The analysis revealed that by participating in CPD for social cohesion, teachers shifted their awareness of themselves, inequalities and injustices, and about people's different perspectives, such as that of their learners.

In some CPD programmes, teachers learned about in- and out-group biases and how this could lead to creating negative stereotypes. They learned about their prejudice and implicit bias and how this may perpetuate violence through unconscious favouritism or prejudice in their classrooms (Kuppens and Langer, 2019). Teachers' CPD participation furthermore enabled them to critically reflect upon their own experiences. Such self-reflection could potentially support teachers to become more critically conscious (Freire, 2000) of themselves and the multiple realities of others. Engaging in critical reflection made teachers aware that their worldview is not similar to that of their learners:

> remember, they [learners] walk here to school and are dealing with gang violence. Teachers did not feel threatened at all because they come to school in cars, while the learners are walking. (Afrikaans teacher (1), CPD1 (Government), 2017)

The male teacher in the aforementioned quote became increasingly aware how systemic inequalities such as race, class or gender may affect learners' behaviour, both personally and academically differently. This is important, as pedagogies of hope locate challenges in real-world experiences (Bourn, 2021). A limited understanding of their learners' social realities could potentially weaken teachers' efforts to social justice and hope. Through critical reflection, teachers increased their understanding of how history influences potential negative stereotypes, prejudice and implicit bias. Their renewed insights influenced how teachers view power dynamics and systemic challenges regarding race and inequalities, by understanding the multiple perspectives and different backgrounds of learners. However, the agency of the teachers significantly influenced how they internalized this process of raising awareness. The teachers identified themselves in different ways, in relation to their gender, race, class and work in different schooling contexts. These intersectional identities play a significant role in how the teachers perceived forms of privileges and oppression (Le Grange, 2011) through their personal or professional lives, which can influence their critical awareness and enactment towards social justice and hope.

Classroom level

The teachers indicated having become more motivated and confident in incorporating pedagogies suitable to building social justice and cohesion.

Greater levels of motivation and confidence were reported by teachers as a result of using practical methodologies of their CPD materials, to explore controversial issues related to race and inequalities. The teachers' perceived usefulness of such pedagogies was indicated by how learners could share their views about certain topics, through engaging in difficult topics in a less intrusive manner. Without the use of a more authoritarian, 'banking' form of education (Freire, 2000), teachers felt that their learners could arrive at an understanding of social justice and hope, whereby learners equally could express their opinions.

Through using their agency, teachers can influence their practices through curriculum and pedagogy (Horner et al., 2015). An increased motivation of change towards social justice was also indicated by teachers who use dialogue and by having equal relationships with their learners (Waghid, 2008). This view about teaching is similar to 'Teaching as negotiation', one of the five versions of teaching, as identified by Alexander (2009). This version of teaching reflects the Deweyan idea that teachers and learners jointly create knowledge and understanding in an ostensibly democratic learning community, rather than relate to one another as an authoritative source of knowledge and its passive recipients (Alexander, 2009: p. 11). Furthermore, some teachers described their enactment with their curriculum to promote hope:

> Now I'm thinking more about the lesson. Shakespeare for example, when it comes to the like, the black kids, it's so Eurocentric. That is a concern for me, that we don't do enough African literature ... Now it makes the kids who [felt]

less comfortable about their background, predominately non-white kids, a little more empowered. (English teacher, CPD2 (Teachers' union), 2017)

The female teacher just quoted indicated that her current curriculum was too Eurocentric. In South Africa, the colonial and apartheid curricula have always been dominated by Western epistemic ethnocentrism (see Heleta, 2016; Chisholm, 2019). Influenced by her CPD participation, the teacher recognized the importance of connecting the content of her lessons to the lives of her learners. An understanding of different perspectives and voices, whereby teachers and learners can learn from each other through their similarities and differences, can contribute towards greater social justice and hope (Andreotti and De Souza, 2008; Hughes, Loader and Nelson 2018; Freire, 2014). Heleta (2018: p. 58) argues that the use of African literature alone might not be sufficient, as one's attitudes to these materials in the curriculum are important too. However, the current curriculum is highly prescriptive and narrowly focused, which limits teachers' agency to recontextualize the content they teach (Hoadley, 2018). This can potentially pose significant difficulties for teachers to enact their newly acquired CPD learnings in their classroom settings in an effort to promote social justice and hope.

Raising an awareness of themselves significantly influenced the teachers' enactment within their classrooms. The teachers in this study felt hopeful and motivated to actively contribute towards change through their classroom practices. In some contexts, this included the use of CPD materials which supported the discussion of controversial topics, and in other contexts it was the teachers' critique of a banking model of education. Furthermore, teachers revealed that an increased awareness of the importance to recontextualize their knowledge to the lives of their learners. However, the prescribed curriculum might limit teachers in the enactment of their new CPD learnings to promote social justice and hope in their classrooms.

School level

The majority of teachers in this study stated that their CPD participation raised awareness of themselves, shifted beliefs and classroom practices. However, their action towards social justice and cohesion was highly influenced by institutional factors. Learner-centred pedagogies, such as group work, are often viewed to be conducive to social justice and cohesion (Tikly, 2020; UNESCO-IICBA, 2017). However, teachers' abilities to incorporate such pedagogies are influenced by contextual factors relating to the schools' infrastructure and working conditions (Hatch, Buck and Omoeva, 2017; FHI360 and UNICEF, 2015). As a legacy of apartheid, such factors still influence the quality of teaching (Sayed et al., 2017). Therefore, to provide teachers with pedagogies towards hope, it is essential that CPD is context-specific and applicable to a range of schooling environments.

Furthermore, time constraints hampered teachers' efforts to share their new CPD learnings with peers. Most teachers indicated to have discussed the content of the programme with other colleagues. However, only a few teachers said that the CPD content was disseminated to the rest of their peers, which highlights the potential shortfalls of peer learning through informal or formal CPD initiatives in the school (Evans, 2018), and risks the 'fading-out' of newly acquired CPD learnings (Wolf and Peele, 2019). If teachers are unable to share their new CPD strategies with peers, it can be difficult to embark on transformation that goes beyond personal and classroom practices:

> There are times when I'm very much confronted when I do stuff where . . . remember the predominant culture here is the English and white culture. [. . .] So, but at the end of the day the person who is coming into the dominant culture must be brave enough to stand up, but also respectful enough. (Afrikaans teacher (2), CPD2 (NGO), 2017)

The female teacher just quoted describes her experiences as a minority within her school. This institutional context can significantly influence the utilization of newly acquired CPD learnings (Raanhuis, 2021; Zembylas and Bekerman, 2012). Implementing CPD strategies whereby hegemonic school cultures and traditions need to be changed might be even more challenging, as personal and institutional change requires time (Darling-Hammond, Hyler and Gardner, 2017; Mogliacci, Raanhuis and Howell, 2016). To navigate this change process, ongoing support from school leaders is essential to foster this process within the school (Molla and Gale, 2019).

Whereas awareness on a personal level may influence teachers' pedagogical enactment towards global social justice and hope, institutional influences, such as the school culture or resources, may hinder teachers in their efforts towards social change. As a sense of hope is to arrive at a cohesive society that unites teachers by shared commitment to principles of diversity, equality and injustice (Chipkin and Ngqulunga, 2008), it is key that CPD includes components that focus on the opposite of hope, leading to greater global social justice. This includes teachers' critical reflections on their own discomfort of their painful and traumatic past, and the ability to redress inequalities and dispossessions within education (see Moosa, 2021; Tibbitts and Weldon, 2017. It should not be the burden of individual teachers and requires collective action of all teachers, as it is often difficult to transform institutional cultures. In addition, such CPD programmes should be context-specific and include guided approaches on how to dismantle institutional cultures (see Raanhuis, 2021). As the transformation of institutional cultures requires time, long-term efforts towards institutional change and follow-up support are essential.

Conclusion

The chapter showed how the participation in CPD has played an influenced role for teachers at a personal, classroom and school level, to act as agents of change towards social justice and hope. In countries with a divided past, such as South Africa, it is essential to be aware of their traumatic past and focus on hope through their pedagogical practices. The content of CPD programmes may provide teachers with sources of hope. Similarly, their participation in such CPD programmes has the potential to provide teachers with a sense of hope in order to learn the knowledge, skills, attitudes and dispositions to bring about social change.

This study did not look at the long-term outcomes of the CPD programmes. Further research could investigate the long-term effects of such CPD programmes. The study found that CPD programmes focusing on beliefs and attitudes can support teachers to become more cognisant of their prejudice and implicit biases. However, teachers' oppression and privileges need to be viewed in relation to their intersectional identities, including race, class, gender and location. These identities significantly influence their ability or inability to bring about social change that goes beyond awareness-raising and classroom practices.

Renewed insights about understanding multiple viewpoints, power dynamics and inequality are essential aspects for social justice and hope. The implementation of newly acquired CPD learnings supported teachers in discussing controversial topics in a non-intrusive manner. However, the current prescribed curriculum might pose difficulties to teachers' abilities to recontextualize the content of their curriculum. This may hamper teachers' efforts to jointly construct knowledge with learners, by using real-world experiences to enable learners to understand the complexity of global problems through different perspectives. Teachers highlighted their role as facilitators in guiding classroom discussions and described their awareness and enactment to change their curriculum by including different forms of knowledges. However, they may feel a sense of despair when they are unable to implement their newly acquired CPD learnings due to their institutional context and structures.

As CPD aims to equip teachers with tools for social justice and hope, it is important that all teachers are trained to take collective actions in these ways. CPD programmes need to be mindful of the contexts in which teachers work. This includes how hegemonic institutional cultures and power dynamics within the school influence their ability to act as agents of social justice and hope. As part of CPD programmes for social justice and hope, a whole-school approach with guided approaches on how to dismantle institutional cultures is therefore essential. Furthermore, the CPD programmes in this study were designed and facilitated by different providers. As CPD providers emphasize different aspects of social justice and cohesion, it may take a limited approach to adequately support teachers with competences of social justice and hope, in line with the governments' objectives. Therefore, CPD programmes may potentially be more beneficial when CPD providers unify efforts and goals towards social justice and cohesion.

Funding

The work reported in this chapter was supported by the generous financial assistance of the National Research Foundation (NRF), which funds the South African Research Chair in Teacher Education, Centre for International Teacher Education (CITE), Cape Peninsula University of Technology (CPUT). In addition, CPUT provided a further Postgraduate Bursary. Opinions expressed in this chapter and the conclusions resulting from these studies are those of the authors and are not necessarily to be attributed to the South African Research Chair in Teacher Education, National Research Foundation or CPUT.

Note

1 The author understands race to be socially constructed. However, this chapter uses the official categories of 'black', 'coloured', 'Indian' and 'white'. These categories were opposed under apartheid and not set by the author. In self-identifying racial backgrounds, teachers could choose between 'black African', 'coloured', 'Indian',

'white', 'other' and 'I choose not to respond'. The author uses these categories as markers of inequities but does not endorse the use of these categories.

References

Abdi, A. A., L. Shultz and T. Pillay (2015). *Decolonizing Global Citizenship Education*. Rotterdam: Sense Publishers.

Abrahams, C. (2016). 'Twenty Years of Social Cohesion and Nation-Building in South Africa'. *Journal of Southern African Studies* 42(1): 95–107.

Alexander, R. J. (2009). 'Toward a Comparative Pedagogy', in R. Cowen and A. M. Kazamias (eds), *International Handbook of Comparative Education*, 923–42. Dordrecht: Springer.

Andreotti, V. (2011). '(Towards) Decoloniality and Diversality in Global Citizenship Education'. *Globalisation, Societies and Education* 9(3–4): 381–97.

Andreotti, V. and L. M. de Souza (2008). 'Translating Theory into Practice and Walking Minefields: Lessons from the Project "Through Other Eyes"'. *International Journal of Development Education and Global Learning* 1(1): 23–36.

Anonymous (2016). Programme document CPD1.

Anonymous (2017a). Programme overview CPD2.

Anonymous (2017b). Programme overview CPD3.

Barrett, A. M. (2007), 'Beyond the Polarization of Pedagogy: Models of Classroom Practice in Tanzanian Primary Schools'. *Comparative Education* 43(2): 273–94.

Bekerman, Z. and M. Zembylas (2012). *Teaching Contested Narratives: Identity, Memory and Reconciliation in Peace Education and Beyond*. Cambridge: Cambridge University Press.

Booyse, J. J., C. S. Le Roux, J. Seroto and C. C. Wolhuter (2011). *A History of Schooling in South Africa: Method and Context*. Pretoria: Van Schaik.

Bourn, D. (2016). 'Teachers as Agents of Social Change'. *International Journal of Development Education and Global Learning* 7(3): 63–77.

Bourn, D. (2021). 'Pedagogy of Hope: Global Learning and the Future of Education'. *International Journal of Development Education and Global Learning* 13(2): 65–78.

Bourn, D., F. Hunt and P. Bamber (2017). 'A Review of Education for Sustainable Development and Global Citizenship Education in Teacher Education', in *Paper Commissioned for the 2017/8 Global Education Monitoring Report, Accountability in Education: Meeting Our Commitments*. UNESCO.

Britzman, D. P. (1988). *Lost Subjects, Contested Objects: Toward a Psychoanalytic Inquiry of Learning*. Albany: State University of New York Press.

Charalambous, C., M. Zembylas and P. Charalambous (2020). 'Reconciliation Pedagogies and Critical Ambivalence in Teacher Professional Development: Insights from a Case Study in Cyprus'. *Journal of Peace Education* 17(2): 208–33.

Chipkin, I. and B. Ngqulunga (2008). 'Friends and Family: Social Cohesion in South Africa'. *Journal of Southern African Studies* 34(1): 61–76.

Chisholm, L. (2019). *Teacher Preparation in South Africa: History, Policy and Future Directions*. Bingley: Emerald Group Publishing.

Darling-Hammond, L., M. E. Hyler and M. Gardner (2017). *Effective Teacher Professional Development*. Palo Alto: Learning Policy Institute.

Day, C. (1999). *Developing Teachers: The Challenges of Lifelong Learning*. London: Falmer.

Desimone, L. M. (2009). 'Improving Impact Studies of Teachers' Professional Development: Toward better Conceptualizations and Measures'. *Educational Researcher* 38(3): 181–99.

Dover, A. G., N. Henning, R. Agarwal-Rangnath and E. K. Dotson (2018). 'It's Heart Work: Critical Case Studies, Critical Professional Development, and Fostering Hope among Social Justice–Oriented Teacher Educators'. *Multicultural Perspectives* 20(4): 229–39.

Evans, L. (2018). 'Implicit and Informal Professional Development: What it "looks like", How It Occurs, and Why We Need to Research It'. *Professional Development in Education* 45(1): 3–16.

FHI 360 & United Nations International Children's Emergency Fund (UNICEF) (2015). *Investment in Equity and Peacebuilding: South African Case Study*. New York: Learning for Peace; UNICEF.

Fonseca, X., S. Lukosch and F. Brazier (2019). 'Social Cohesion Revisited: A New Definition and How to Characterize It'. *Innovation: The European Journal of Social Science Research* 32(2): 231–53.

Freire, P. (2000). *Pedagogy of the oppressed*. New York: Continuum.

Freire, P. (2014). *Pedagogy of Hope. Reliving Pedagogy of the Oppressed*. London: Bloomsbury Publishing.

Fullan, M. (2007). *The New Meaning of Educational Change*. New York: Routledge.

Gee, J. P. (2014). *How to do Discourse Analysis: A Toolkit*. London: Routledge.

Govender, L. (2015). 'Teacher Unions' Participation in Policy Making: A South African Case Study'. *Compare: A Journal of Comparative and International Education* 45(2): 184–205.

Hatch, R., E. Buck and C. Omoeva (2017). 'The Limits of Redistributive School Finance Policy in South Africa'. *Journal on Education in Emergencies* 3(1): 79–105.

Heleta, S. (2016). 'Decolonisation of Higher Education: Dismantling Epistemic Violence and Eurocentrism in South Africa'. *Transformation in Higher Education* 1(1): 1–9.

Heleta, S. (2018). 'Decolonizing Knowledge in South Africa: Dismantling the "pedagogy of big lies"'. *Ufahamu: A Journal of African Studies* 40(2): 47–65.

Hoadley, U. (2018). *Pedagogy in Poverty: Lessons from Twenty Years of Curriculum Reform in South Africa*. Oxon: Routledge.

Horner, L., L. Kadiwal, Y. Sayed, A. Barrett, N. Durrani and M. Novelli (2015). *Literature Review: The Role of Teachers in Peacebuilding*. London: UNICEF–ESRC.

Hughes, J., R. Loader and J. Nelson (2018). 'Fostering Harmony and Dealing with Difference in Education: A Critical Review of Perspectives on Intergroup Relations', in A. Keet and M. Zembylas (eds), *Critical Human Rights, Citizenship, and Democracy Education: Entanglements and Regenerations*, 123–38. London: Bloomsbury.

Jansen, J. (2009). *Knowledge in the Blood: Confronting Race and the Apartheid Past*. Stanford: Stanford University Press.

Kohli, R., B. Picower, A. N. Martinez and N. Ortiz (2015). 'Critical Professional Development: Centering the Social Justice Needs of Teachers'. *The International Journal of Critical Pedagogy* 6(2): 7–24.

Kuppens, L. and A. Langer (2019). 'Building Social Cohesion through Education in Africa? Lessons from Côte d'Ivoire and Kenya', in H. Hino, A. Langer, J. Lonsdale and F. Stewart (eds), *From Divided Pasts to Cohesive Futures. Reflections on Africa*, 322–45. Cambridge: Cambridge University Press.

Le Grange, L. (2011). 'A Pedagogy of Hope after Paulo Freire'. *South African Journal of Higher Education* 25(1): 183–9.

Mezirow, J. (2000). *Learning as Transformation: Critical Perspectives on a Theory in Progress. The Jossey-Bass Higher and Adult Education Series*. San Francisco: Jossey-Bass Publishers.

Mogliacci, R. J., J. Raanhuis and C. Howell (2016). 'Supporting Teachers in Becoming Agents of Social Cohesion: Professional Development in Post-apartheid South Africa'. *Education as Change* 20(3): 160–79.

Molla, T. and T. Gale (2019). 'Positional Matters: School Leaders Engaging with National Equity Agendas'. *Journal of Education Policy* 34(6): 858–76.

Moosa, M. (2021). *SA Reconciliation Barometer Survey: 2021 Report*. Cape Town: Institute for Justice and Reconciliation.

Morrow, R. A. and C. A. Torres (2002). *Reading Freire and Habermas: Critical Pedagogy and Transformative Social Change*. New York: Teachers College Press.

Navarro, N. (2018). 'We Can't do this Alone: Validating and Inspiring Social Justice Teaching through a Community of Transformative Praxis'. *Curriculum Inquiry* 48(3): 335–58.

Pantić, N. (2015). 'A Model for Study of Teacher Agency for Social Justice'. *Teachers and Teaching* 21(6): 759–78.

Pickett, K. and R. Wilkinson (2011). *The Spirit Level: Why Greater Equality Makes Societies Stronger*. New York: Bloomsbury Press.

Raanhuis, J. (2021). 'Empowering Teachers as Agents of Social Cohesion: Continuing Professional Development in Post-apartheid South Africa'. *Policy & Practice: A Development Education Review* 33: 28–51.

Raanhuis, J. (2023). 'Teachers' Views of Continuing Professional Developmenbt Related to Social Cohesion in the Western Cape, South Africa', Unpublished doctoral thesis, Cape Town: Cape Peninsula University of Technology.

Sancar, R., D. Atal and D. Deryakulu (2021). 'A New Framework for Teachers' Professional Development'. *Teaching and Teacher Education* 101: 1–12.

Sayed, Y., A. Badroodien, Y. Omar, L. Balie, Z. Mcdonald, T. De Kock, T. Salmon, J. Raanhuis, M. Singh, N. Robinson and T. Nakidien (2017). 'Engaging teachers in peacebuilding in post-conflict contexts: Evaluating education interventions in South Africa'. South Africa Country Report: ESRC/DFID Research Report. Brighton: University of Sussex.

South African Council for Educators (SACE) (2013). 'Continuing Professional Teacher Development (CPTD) Management System Overview'. http://www.sace.org.za/upload/files/CPTD%20Handbook.pdf (accessed 7 February 2017).

Spaull, N. (2019). 'Equity: A Price Too High to Pay', in N. Spaull and J. Jansen (eds), *South African Schooling: The Enigma of Inequality*, 1–24. Cham: Springer Nature.

Tarozzi, M. (2022). 'Implementing Global Citizenship Education Policy: The Bargaining Process of NGOs in Some European Countries'. *Journal of Global Education and Research* 6(1): 82–97.

Taylor, N. (2019). 'Inequalities in Teacher Knowledge in South Africa', in N. Spaull and J. Jansen (eds), *South African Schooling: The Enigma of Inequality*, 1–24. Cham: Springer Nature.

Tiainen, K., A. Leiviskä and K. Brunila (2019). 'Democratic Education for Hope: Contesting the Neoliberal Common Sense'. *Studies in Philosophy and Education* 38(6): 641–55.

Tibbitts, F. and G. Weldon (2017). 'History Curriculum and Teacher Training: Shaping a Democratic Future in Post-apartheid South Africa?' *Comparative Education* 53(3): 442–61.

Tikly, L. (2020). *Education for Sustainable Development in the Postcolonial World: Towards a Transformative Agenda for Africa*. Oxon: Routledge.

Tikly, L. and A. M. Barrett (2011). 'Social Justice, Capabilities and the Quality of Education in Low Income Countries'. *International Journal of Education Development* 31: 3–14.

UNESCO-IICBA (2017). *Transformative Pedagogy for Peace Building: A Guide for Teachers*. Addis Ababa: UNESCO-IICBA.

Waghid, Y. (2008). 'Higher Education Transformation and a Pedagogy of Hope'. *South African Journal of Higher Education* 22(4): 745–8.

Walker, J. and C. Palacios (2016). 'A Pedagogy of Emotion in Teaching about Social Movement Learning'. *Teaching in Higher Education* 21(2): 175–90.

Wolf, S. and M. E. Peele (2019). 'Examining Sustained Impacts of Two Teacher Professional Development Programs on Professional Well-being and Classroom Practices'. *Teaching and Teacher Education* 86: 102873.

Zembylas, M. and Z. Bekerman (2018). 'Engaging with Teachers' Difficult Knowledge, Seeking Moral Repair: The Entanglement of Moral and Peace Education'. *Journal of Peace Education* 16(2): 155–74.

Conclusion

Pedagogy of Hope for Global Social Justice

Douglas Bourn

Introduction

This final chapter of the volume aims to remind the readers of why the themes of hope and global social justice are so important to education in the third decade of the twenty-first century. Central to the themes of this chapter is the need to develop and implement a pedagogical approach that situates learning within real-world issues and contexts and give suggestions as to ways these points can become an essential component of education around the world.

The 2020s have already included some major global events that have questioned every optimistic notion and hope we may have. The climate emergency already evident in the earlier decades of the century has become heightened by the increases in global temperatures, the rise in weather extremes and consequential impacts upon many societies and cultures. The global pandemic as a result of Covid-19 has had an impact upon all societies around the world. It has shown the extent to which we are all globally connected but, as noted in earlier chapters in this volume, the poor and vulnerable have been disproportionately affected by it (Kharas, 2020). In 2022, war in Europe returned through the invasion by the Russian army to Ukraine which potentially could lead to wider conflicts across the continent.

There was evidence in many countries of increased anxieties by young people particularly of the consequences of these events (Duarte, 2020; UK Council for Psychotherapy, 2020).

The assumption of social and economic progress for all was being challenged. Educationalists were faced with having to adapt quickly to addressing these issues, having to promote a sense of optimism and that change is possible against a barrage of pessimistic media comments.

The engagement of many thousands of young people to addressing the climate emergency through Fridays for the Future has been one example of the positive responses that have taken place around the world (UKSCN, 2020). Similar social movements can be seen around Black Lives Matter and the #MeToo campaign.

What this shows is that through a sense of solidarity and collective social action, not only can policies which harm the planet and discriminate against social groups be challenged, there can also be change through the popular engagement of people regardless of the positioning and policies of governments and international institutions.

Education is, however, more than acting as the fuel for social action. It must have value in itself in providing learners with the knowledge, skills and values base to address the challenges they are facing. This means, as this chapter will now aim to show, that education needs to have a social purpose at its heart. There is a need to move from the neoliberal emphasis on individualism, competition, testing and assessment to an educational approach that is based on a sense of collectivism, of social and public good and that puts social justice at its heart.

Relevance of ideas of Paulo Freire

Several of the early chapters in this volume made reference to the ideas of Paulo Freire and his pedagogy of hope. To Freire, education has to have social meaning and be relevant to the needs of the world. Only through a process of dialogue and social engagement can education play a role in building new societies. Hope to Freire has to be central to this approach, but it should be grounded in social realities and not in some idealistic notions. This means understanding issues and showing how change is possible. Climate change, for example, should be understood first before engaging in forms of social action. It also means in the process of engagement addressing the fears that many people may have about a climate crisis.

As Freire himself stated (2004: p. 9), 'One of the tasks of the progressive educator is to unveil opportunities for hope, no matter what the obstacles may be.' For Freire, however, hope had to be related to social change and forms of collective action.

Henry Giroux (2011), in developing Freire's ideas, suggested the term 'educated hope'. Only through education can people see what is possible to achieve within the existing social conditions.

An earlier chapter in this volume by Greg Misiaszek develops these ideas further by showing their relevance to environmental concerns and what he calls ecopedagogy. Misiaszek (2021) had also emphasized that for change to take place within societies, hope was essential. While he notes that students can dream of environmental utopias their thinking must be grounded in real-world issues and a sense of justice.

It is this connection between hope and social justice that has been the main theme of this volume. Linking hope and social justice ensures moving beyond idealistic and individualistic notions of improvement to an approach to learning that ensures engagement with real-world dilemmas.

From despair to sense of hope

Education should be seen as a 'future-orientated project' (Halpin, 2003: p. 16), but for many teachers this promotion of a sense of optimism may not be easy with the many constraints they have as a result of the influence of neoliberalism and emphasis on performance, accountability and examinations (Giroux, 2011; Beck, 2000). There is also the view that hope can create a sense of unrealism and feel good feelings (Levitas, 1990; Zaleski, 1994). Lazarus, however, suggests that if hope also includes a sense of commitment and enthusiasm for change and has a clear educational function, then there is greater possibility for social change (Lazarus, 1991).

As Giroux has commented if this sense of hope is located within real social experiences then it can be seen as distinctly pedagogical approach (Giroux, 2002: p. 102). This also means ensuring that the process of learning engaged with a range of desirable futures, assessed them critically and gave the learner the appropriate skills to actively engage in processes of change.

Futures thinking should therefore be seen as a central component of moving from despair to a pedagogy of hope. As Kool (2017) notes:

> Our work as educators is not to lead our students to face the future with despair, nor is it to live in a Panglossian sense of optimism. The future is going to pose serious dangers to our societies and the diversity of life in earth, and we need ways of imagining the future(s) our children will want to live in, grounded in the realities of today. (Kool, 2017: p. 141)

Dave Hicks, a leading UK figure in the development of global education, summarized this approach as sharing, listening, understanding and acting. He used the example of climate change of the context for this approach to learning, enabling learners to share their feelings about climate change, to listen to range of views, understand what climate change means and finally knowing what could be done to secure change (Hicks, 2018: p. 8). A key component of his approach was the development in learners the skills to engage in movements for change (Hicks, 2014).

Perhaps these comments from Kelly summarize well the role of educators in addressing this theme of hope:

> In re-thinking young people's futures, we need to plan and act in terms beyond the simplicity of being either optimistic or pessimistic. What we need is an exercise in HOPE. . . . Hope is a much more radical and productive act. Hope enables us to look critically at the past, whilst simultaneously acknowledging the reality of present, and, in so doing, providing us with the capacity to envision and radically transform our future. (Kelly, 2021)

Role of the Sustainable Development Goals and Target 4.7

Several of the chapters in this volume have made reference to the opportunities created by the UN Sustainable Development Goals which were launched in 2015 and were seen as providing a common goal for a more just and sustainable world. However, despite some marginal impact on some countries (United Nations, 2020), they have not so far led to any significant discussions or policy changes or discussions on the purpose of education. The lack of progress has not been helped by the failure to tackle the dominance of neoliberalism within education resulting in continued dominance of market forces (Belda-Miguel, Boni and Calabuig, 2019).

Target 4.7 within the Goals has been seen, however, as a potential focus for mobilizing educationalists around the world towards putting sustainable development and social justice themes at the heart of learning. The Target states:

> By 2030, ensure that all learners acquire the knowledge and skills needed to promote sustainable development, including, among others, through education for sustainable development and sustainable lifestyles, human rights, gender equality, promotion of a culture of peace and non-violence, global citizenship and appreciation of cultural diversity and of culture's contribution to sustainable development.[1]

In England this focus on Target 4.7 has galvanized over 300 civil society organizations to engage in debate and promoting to policymakers a vision of education in the future that not only connects to real-world issues but also provides opportunities for a new pedagogy based on participatory and learner-centred approaches to the school curriculum (Bourn and Hatley, 2022).

This focus on Target 4.7 also resulted in a major civil society organizations initiative across Europe which, while promoting the importance and value of global citizenship education, suggested moving towards a more transformative approach to learning. This initiative was called Bridge 47 (https://www.bridge47.org).

What is significant about both of these initiatives has been a more holistic and intersectional approach to learning which has led to discussions about the purpose of education. For example, one of the key publications from the Bridge 47 network suggests that Target 4.7 provides an opportunity to bring together what have tended to be separate educational fields into an overarching transformative learning approach (Arbeiter and Bucar, 2021). The evidence in England for the network of civil society organizations, Our Shared World, demonstrates the growing interest in encouraging a move away from an economically driven educational agenda to one that focused more on needs of society (Bourn and Hatley, op.cit). These themes also connect to debates within UNESCO who have been referring to moral purpose and a sense of hope (Sobe, 2021). These themes, as noted by UNESCO, were brought into greater relief during the global pandemic and the need to respond to the climate change crisis:

> The current crisis is reminding us how crucial public education is in societies, communities, and in individual lives. We have been reminded that education is a bulwark against inequality—and of the importance of schooling in enabling lives of dignity and purpose. As we embrace this exceptional opportunity to transform the world, and as we reimagine the organization of our educational institutions and learning environments, we will need to think about what we want to become. We have arrived at a moment—however unexpectedly—where collectively revisiting the purposes of education and organization of learning has become imperative. (UNESCO, 2020: p. 11)

Challenges from climate change

As suggested earlier, an influential driver in these calls for changes within education has been the growth in interest and engagement in climate change issues. Around the world as a result of campaigns and awareness-raising initiatives by many thousands of young people, policymakers, academics, researchers and practitioners have recognized not only how important it is to raise awareness of the threat of climate change but also the central role education should play. In England, which for a long time resisted calls for climate change to have a higher status within the school curriculum, the Ministry for education produced a strategy that calls for climate change and sustainability be part of the learning of all school pupils. The Minister for Education in launching the draft strategy stated:

> Education is critical to fighting climate change. We have both the responsibility and privilege of educating and preparing young people for a changing world – ensuring they are equipped with the right knowledge, understanding and skills to meet their biggest challenge head on. (Department for Education, 2021: p. 5)

This draft strategy goes no further than focusing on greater emphasis on themes in geography and science. However, such strategies do by their very existence pose questions about the role of education in addressing social themes, of playing a proactive role in equipping learners to be actively engaged in processes of social change regardless of the aims of the politicians.

The actions of many thousands of young people in 2018 and 2019 not only wished to raise awareness of the climate emergency with policymakers, they believed they had a broader educative function that change was possible and a more just and sustainable future is a realistic goal to work towards (UKSCN, 2020; Yeung, 2020).

Contribution of global education and learning

All of the chapters in this volume have made reference to the role of global education and learning and global citizenship education as providing the tools and framework to encourage a pedagogy of hope for global social justice. These fields of learning have common conceptual roots around global social justice, learner-centred and participatory-based pedagogies, challenging dominant orthodoxies and a sense of empowerment to be active global citizens (see Bourn, 2020; Hartmeyer and Wegimont, 2016; Tarozzi and Torres, 2016; Sant et al., 2018).

What is also evident from a number of chapters in this volume is that what were once regarded as European- and North American–based fields have become much more global and relevant to educational and social debates in Latin America, sub-Saharan Africa and East Asia. Global education and learning and global citizenship education provide a pedagogical approach grounded in social justice.

But perhaps what has been neglected within some of the discourses in and around global education and learning is a future-orientated approach, giving a sense of hope and optimism and located this engagement in real-world issues. This means that in bringing into debates postcolonial thinking for example, it needs to be done in a way that moves beyond a 'guilt mentality' approach to one of showing not only that change is possible but also how this change can be achieved.

Numerous examples from the practices of civil society and international organizations show the connections between learning, understanding, engagement and social action. One example from the UK that shows this approach is that of UNICEF and their Youth Advocacy Toolkit which aims to support 'young people to speak up' and help 'them actively take part in the decisions that affect them' through the following pedagogical approach:

> Explore: identify the problem in terms of what needs to change. Outline your vision and research and analyse the issue.
>
> Think: what steps need to be taken to progress the issue and identify who has the power and who can make a difference.
>
> Act: what do you need to do and what do you need to say and devise an advocacy plan.
>
> Evaluate: what were the lessons from the actions? (UNICEF UK, 2020: p. 3).

Another example is Oxfam UK, who through their education for global citizenship programme make reference to themes such as transformation, understanding different worldviews, being critical thinkers and acting as agents of change. A feature of their pedagogical approach is a learner-centred and participatory methodology:

> Education for global citizenship uses a multitude of participatory teaching and learning methodologies, including discussion and debate, role play, ranking exercises, cause and consequence activities, and communities of enquiry. These methods are not unique to education for global citizenship but, used in conjunction with a global perspective, they can advance global understanding while fostering skills such as critical thinking, questioning, communication and cooperation. (OXFAM, 2016: p. 9)

A criticism that has made of the activities of some civil society organizations is that their educational materials can be too prescriptive, encouraging learners to follow a linear path of engagement in an uncritical way. What is significant about

Oxfam's approach is the emphasis it gives to 'learning- thinking- action', giving emphasis to critical thinking and multiple perspectives.

Importance of research

The field of global education and learning, while having a long tradition among civil society organizations, particularly in Europe and North America, has only became recognized within educational research in more recent times. A number of academic journals have been created since 2000 that cover the field. The creation of the Academic Network of Global Education and Learning (ANGEL)[2] in 2017 and its engagement with several hundred academics around the world demonstrates the extent to which the field is now global. This can be seen by the range of contributions in this volume.

What a number of the chapters in this volume also demonstrate is the importance of research. Policymakers who have supported global education and learning have tended to focus on evidence provided by civil society organizations. With the creation of a number of academic journals,[3] the existence of ANGEL and major expansion of articles, books and doctoral theses in the field, there is now a strong body of independent research as can be seen in the annual *Global Education Digest*.

The value and importance of research can be seen in a number of chapters in this volume particularly the ones from Menzie-Ballantyne et al., Shultz and Tarozzi, Frantz, Saude and Ferro, Scheunpflug et al. and Hunt and Blum. They demonstrate in different ways how the global education and learning sector is reflecting broader debates within education regarding the quality of teaching, relevance to social issues and value of participatory approaches. This independent approach to research as opposed to providing evidence to support evaluations of projects is a theme of many of these chapters.

Theoretical clarity

For research in global education and learning to be valued and recognized within mainstream debates, the field needs to have distinctive theoretical frameworks and models upon which any empirical research is based. The field of global education and learning has in the past been rightly criticized for its lack of a theoretical basis (Reimers, 2020; Marshall, 2007), but, as several of the chapters in this volume show, there is today considerable progress from a range of perspective on the influences and themes of its conceptual development.

What is evident from the theoretical debates are the continuing references to terms such as 'global social justice', 'postcolonialism', 'connections to sustainable development', 'peace' and 'human rights'.

Global social justice can only be effective, as this chapter has aimed to highlight, if it is linked to a pedagogical approach that is participatory, progressive and optimistic. This is where hope comes in as more than just an ideal goal but as part of the process of learning.

Conclusion

This final chapter has aimed to demonstrate how key a pedagogy of hope and global social justice are to education today. In doing so, this chapter has shown why and where the field of global education and learning contributes to this. But above all at a time of increased uncertainty and insecurity in the world and rise in anxieties about the future particularly among young people, then encouraging and support a distinctive pedagogy of hope based on global social justice has become more relevant and important than it has ever been before.

Educators have a challenge and a major role to play as optimists, facilitators, energizers and perhaps even inspirers to all learners in promoting and delivering this pedagogy. This is not an easy task but as all the chapters in this volume demonstrate, there is a clear desire from leading educationalists around the world for this to happen, and there is evidence of a thirst for knowledge and skills to bring about a more just and sustainable planet.

Notes

1 https://unstats.un.org/sdgs/metadata/?Text=&Goal=4&Target=4.7
2 www.angel-network.net
3 These include *International Journal of Development Education and Global Learning*; ZEP: Die Zeitschrift für internationale Bildungsforschung und Entwicklungspädagogik; Sinergias; *Journal of Global Education and Research* and *Journal of Global Citizenship and Equity Education*.

References

Arbeiter, J. and M. Bucar (2021). *Transformative Education- Bridging Education for Change*. Helsinki: Bridge 47.

Beck, U. (2000). *What Is Globalization?* Cambridge: Polity.

Belda-Miquel, S., A. Boni and C. Calabuig (2019). 'SDG Localisation and Decentralised Development Aid: Exploring Opposing Discourses and Practices in Valencia's Aid Sector'. *Journal of Human Development and Capabilities* 20(4): 386–402.

Bourn, D. and J. Hatley (2022). 'Evidence of Impact of Target 4.7 of the Sustainable Development Goals in Schools in England'. Development Education Research Centre Paper 22, London, UCL and Our Shared World. Available at https://discovery.ucl.ac.uk/id/eprint/10147491/1/OSW%20report_Revised.pdf

Bridge 47 (2020). 'Envision 4.7 Road Map'. https://www.bridge47.org/sites/default/files/2020-01/envision_4.7_roadmap_0.pdf (accessed 3 March 2021).

Department for Education (2021). *Education for Climate Change and Sustainability Draft Action Plan*. London: HMSO.

Duarte, C. (2020). *Don't Despair: Use the Pandemic as a Springboard to Environmental Action*. www.theguardian.com/commentisfree/2020/jul/11/pandemic- (accessed 2 March 2021).

Freire, P. (2004). *Pedagogy of Hope*. New York: Continuum.

Giroux, H. (2002). 'Educated Hope in Age of Privatized Visions'. *Cultural Studies-Critical Methodologies* 2(1): 93–112.

Giroux, H. (2011). *On Critical Pedagogy*. New York: Continuum.

Halpin, D. (2003). *Hope and Education: The Role of the Utopian Imagination*. London: Routledge-Falmer.

Hartmeyer, H. and L. Wegimont, eds (2016). *Global Education in Europe Revisted*. Munster: Waxmann.

Hicks, D. (2014). *Educating for Hope in Troubled Times. Climate Change and the Transition to a Post-carbon Future*. London: Trentham Books.

Hicks, D. (2018). 'Why We Still Need a Geography of Hope'. *Geography* 103(2): 78–85.

Kelly, P. (2021). 'Covid-19 and Young People's Recovery: An Exercise in Hope, RSA'. https://www.thersa.org/comment/2021/03/covid-19-young-peoples-recovery

Kharas, H. (2020). 'The Impact of COVID-19 on Global Extreme Poverty'. https://www.brookings.edu/blog/future-development/2020/10/21/the-impact-of-covid-19-on-global-extreme-poverty/ (accessed 2 Marsh 2020).

Kool, R. (2017) 'If the Past Is a Foreign Country, What Is the Future? The Necessity of Understanding the Past, Confronting the Present, and Envisioning the Future', in P. Corcoran, J. P. Weakland and A. Wals (eds), *Envisioning Futures for Environmental and Sustainability Education*, 141–50. Wageningen: Wageningen Publs.

Lazarus, R. S. (1991). *Emotion and Adaptation*. New York: Oxford University Press.

Levitas, R. (1990). 'Educated Hope: Ernst Bloch on Abstract and Concrete Utopia'. *Utopian Studies* 1(2): 13–26.

Marshall, H. (2007). 'Global Education in Perspective: Fostering a Global Dimension in an English Secondary School'. *Cambridge Journal of Education* 37(3): 355–74.

Misiaszek, G. (2021). *Ecopedagogy*. London: Bloomsbury.

Oxfam (2016). *Education for Global Citizenship: Guide for Schools*. Oxford: Oxfam.

Reimers, F. (2020). *Educating Students to Improve the World*. Singapore: Springer.

Sant, E., I. Davies, K. Pashby and L. Shultz (2018). *Global Citizenship Education*. London: Bloomsbury.

Sobe, N. W. (2021). 'Reworking Four Pillars of Education to Sustain the Commons'. *UNESCO Futures of Education Ideas LAB*. https://en.unesco.org/futuresofeducation/ideas-lab/sobe-reworking-four-pillars-education-sustain-commons

Tarozzi, M. and C. Torres (2016). *Global Citizenship Education and the Crises of Multiculturalism*. London: Bloomsbury.

UKSCN (2020). 'Our Demands'. https://ukscn.org/our-demands/ (accessed 19 September 2020).

United Nations (2020). 'Sustainable Development Goals Progress Report'. https://www.un.org/sustainabledevelopment/progress-report/ (accessed 20 September 2020).

UNESCO (2020). 'International Commission on the Future of Education'. Available at https://unesdoc.unesco.org/ark:/48223/pf0000373717/PDF/373717eng.pdf.multi

UNICEF UK (2020). *Youth Advocacy Toolkit*. London: UNICEF UK.

Yeung, P. (2020). 'How Young People Are Tackling the Climate Crisis and Five Ways to Help Them'. *Positive News*. https://www.positive.news/society/youth/how-young-people-are-tackling-the-climate-crisis-and-five-ways-to-help-them/ (accessed 3 March 2021).

Zaleski, Z. (1994). 'Personal Future in Hope and Anxiety Perspective', in Z. Zaleski (ed.), *Psychology of Future Orientation*, 174–94. Lublin: Towarzystwo RRSANaukowe KUL.

Index

Note: Page locators followed by 'n' refer to notes.

abstract idealism   2, 4, 5
Academic Network of Global Education and Learning (ANGEL)   248
Africa, youth populations in   181–2
African Institute for Development Policy   181
African Union Agenda 2063   181, 188
African Youth Charter   181
Afrodescendants   142, 149, 152
Agenda 2030   21, 105
Agyeman, J.   186
Aktas, F.   87
Akudolu, L. R. I.   91
Alexander, R. J.   232
Alice Springs (Mparntwe) Education Declaration   112
ANGEL. *See* Academic Network of Global Education and Learning (ANGEL)
apartheid   226, 228, 234
Apple, M.   19, 24
Aronsson, K.   131
artificial intelligence (AI)   167, 184
Asia Education Foundation   113
Australia
   educational context   111–13
   educational initiatives   113
   global citizenship education in   113
   global competence (*see* global competence)
   Global Education Project   113
   national curriculum   111, 113
authoritarianism   24
authoritarian populism   19
Autor, D.   184

Baixo Alentejo region
   gender equality   216–18
   social representations on existing practices   217, 219

Bamber, P.   195
banking education model   45, 47, 148, 168, 176, 232
   teachers' critique of   233
Bavaria, global curricula values in   67–71
Bayne, S.   167
Beck, U.   30, 31, 186
Behavioural Insights Team (BIT)   160–2
behavioural science   161, 162, 167
behavioural/soft skills   184
behaviour change   161–3, 170 n.6
Bell, L. A.   178
Belle, C.   177
Benavot, A.   135
benevolence   132–4
Berlin Declaration   162
Bernstein, B.   23
Bertolini, P.   4
Bhabha, B.   146
Biesta, G.   163
BIT. *See* Behavioural Insights Team (BIT)
#Black Lives Matter   165, 179, 180, 242
Bloch, E.   4
Boggs, D. L.   185
Bourdieu, P.   23, 24
   concept of field   98
Brazil
   citizenship in   143–4
   educators   144–5
   planetary citizenship (*see* planetary citizenship)
   Popular Healers   152
   universities   144
Bridge 47 initiatives   245
Buddhism   131, 134, 136, 137. *See also* Confucianism; Taoism
Building Kinder Brains   160, 170 n.2
Bullard, D.   186
Burningham, K.   186

care work 37
CASEL 165
Chuang Tzu 134–5, 138, 139 n.5
citizenship
　in Brazil 143–4
　building 22
　concept of 32–3
　defined 81
　development and 50–2
　global (*see* global citizenship)
civic
　education 21–2
　knowledge 22
　skills 22
　virtues 22, 83
civil society organizations 229
class 231, 232, 235
　struggles 168
Clifford, V. A. 82, 89
climate change 242
　challenges 245–6
　crisis 245
　nature and 68–9
　and pedagogy of hope 184–5
climate protection 69
collective agency 85–6
Colombia, ecopedagogy case study 52–5
colonization 146, 149
Confucianism 131–4
Confucius 133–6
contingent pedagogy 130–2
continuing professional development
　　(CPD) 193–5, 201,
　　225–9, 235–6
　description of 229–30
　for hope 227–9, 231–4
　providers 229–30, 236
　for social cohesion 228–34
　for social justice 227–9, 231–4
　strategies 234
　teachers' experiences
　　classroom level 232–3
　　personal level 231–2
　　school level 233–5
core-periphery network map 102–5
Cornwall, A. 214, 215
Cortina, A. 33
cosmopolitan democracy 33
Cosmos 134, 135

Covid-19 pandemic 241
　in Ghana 178–81
　MOOC enrolment in 196
　online learning 161, 196
　social justice education in 178–9
CPD. *See* continuing professional
　　development (CPD)
critical consciousness 147–9
critical global citizenship education
　　(GCE) 51, 52, 54
critical hope 1, 2, 5, 178, 220
　pedagogy of 184, 186, 187, 213,
　　221–2, 228, 231
critical pedagogy 45, 49, 120, 177, 185
cultural diversity 35, 85
curricula
　for Bavarian Gymnasium 67, 68, 70
　global values in 61
　　equality 65, 67–8
　　justice 65, 67–8, 71
　　methodology 63–4
　　security 65, 67–8
　　universal values 64–72
　research on global learning 60–2
cynical fatalism, of neoliberalism 15, 49

datafication of education 164–7, 169
data science 162, 167
Davies, L. 82
DE. *See* development education (DE)
decentralization 19
dehumanization 44–5
deplanetarization 45
development
　and citizenships 50–2
　ecopedagogy and 47–52
　teaching for praxis for 49–50
development education (DE) 182
　achievement of the learning
　　outcomes 186–7
　contributions 186
　improving the quality of
　　teaching 186–7
　as pedagogical approach, role
　　of 185–7
　quality education 186
　for social justice 177–8, 186–7
　University of Ghana 176–7
dialogue 148, 149

digitalization 184
digital learning 159–62
  transformative 168–9
digital skills 184
Dill, J. S. 83
diversity 35, 134–5, 139
  cultural 35, 85
  of knowledge 37

ecologies of knowledges 52
economic crisis 2008 31
economic development 79, 177, 178
economic inequality 40, 144, 183
economic interventionism 16–17
economic rationality 130–1
ecopedagogy 44–7
  Colombia 52–5
  and development 47–52
  praxis 49–50
education 212, 213
  concept of 32
  datafication of 164–7, 169
  to fighting climate change 245–6
  for global competence 113
  happinisation of 164–7, 169
  learnification of 163–7, 169
  neoliberalism of 50, 168
  political sociology of 16–18
  privatization and decentralization 19
  promoting gender equality
      through 218–21
  schooling 23–4
  social and cultural theories 23–5
  for social justice 178
  in South Africa 226
  technological conception of 163
  and utopia 14–15, 47, 55
educational equity 67
educational inequalities 31
educational opportunities 67–8
Educational Testing Service (ETS) 166
Education for Sustainable Development
    (ESD) 159–63, 170 n.6, 195
elective affinity 21, 22
  defined 26 n.3
Eloundou-Enyegue, P. M. 181
Emcke, C. 35
emotional intelligence 167
environmental consciousization 45

environmental justice 185
environmental preservation 136
environmental sustainability 68, 120
epistemology 52, 144, 147
equality 65, 67–8
  gender (*see* gender, equality)
equitable education 168
equity 38, 62, 85, 87, 113, 116, 117, 159,
    165, 166, 178, 220
Espada, Martin 26
ETS. *See* Educational Testing Service
    (ETS)
Europe and North America (EUNA)
    96–7
  critical global citizenship education
      (GCE) 98–9, 101–2, 105–7
  division of two geographical
      areas 101–2
  social network analysis 98–9
Evans, B. 186
Every Student Succeeds Act (ESSA) of
    2015 164
extreme right-wing groups 37, 40

faith 148
fatalism 2, 3, 44–5, 52–5
  cynical 15, 49
  of development 50
  neoliberal 5, 7, 15
  Western 7
fatalistic education 45, 49
fatalistic pedagogies,
    deplanetarizing 46–7
Federal University of Ceará (UFC)
    142, 150
Floresta, N. 144–5
Foaleng, M. 177
Fourie-Malherbe, M. 84
Frantz, J. M. 87
Fraser, N. 213, 215
freedom 134
Freire, P. 1–3, 5, 6, 13, 44, 45, 50–1, 80,
    87, 110, 117, 144, 146, 147
  critical pedagogy 120
  critics on banking model of
      education 176
  development 47–8
  dialogue 148–9
  ecopedagogy 44–7

education   214, 242
fatalistic education   45, 49
hope-in-action   142, 143, 148-9
humanizing pedagogy   148, 149, 152
neoliberalism   49
pedagogy in curriculum practice   150-1
pedagogy of hope   3, 175-8, 186, 228, 242
pedagogy of the oppressed   2, 45, 50
planetary citizenship   147, 149-51
unfinishedness   44, 48
untested feasible   15
utopia   14, 15
functional literacy and numeracy   183
FutureLearn platform   194, 200

Gadotti, M.   50
Galeano, E.   26
Galtung, J.   38
Gamal, M.   196-7
Garwe, E.   89
Gaudelli, W.   83
GCE. *See* global citizenship education (GCE)
GCED. *See* global citizenship education (GCE)
gender   231, 232, 235
   equality   37, 211-12
      Baixo Alentejo   216-18
      combating the   221
      discrimination   213, 214, 216-19, 221
      men and women   214-16, 221
      promoting through education   218-21
      and social justice   214-16, 219-22
      transformation   219, 220
      UN report on the Sustainable Development Goals   215
      wage gap   216
   stereotypes   219, 222
GET course. *See* Global Education for Teachers (GET) course)
Ghana
   Covid-19 and social justice education   178-81
   youth populations in   181-2
   youth unemployment   182-3

Giroux, H.   5, 212, 242
global awareness   82
global citizenship   33-4, 97, 105, 107, 168
   competencies   128-9, 131, 138
   defined   33
   gender perspective   34
   neoliberal view of   84
   traditional conceptualizations of   81-2, 84
   transnational and cosmopolitan   34
   through virtual learning   91
global citizenship education (GCE)   13, 16-18, 25, 41, 80-4, 96-7, 105, 159, 161, 162, 195, 219-20
   in Australian curriculum   113
   conceptualizations across the network   105-7
   critical   51, 52, 54
   critics   83
   dilemmas and proposals   34-5
   elements of   114
   Europe and North America (EUNA)   98-9, 101-2, 105-7
   new interpretative frameworks   36-8
   organizations   99-102, 104-6
   policy and practice   98
   promotion   99, 101
   response to pandemic   38-40
   rights of the people and   34-5
   social network analysis (SNA)   98-101
   in sub-Saharan Africa (SSA)   84
      credit-bearing programmes   87-8
      engagement and service-learning   88
      institutional objectives and culture   86-9
      international travel   87-8
      language requirements   88
      student development   89-91
      theory of change for   84-6
   and sustainability   13, 16-18, 20-3, 25
   Sustainable Development Goals (SDGs) for   20-3
global competence   83, 111-13, 119-22
   collaborative approach for   120
   defined   128
   framework   114, 166
      design and consultation   118-19

pilot programme   114–18
    interpreting and
        contextualizing   115–17
    observations from
        workshops   117–18
  pilot schools
    action research projects   119–20
    barriers   120–1
    enablers   121–2
global consciousness   83
global education
  defined   82–3
  globalizing access to the training
        of   195–7
  hope through   202
  ideas of hope in   196–7
  and learning
    contribution of   246–8
    research   248
  qualitative and quantitative
        analysis   197–8
  and teacher education   192–5
  teachers' experiences and engagement
        in   200–1
Global Education for Teachers (GET)
        course   193–7
  exploring ideas of hope
    through children and young
        people   204–6
    through global education   202
    through online teacher
        education   202–3
    through teachers and
        teaching   203–4
  participants
    overview profile of   198–200
    survey   197–8
Global Education Project, Australia   113
globalization   33, 36, 71
global learning, on curriculum
        research   60–2
global pandemic   241, 245
global risks   31
global social justice   3, 5, 6, 20, 96, 97,
        101, 106, 211
  pedagogy of critical hope and
        212–14, 221, 234, 241, 246
global values   61–2
  in curricula   64–71
    in Bavaria   67–71

Gonzalez, L.   146
Goos, M.   184
governability, utopia of   18–19
Gramsci, A.   4, 25
grassroots movements   229
Guanxi   132
Gutiérrez, F.   51, 53
Gutierrez, J.   39

Hackman, H.   178
Haigh, M.   82
Hanson, L.   82
happinisation of education   164–7, 169
HEE. *See* higher education enrolments
        (HEE)
hegemonic institutional cultures   234, 236
HEIs. *See* higher education institutions
        (HEIs)
Heleta, S.   244
Herman, C.   90–1
Hicks, D.   179
higher education
  internationalization   87–9
  sub-Saharan Africa (SSA)   79–80
    internationalizing   89
    programmes   80–1
higher education enrolments (HEE)   79–80
higher education institutions (HEIs)
  North-South collaborations   87
  in sub-Saharan Africa (SSA)   79–80,
        84–7, 89, 91
Hodson, D.   185
Hofstede, G. J.   131
hooks, b.   5–6, 86, 178
hope   1–3, 148–9, 227
  through children and young
        people   204–6
  concept of   3
  CPD programmes for   227–9, 231–4
  critical   1, 2, 5
  in global education   196–7
  through global education   202
  through online teacher
        education   202–3
  optimism   4–5
  pedagogy of   3, 5–6, 72, 80, 91, 122, 152,
        168–9, 175–82, 184, 186–7, 196,
        213, 221–2, 228, 231, 242, 243
  through teachers and teaching   203–4
  utopia   5

Hopgood, S.   178, 180
house of modernity   216
Hsing Yun   134, 136
human
    heart   132-3
    nature   133
    rights   20, 40, 62, 167, 214, 215, 221
human-centric skills   167
humanization   152-3
humanizing pedagogy   148, 149, 152
humility   148
Hunt, F.   195

imagination   15, 26
Imagination Declaration   119
inclusive education   168
inclusiveness   215
indigenous peoples   142, 143, 149, 151, 152
Indigenous Young Leaders
        programme   119
inequalities   6, 23, 32, 85, 86, 88, 151,
        165, 167, 168, 177, 179, 186,
        212-14, 231, 232, 234, 235
    educational   31
    gender   218, 221
    race and   232
    structural   165, 168, 228
    systematic   221, 231-2
information and communications
        technology (ICT) skills   183
information sharing   101
innate knowledge   133, 137
institutional objectives and culture   86-9
interconnectedness   129, 138
intercultural understanding   111, 113,
        114, 119
internationalization of higher
        education   87-9
intersectional identities   232, 235
intertransculturality   50
Ivanhoe, P. J.   133, 137

Karma   131-2, 134
    body, speech and mind   136
'Kindness Matters for the SDGs'   160
knowledge   24, 36
    diversity of   37
    ecologies of   52
    network   102, 106
    sharing   101, 102, 105, 106

Knox, J.   167
Kool, R.   179
Kuaba Indigenous Intercultural
        Degree   151

Lao Zi   135
Laporte, P. F.   182
Latour, B.   184
Lauwerier, T.   177
learnification, of education   163-7,
        169
learning about development   185
Lederach, J. P.   39
Lee, W. O.   135
Levy, F.   184
liangzhi (pure knowing)   133
liberalism   19
liberating pedagogy   50
Lin, N.   132
Loots, S.   89-90
love   148

Maastricht Declaration of the 2002   61
McGrath, S.   89
Machado de Assis, J. M.   145, 146
Machado de Oliveira, V.   222
Mahatma Gandhi Institute of Education
        for Peace and Sustainable
        Development (MGIEP)
        159-63, 170 n.2
Manning, A.   184
Mansilla, V. B.   128
market fundamentalism   20
Martinez-Guzmán, V.   38
Massive Online Open Course (MOOC)
        194-6, 200, 203
Mayor Zaragoza, F.   41
Meireles, C.   145
Meki Kombe, C. L.   90, 91
men, gender equality in   214-16, 221
Mencius   133
Meneses, M. P.   144
#MeToo   165, 242
MGIEP. *See* Mahatma Gandhi Institute
        of Education for Peace and
        Sustainable Development
        (MGIEP)
Miceli, S.   146
'Middle Way' (Buddhist idea)   134
Millennium Development Goals   113

Index

Misiaszek, G. W.   47–9, 51, 242–3
Monteiro, F.   176
Montgomery, C.   89
MOOC. *See* Massive Online Open Course (MOOC)
moon, Ban-Ki   17, 23
moral imagination   39
multiculturalism   22, 23
multi-stakeholder collaborations   105
Murnane, R. J.   184

nationalism   35
national literacy and numeracy assessment (NAPLAN)   112
nature and climate change   68–9
neoliberalism   5, 20, 49, 50
   cynical fatalism of   15, 49
   of education   50, 168
   fatalism   5, 15
   of global citizenship   84
   political economy of   19
   utopia of   18
networked keyword analysis   105
networking   104–5, 107
network properties   101
neuromania   169
NGOs   229
Nolan, M.   20
non-citizen   51
North-South collaborations   87
Novo, M.   36
nudge   161, 162, 169

occidental cultural tradition   69
O'Dowd, R.   82, 91
OECD. *See* Organisation for Economic Co-operation and Development (OECD)
Offe, C.   17
Olibie, E. I.   91
Oneness   137–8
online learning, Covid-19 pandemic   161, 196
online teacher education, hope through   202–3
oppression   2, 5, 14, 45, 46, 48–51, 55, 85, 86, 146, 150, 165, 168, 177, 196, 232, 235
optimism   4–5
organizational field   98

Organisation for Economic Co-operation and Development (OECD)   111, 116, 164, 166, 179
Owusu-Agyeman, Y.   84
Oxfam UK   247–8

pacifism   37, 41
pandemic   30–1
   and educational inequalities   31
   global citizenship education response to   38–40
   women in care work   37
Paris Agreement   21
Parmenter, L.   82
Passeron, J. C.   23
pay for success   164
PCE. *See* planetary citizenship education (PCE)
peace   38–9, 83, 85, 160, 202
Peace and Human Rights Education   161
pedagogy
   critical   45, 49, 120, 185
   of hope   3, 5–6, 72, 80, 91, 122, 152, 168–9, 175–82, 184, 186–7, 196, 213, 221–2, 228, 231, 242, 243
      climate change and   184–5
      Covid-19 effect on   178–81
      global learning as   196
      pre-employment support   182–3
   of the oppressed   2, 45, 50
Pedagogy of Hope (Freire)   2, 168–9
Pedagogy of the Oppressed (Freire)   1, 2
Pérez Cubero, M. E.   54
personal agency   85
pessimism   4
Peterson, C.   62
pilot programme, for global competence   114–18
   interpreting and contextualizing   115–17
   observations from workshops   117–18
pilot schools
   action research projects   119–20
   barriers   120–1
pingdeng (equality)   134
PISA. *See* Programme of Student Assessment (PISA)

planetary citizenship   142, 147, 149
    curriculum   150-1
    e-book   152
    projects and publications for   151-2
planetary citizenship education
        (PCE)   51, 52, 54
planetary sustainability   45, 48, 55
planetary unsustainability   45, 49
political economy   16
    of neoliberalism   19
political sociology of education
        16-18
Popescu, F.   86-7
post-Cold War   168
postcolonialism   185
poverty alleviation   183
power dynamics   232, 235, 236
Prado, C.   51, 53
precarious care   37
privatization   19
    of education   19
privileged students   68
pro-environmental behaviour   162
Programme of Student Assessment
        (PISA)   111-13, 119
    Global Competence Framework   115, 116
    2018 frameworks   166
pro-social behaviour   161-2

Quigley, B. A.   185
Quimbayo Ruiz, G. A.   54

race   231-2, 235
radical behaviourism   164
randomized controlled trials   162
real utopias   14
Regan, C.   176
Reimers, F. M.   110, 122
relational rationality   130-2
Relational Rationality Theory
    diversity   134-5, 139
    interconnectedness   129, 138, 139
    Oneness   137-8
    respect for all   134-5, 139
    self-cultivation   133, 135-6, 139
    universal compassion   136-7
religious network   90
renxin (human heart)   132-3
Report, D.   32

respect for all   134-5, 139
Ribeiro, D.   145
Ricoeur, P.   15
right to education   67
Rivas, A.-M.   214, 215
Rosa, H.   24
Rowson, J.   169

'Salzburg Statement for SEL'   166
Santos, B de S.   36, 39, 52, 144, 146, 212
Santos, M.   145
Sauvé, Lucie   53
Schattle, H.   83
schooling   23-4
School Strike 4 Climate Change   112
Schwartz's value theory   62-5
scientific literacy   185
SDGs. *See* Sustainable Development Goals (SDGs)
security   38, 65, 67-8
SEL. *See* Social and Emotional Learning (SEL)
self-cultivation   133, 135-6, 139
Seligman, M.   62
Shackley, S.   185
Shared World   245
Shiva, V.   212
SIBS. *See* social impact bond schemes (SIBS)
Silveira Gorki, H.   34
Sinclair, S.   176
skills   183-4
    civic   22
Skinner, B. F.   164
slavery   143, 145-7, 149
SNA. *See* social network analysis (SNA)
social
    capital   98
    change   14, 59, 168, 169, 187, 188, 224, 227, 228, 234, 235
    cohesion   18, 226, 228-31, 233, 234, 236
    and emotional skills   164-7
    heterogeneity   71
    inequalities   186, 212-14
    networks   90
    responsibility   85
    transformation   35
    values   59, 61, 65, 67-8

Social and Emotional Learning
    (SEL)   159–67
  transformative   168–9
social impact bond schemes (SIBS)   164
social justice   3, 5, 6, 14, 35, 38, 44, 45,
    62, 65, 67–8, 71, 79–80, 83, 85,
    86, 89, 91, 113, 116–18, 122,
    152, 159, 164–5, 168, 175–8,
    182, 183, 213, 244
  continuing professional development
    (CPD) programmes for   227–9,
    231–4
  defined   33–4
  development education (DE)
    for   177–8, 186–7
  education   179–81, 187
    for climate change   184–5
    for pre-employment support
      182–3
    to provide basic skills   183–4
  gender equality and   214–16, 219–22
  global   3, 5, 6, 20, 96, 97, 101, 106,
    211
    pedagogy of critical hope
      and   212–14, 221, 234, 241, 246
  pedagogy   177–8, 181
    Covid-19 effect on hope and
      178–81
  in South Africa   226, 228
social movements   54–5
social network analysis (SNA)   97–101
  core-periphery maps   102–5
  global citizenship education
    (GCE)   98–101
  methodological framework   99
  structural properties   101
social representations on existing
    practices, Baixo Alentejo
    region   217, 219
social service education   182
socio-economic inequality   31, 144
socio-economic integration   181–2
socio-environmental (in)justices   45–8,
    52, 54
South Africa
  apartheid   226, 228, 234
  colonial and apartheid curricula   233
  CPD (see continuing professional
    development (CPD))
  education   226

social cohesion   226, 228
social justice   226, 228
teachers in   226
South African National Development Plan
    2030   80
SSA. See sub-Saharan Africa (SSA)
state
  capital accumulation   17–18
  concept of   16
  economic interventionism   16–17
  political economy   16
  political legitimation   17–18
  role in promoting social cohesion   18
Stoner, L.   82
structural inequalities   165, 168, 228
structural violence   38, 228
student
  development   89–91
  voice   111, 113, 118, 120
study-abroad programme   90
sub-Saharan Africa (SSA)
  global citizenship education
    (GCE) in   84
    credit-bearing programmes
      87–8
    curriculum content   89
    engagement and service-
      learning   88
    institutional objectives and
      culture   86–9
    international travel   87–8
    language requirements   88
    learning outcomes   88–9
    student development   89–91
    theory of change for   84–6
  higher education institutions (HEIs)
    in   79–80, 84–7, 89, 91
  higher education participation
    in   79–80
  'Undergraduate Leadership
    Programme'   89–90
Sueña Colombia   54–5
sustainability   46, 53, 68, 72, 85, 228,
    246
  environmental   68, 120
  global citizenship education and   13,
    16–18, 20–3, 25
  planetary   45, 48, 55
  policies   14, 16
  unplanetary   49

sustainable development (SD)   17, 21, 22, 25, 54, 60, 68, 128, 143–4, 160, 162, 177–8, 192–3, 196, 206, 244
Sustainable Development Goals (SDGs)   17, 20–3, 26 n.4, 53, 168, 180, 181, 206, 215
   Target 4.7   105, 159–62, 192–3, 244–5
Sustainable Development Goals Center for Latin América (CODS)   52–6
Swanson, D. M.   196–7, 206
systemic inequalities   221, 231–2

Tan, C.   138
Taoism   131, 134–5, 137–8
teacher education   192–3
   continuing professional development (CPD) course   193–5, 201
   global education and   192–5
      teacher's experiences and engagement   200–1
   Global Education for Teachers (GET) course   194
   Massive Online Open Course (MOOC)   194–6, 200, 203
   training and   195, 196
teachers
   agency for social justice and hope   228
   continuing professional development (CPD)   225–9
      classroom experiences   232–3
      learnings   233–5
      personal experiences   231–2
      school experiences   233–5
   critical reflection   231, 234
   critique of banking model of education   233
   curriculum and pedagogy   232–3
   difficult knowledge   228
   emotions and traumas   228
   experiences and engagement in global education   200–1
   prejudice and implicit bias   231, 232, 235
   promoting hope and social justice to learners   228, 232–3
   self-reflection   227
   social justice   228
   in South Africa   226
   unions   228

technical skills   183
technological conception of education   163
technological development   184
technology   184
Teixeira, A.   145
Teodoro. A.   44
Thondhlana, J.   89
tianxia (global)   129, 132, 133
tolerance values   69–70
Torres, C. A.   5, 44, 83
Torres-Olave, B.   176
transformation of institutional cultures   235
transformative approach   213
transformative learning approach   245
trust   148

Ugochukwu, S. E.   91
UN Behavioural Science Report of 2021   161
'Undergraduate Leadership Programme'   89–90
UNESCO. *See* United Nations Educational Scientific and Cultural Organisation (UNESCO)
Unger, R.   212
UNICEF   247
United Nations Educational Scientific and Cultural Organisation (UNESCO)   13, 20, 22, 81, 96, 98, 245
universal compassion   136–7, 139
Universal Declaration of Human Rights   20
universalism values   64, 71–2
   climate change   65, 68–9
   nature   65, 68–9
   social concern   67–8
   tolerance   65, 69–70
university civic environment   84
University of Ghana   180
   development education   176–7
   social justice education   180
UN Sustainable Development Goals (SDGs)   17, 20–3, 26 n.4, 53, 168, 180, 181, 206, 215
   Target 4.7   105, 159–62, 192–3, 244–5
untested feasible   15

utopia   5, 13–15, 26, 46, 48–52
  of conviviality
    human rights   20
  defined   14
  education and   14–15, 47, 55
  Freire, P.   14, 15
  of governability   18–19
  of neoliberalism   18
  real   14
  Sustainable Development Goals and   20–3
utopian pedagogies, planetarizing   46–7
utopic ecopedagogy   52–3
utopistics   15

values   59–62
  global (*see* global values)
  levels of manifestation   66–7
  openness to change   65–6
  research   61
  Schwartz's theory of   62–5
  self-transcendence   65–6
  social   65, 67–8
  universalism values (*see* universalism values)
Vincent, K.   82
virtual learning   91

wage gap   216
Waghid, Y.   178
Walker, G.   186
Walker, M.   89–90
Wallerstein, I.   15
Wang Yang-ming   133, 137–8
Weiss, Cora   41
'well-being is a skill'   162–5
whole network design   101
whole-school approach   120, 122
Williamson, B.   167
Wilson, D.   128
women
  abuse and domestic violence against   216
  gender equality   214–16, 221
  rights and equality   37
World Economic Forums (WEF)   167
Wright, E. O.   13–14
Wynne, B.   185

Youth Advocacy Toolkit   247
youth in Ghana
  populations   181–2
  socio-economic integration   181–2
  unemployment   182–3

Zemach-Bersin, T.   84
Zembylas, Michalinos   165
Zhai, X.   131
Zhe, M.   136, 137
Zhuang Zi. *See* Chuang Tzu

www.ingramcontent.com/pod-product-compliance
Lightning Source LLC
Chambersburg PA
CBHW071812300426
44116CB00009B/1283